# STUART ENGLAND

By the same author
*Robert Spencer Earl of Sunderland*
*The Stuarts: a study in English Kingship*
*The Stuart Constitution: Documents and Commentary*
*Halifax: Complete Works* (ed.)
*The Popish Plot*
*Revolution Principles*

J. P. KENYON

# STUART ENGLAND

ST. MARTIN'S PRESS
NEW YORK

# CONTENTS

Preface    7

I Introduction    13
II James I and Peace, 1603–18    48
III Buckingham and War, 1618–29    75
IV Charles I Alone, 1629–40    107
V The Great Rebellion, 1640–42    123
VI The Civil Wars and Interregnum, 1642–60    146
VII The Restoration, 1660    181
VIII Charles II, 1661–85    198
IX The Revolution, 1685–8    228
X The Revolution Settlement, 1689–90    254
XI War and Politics, 1690–97    268
XII Peace and Material Progress, 1697–1702    282
XIII The Whig War, 1702–10    298
XIV The Tory Peace, 1710–14    321
XV Artistic and Literary Trends, 1603–1714    336
XVI Conclusion    352

Bibliography    357
Index    373

FOR
DANIEL

# PREFACE

At the beginning of the present century, the accepted interpretation of English seventeenth-century history was disarmingly straightforward and sentimental, and at the same time perfectly self-assured. Naturally, since it was a distillation of nearly two hundred years of Whiggism, topped up with Liberalism.

According to this interpretation, disaster at once became inevitable when that remarkable woman Queen Elizabeth, who had maintained the equilibrium of Tudor government with consummate skill, gave way in 1603 to the feckless and incompetent Stuarts, who frittered away their money on unworthy ends, tried to establish an un-English despotism based on the doctrine of the Divine Right of Kings, and by so doing broke the delicate compromise imposed by the Queen in politics as well as religion.

However, the parliamentary gentry, fearless upholders of personal liberty and constitutional government, found in Puritanism not only an assurance of their individual rectitude but the moral authority to oppose the tyranny of the Stuarts and eventually defeat it; a process which was later dubbed 'The Puritan Revolution'. Unfortunately, these sterling men then made the mistake of executing Charles I, thus granting him a posthumous credibility to which he could not aspire in life, and not even Oliver Cromwell could fill the constitutional vacuum thus created, especially since he was beleaguered by risible religious cranks and unrealistic radicals. (Though these radicals were soon swept into the socialist pantheon as precursors of the Labour Party.)

7

Altogether, Cromwell's undeniable greatness posed considerable problems of interpretation – some of the most teasing in Whig–Liberal historiography; it was not clear whether he was on the 'right side' or not, or whether or not he ought to be on the 'right side'; and this raised unpleasant doubts as to whether there was in fact a 'right side' at all. Certainly he could not measure up to events, and in the end he lapsed into the decidedly un-English practice of military rule. So, the Restoration was on balance a 'good thing'. (In any case, it was mind-wrenching for an early twentieth-century Englishman to imagine the country developing into anything but a constitutional parliamentary monarchy.)

The later Stuarts, the sons of Charles I, soon showed that they had learned nothing from their father's fate. True, Charles II was clever and adaptable; after all, he was credited with the invention of the British Empire, the Army and the Navy, not to mention Science and the Theatre. But he was cynical and dissolute; he wasted money on women, just as his father had wasted it on paintings and his grandfather on boys. He managed to evade an enlightened and patriotic parliamentary opposition led by the great Earl of Shaftesbury, with the even greater John Locke as his ideas man, but the event proved Locke and Shaftesbury right. James II, not only an autocrat but a Catholic to boot, showed the Stuarts up in their true colours again, and he was painlessly removed by William of Orange, who was called in by the Whigs, assisted by a few unusually enlightened Tories. It was they and he who established a form of government which proceeded, subject to various trifling adjustments, down to the present day, and which not only made the nation Free and Rich but showed it to be Great and Right.

* * * * *

Now it is easy to make fun of this rather innocent construct, but from a technical point of view its passing in the 1920s and 1930s was a great loss to historians. It was an ideal apparatus on which to hang a narrative of events, and without it Samuel Rawson Gardiner, for instance, could never have produced his unrivalled month-by-month, almost day-by-day account of the years 1603 to 1656. Its absence has undermined the gallant attempts of later historians, such as C. V. Wedgwood, to produce a more up-to-date history of the period on anything approaching the same scale.

The teleological approach of the Whig–Liberal historians has rightly been dismissed by our present generation, but it has not been easy to replace it, except by an equally teleological Marxist approach, which has now been discredited in its turn. Meanwhile, the emergence of economic and social history, of demography, sociology and even anthropology, has thrown a clearer light on some areas, but at the cost of throwing others into shadow. In a way they only serve to expose our ignorance. Instead of striding along a brightly illuminated high road, the historian now shuffles uneasily in a thick fog from one lamp-post to another, the lamp-posts wide apart and eccentrically sited, and frequently shifting their position. The interpretation of the seventeenth century, certainly of the first half of it, is in a state of flux, and there are no immediate signs of it hardening out. Attempts to rationalize the matter by sweeping schematic interpretations, like Tawney's theory of 'the rise of the gentry', or Trevor-Roper's theory of a 'General Crisis', exhibit the brilliance of the human imagination and are a stimulus to clearer thinking, but they are by their nature subjective, procrustean and essentially superficial. It is significant that the latest attempt to produce a working synthesis on the causes of the Great Rebellion, by Lawrence Stone, has been dismissed, with some plausibility, as a retreat on the ideas of Gardiner.

However, most historians now start from the premise that there is nothing necessarily evil about the growth of monarchical power in the seventeenth century, that it was in fact the natural line of governmental development, and that the Stuart kings must be placed in context with their contemporaries in Europe. So the question becomes not, 'Was Charles I aiming at absolute power?' nor, 'Why was he aiming at absolute power?' but, 'Why did he not succeed?' Similarly, historians are much less inclined to view Parliament and all its works with the awestruck veneration of their fathers and grandfathers, and there is much less disposition to stamp its actions and achievements with automatic approval. Its motives have been re-examined in no very charitable spirit, its tactics reassessed and often found wanting. Even the sacred cow of personal liberty and freedom under the law has been pushed hither and thither by impatient and sacrilegious hands. Yet it is still not certain how we should view seventeenth-century England as a whole, nor even whether we are standing in the right place from which to view it. Should we, for instance, stand in the centre and look outwards to the provinces, as we naturally tend to do anyway; or should we look in from the provinces towards the centre, as some of the new school of local historians think we ought? Was Parliament basically a legislative organ at all, and if not, what? How did men who sat in Parliament regard it? – almost certainly not as we do at all, except perhaps at the very end of the period, under Queen Anne. Then there are two whole categories of question which are notoriously difficult to answer, the economic and the moral. Given the evidence available, its nature and extent, it is extraordinarily difficult to answer the simplest economic questions.

For instance, was England a prosperous country in such-and-such a decade? And how would contemporaries have defined the word 'prosperous' anyway? What was the standard of living of the people at any given time? What constituted an acceptable standard of living? (And who were 'the people'?) Finally there are such straightforward moral questions as, 'Was Cromwell a good man? Did he mean well?' Or, 'Was Charles I right?' Or, 'Was Charles II's policy in the country's best interests?' Of course, by their very nature it is impossible to answer such questions in an objective way, and lately it has become unfashionable, even disreputable, to pose them at all, unless it is to dismiss them with a frisson of moral disapproval, as 'value judgements'; and historians who give value judgements are referred to as if they had a social disease. But these are the basic questions which most readers ask of history – not in any naïve expectation, usually, that they can be answered, but to see them discussed by professionals and to think about them themselves; to most people this is what history is all about. So I have not shirked such questions, though my answers are really no more valid, and no less valid, than anyone else's.

If these remarks seem a poor introduction to yet another survey of this much-surveyed period, this is something for which I make no apology. Historians are often loath to admit to their readers the limitations on their powers. But no historian can provide a definitive account, even of one historical figure, in anything but strictly factual terms. He can state without fear of contradiction that civil war broke out in England in 1642, but he cannot state categorically why, and even his choice of terms – whether he calls this event a rebellion or a revolution, for instance – is often open to serious objections. He commonly uses terms like

'gentry' or 'Puritanism' which have no accepted definition, or terms like 'Whig' and 'Tory' whose meaning was
disputed even by contemporaries, and is disputed still. In
the seventeenth and earlier centuries these problems are
the more acute for being disguised much of the time. For
instance, it is fairly well known that seventeenth-century
Englishmen rarely used our political term 'revolution',
and when they did they usually attached a different
meaning to it; but recent research has even cast doubt on
the meaning in a seventeenth-century context of the word
'election' (in a parliamentary sense). The very concept of
majority election, it seems, was rudimentary and confused.
Yet for want of anything better we have to go on using
such terms, and other terms which would almost certainly
have been meaningless to contemporaries, like 'representation', 'constituency' or 'mandate'. Any interpretation of
the past is not only anachronistic, but often written in
anachronistic terminology.

In these circumstances the best I can offer is my own
account of men and events as I see them, while trying to
do justice to contrary or conflicting interpretations. Each
chapter is furnished with a critical bibliography, printed
at the end of the book, which will enable the studious or
curious to proceed much further.

*

Anyone attempting a book like this incurs a multitude of
debts, and it is impossible to acknowledge all of them.
However, it would be spectacularly ungrateful of me not
to mention Professor J. H. Plumb, who read the book in
typescript and had many constructive suggestions to make,
or Dr A. H. Lloyd, who read it in proof and saved me from
many errors, great and small.

J.P.K.

# INTRODUCTION

The current reputation of Queen Elizabeth exemplifies the flux in sixteenth- and seventeenth-century history. The picture of an all-wise, all-competent national leader created by Sir John Neale's classic biography, published in 1934, held the field for nearly thirty years, but it is now coming under increasing fire. Elizabeth is dismissed as a chronic procrastinator, even a fiddling Nero, and her failure to solve, or even tackle, major problems such as taxation, church reform and parliamentary privilege is blamed for most of the troubles which beset her successors. She has been compared, in the words of a later Fifth Monarchist, to 'a sluttish housewife, who swept the house but left the dust behind the door'. This decline in her reputation may be expected to continue, and the appearance of a 'debunking' biography is only a matter of time.

Certainly Elizabeth left many problems for her successor, and if she could not solve them, with her resplendent reputation and her powers of manipulation, few rulers could. Moreover, these problems reached their climax just at a time when the national unity which had been the keystone of her reign was beginning to crumble.

To a great extent this was a result of natural causes. The death of Philip II in 1598 removed England's principal enemy. (It also removed the principal bogeyman of 'The Black Legend', which told of the implacable carnivorous lust of the Mediterranean papists for the flesh of the

Protestant North.) In the same year of 1598, Henry IV of France promulgated the Edict of Nantes, granting the French Protestants protected status. The peace of 1604 between England and Spain was a natural corollary to these events, and owed little to James I's enthusiastic support. Unfortunately, he associated himself with an event which was generally unpopular, though accepted as necessary, which destroyed any sense of unified national purpose, and which brought to the fore problems in the economy which for the past twenty years had been pushed to one side.

## The Economic Question

The economic consequences of this peace were ambiguous. Despite a severe outbreak of bubonic plague in 1603, trade figures tended to improve: between 1600 and 1614, the export of cloth from London rose from 100,000 to 127,000 pieces a year. But the bad harvests of the 1590s continued into the early 1600s, and hard-pressed landowners could no longer look for quick and easy returns from wartime privateering.

As for legitimate trade, this offered no easy returns at any time, for the gilt-edged sector of the market was firmly in the hands of the Merchant Adventurers, a restricted chartered company who monopolized the wool trade with Flanders, which accounted for four fifths of English exports. The influence of the gilds was similarly still paramount in many leading industries, and was to continue so until 1660 and even beyond. Trade with far outposts was conducted by more loosely organized companies, like the Russia Company (founded 1553), the Levant Company (1581) and the East India Company (1600). In general, England's overseas trade was thin and frail, and only one factor suggested her future greatness as a mercantile nation. This was the disproportionate size of her capital city. By 1600, London and its suburbs embraced 130 parishes and an estimated 250,000 people, at least one twentieth of the population. As a centre of mass consumption, the capital absorbed a significant proportion of the agricultural production of England; the need to heat its hearths and smithies virtually created the Newcastle coal industry; its fogs, sweats and agues eliminated the surplus population of the rural areas sucked in by their need for employment. It already exhibited all the symptoms denounced in the nineteenth century as the cancer of megalopolis, yet it was poised for the leap forward which would make it, by 1700, the commercial centre of Europe. For the rest, England seemed to languish in a chronic state of economic depression from 1590 through to 1650, punctuated by an occasional mild boom and more frequently an outright slump.

Nor is this surprising. She was a small, poor country with a single-crop economy; her dependence on the export of unfinished woollens put her on a par with the modern African cocoa states. Though some historians have affected to see a 'First Industrial Revolution' in England between 1540 and 1640, her industries made a minuscule contribution towards the gross national product: a little mining, a little iron-smelting, some cutlery and small iron-ware, a little shipbuilding, a little of this, that and the other. The great exception was coal mining, especially in the north-east coalfield, where production increased by leaps and bounds; this arose from the need to supplement the supply of wood, which was now prohibitively expensive, especially as a domestic fuel. The principal occupation of the lower classes remained agriculture, and if wool production was to be maintained, it was always in doubt whether

England could feed her rising population, which is estimated to have increased by 40 per cent between 1500 and 1600, and by another 30 per cent up to 1642. A bad summer threatened unemployment and famine; a good summer produced a sudden glut, which forced food prices down, and after them wages. The instability of agriculture because of climatic fluctuations, created a floating population of unemployed which was viewed with alarm by the middle classes, and provoked two new Poor Laws in Elizabeth's last two parliaments, 1598 and 1601. The remedy on the Continent was to draft surplus population into the army or onto the galleys; for England, the only alternative was colonization, in America or Ireland; but it was soon apparent that viable colonies could not be established by society's dropouts. The English, by national legislation and private charity, did more to cope with this problem than most nations at this time; and as we have seen, London and other large cities acted as a demographic regulator. But major uprisings like the Midlands Revolt of 1607 and the Western Rising of 1628–30 were symptomatic of an endemic rural unrest, and when the lower classes were helpless victims of the least climatic fluctuation and a ready prey to disease, they cannot be blamed for absorbing the chiliastic ideas put forward by unlicensed, independent preachers. (Everyone has heard of the plague of 1665, which killed 69,000; very few realize that the less celebrated outbreaks of 1603 and 1625 killed 33,000 and 41,000 respectively.)

The problem of over-population accentuated the parallel problem of chronic inflation (and perhaps vice versa).

For whatever reason – and historians and economists cannot reach entire agreement on the cause – prices rose steadily all over Europe from about 1530 to about 1650, and the real value of money fell in proportion. It has been estimated that between 1539 and 1610 the purchasing power of £100 sterling fell to £72.59: a comparatively slight deviation when measured against the gyrations of twentieth-century currencies over much shorter periods, but devastating in an era when income, whether in wages or rents, was inelastic and slow to respond to monetary changes. The Crown, whose main income still came from its landed estates, was the most important victim of this process, and defective administration and lack of overall control made it slow to adopt measures like rack-renting, enclosure and new agricultural techniques undertaken by lesser landlords. But the Crown's lack of initiative was far from unique, and initial research into the administration of land in the sixteenth and seventeenth centuries suggested that the kind of struggle involved with tenants over realistic rent increases, as well as the investment of capital for long-term improvements, could only be undertaken by large landowners, who stood aloof from their social inferiors, were comparatively untroubled by national taxation, and often enjoyed additional income, from government office, mineral rights or investment in trade. Such men need not be noblemen as such – in fact, it has now been shown that the nobility if anything shared in the Crown's economic decline over this period – but they belonged to the sub-aristocracy of the gentry.

## The Gentry Question

But the attempt to build on such ideas a general theory of 'the rise of the gentry', first formulated by R. H. Tawney in 1941, provoked a controversy which has gone on ever since. Tawney's critics responded with a diametrically opposed theory of 'the fall of the gentry', and almost every variation in between has been proposed at one time or another. But it has now become apparent that none of these theories is entirely acceptable in itself, nor do any of them help historians to solve the key questions of the seventeenth century. As Lawrence Stone admits: 'None of the polarities of feudal–bourgeois, employer–employee, rich–poor, rising–declining, country–parish gentry seem to have much relevance to what actually happened.'

However, the debate has not been in vain. It has established the instability of landed income in a period of inflation, when a comparatively poor country was burdened with an excess of population not trimmed to a sufficient extent by war. Further strain was imposed on landowners by the truly horrid complexities of the land law and the difficulty of establishing legal title, which go far towards explaining the constant and aggressive litigiousness of the English gentry, which was an important factor in the ruin of some families. The maintenance of litigation, it seems, was part of the 'port', the outward display and carriage, appropriate to a gentleman. To an extent unique in Europe, English politics was dominated from the middle of Elizabeth's reign to the middle of Charles II's by one social class, but it is still a class very difficult to define.

A man was a gentleman if he behaved like a gentleman and could afford it. It is customary to regard England, then and now, as a class-conscious society. The truth of this is arguable, but what is certain is that, in the seventeenth century, class was not fixed or defined as it was later. Only a peerage conferred absolute and permanent caste status, and the English nobility, despite the massive creations of the Stuarts, remained only a tiny proportion of the upper classes. There were only 78 peers in 1604, 97 in 1625, 142 in 1661; and as late as 1685 they only numbered 145.

Moreover, an English peerage conferred noble status on one man only; not on his brothers and sons, too, as it did on the Continent. (Even the titles assumed by the heirs apparent to earldoms and dukedoms were 'courtesy titles', not recognized by the law.) The institution of a hereditary knighthood, the knights baronet, in 1611 was only a small addition to the aristocracy, and one which was initially regarded as being of dubious standing.

As a result, the index of social rank was economic status, and the law of the market prevailed. It is now apparent that when the feudal caste system based on military allegiance and homage broke down at the end of the Middle Ages, nothing replaced it; though the attempt to marry military discipline to the cash nexus in 'bastard feudalism' is significant of what was to come. For a generation or two, a concept of the peculiar sanctity and unsaleability of land, glimpsed even today in the term '*real* property', survived, but by the end of the sixteenth century the market in landed estates was quite untrammelled by such considerations. A man who acquired money and land entered the upper classes; a man who lost his land left it. Any other distinction was meaningless. Knowing sociologists, never at a loss for a high-sounding term, have christened this 'status inconsistency' (a sufficiently meaningless term – inconsistent with what?), but it would be more accurate to call it 'lack of status definition'. The increasing willingness of the College of Heralds to issue pedigrees, real or imaginary, for landed families, only provided *ex post facto* rationalization of economic achievement, and was itself a cash transaction; there were none of those distinctions between 'old land' and 'new land', 'old title' and 'new title', or 'trade' and 'land' so evident, for instance, in the novels of Trollope. Nor is it clear that speech or accent was a sufficient class indicator. Dramatists mocked rustic and Celtic modes of speech, but many gentlemen and even noblemen unselfconsciously used a provincial accent, and there was no accepted upper-class norm. The result was a class structure unnervingly fluid in its outlines.

On the other hand, some of our pessimism about the economic state of the middle class is unwarranted. The gentry's latest historian points out that the rise in population and the rise in prices in some sense guaranteed agricultural prosperity, and 'there is no need to invoke the bourgeois capitalist spirit to explain why some landowners rose further or faster'. Men with any common sense and practical ability could improve their fortune; conversely, in a period of stiff competition, when abstract class status provided no buffer, the penalties for failure were absolute. It is this intense polarization which provides different historians with evidence for a rising gentry and a falling gentry at one and the same time; in the same way, there is equally good evidence for the rude prosperity of the working classes and their desperate poverty. Yet, though landowning families could easily disappear without trace, through bankruptcy or failure to produce male heirs – especially in an age of high infant mortality – replacements were always available. Whether these replacements came from the yeomanry below (an even more nebulous class than the gentry), or whether they were drawn from other gentry families, perhaps outside the immediate area, is uncertain. Either way, the impression is one of dynamic stability.

For instance, it has been established that in Yorkshire, between 1540 and 1642, 181 gentry families failed in the male line, 30 disappeared without trace, and 64 sold their estates and left the county, cause unknown. Indeed, further analysis shows that a total of 87 families sold up altogether, and several of these are known to have lapsed back into yeoman status or lower, and another 78 had to sell most of their estates; altogether 397 families (out of a total for the whole period of 963) experienced a degree of financial embarrassment which obliged them to sell at least some of their estates. Yet the number of landed families in the county increased from 557 in 1540 to 679 in 1642.

This was obviously a prosperous class, and a prosperous nation. It is possible for us, at this remove in time, to see this clearly, though few contemporaries could. The 'Commercial Revolution' of the late seventeenth century, leading to the bid for Empire, the hegemony of Europe, dominance of the Mediterranean and fighting control of colonial and eastern markets, had to have a strong agricultural base.

But to seventeenth-century Englishmen this was not apparent. They toiled and moiled in a society in which status depended upon ever-renewed success; to stand still was to fall back. To strive to maintain one's position is not necessarily a sign of economic aggression or social desperation, and the maintenance of that position often depended on the development of local industry or mining, the acquisition of court office, investment in trade, or straight agricultural improvement. This fostered a sense of neurosis which was accentuated by the Crown's clumsy attempts, under the Tudors as well as the Stuarts, to obtain a fair slice of the economic cake by the use of controls in trade and industry, and to restrict its expenditure on court sinecures and even on the offices of central and local government.

*The Church Question*

To economic tension was added religious tension. Puritanism has always been central to any discussion of the causes
of the Great Rebellion – indeed, S. R. Gardiner called it
'The Puritan Revolution', a term which became fashionable for a time and has not fallen entirely into disuse even
now. This is all very well so long as we realize that the
word 'Puritanism' was scarcely used by contemporaries,
'Puritan' very rarely, and then as a term of abuse. Moreover, despite the simply enormous volume of research on
this question, in America as well as in England, no one
has come up with any acceptable definition of Puritanism
more specific than Lawrence Stone's, which is 'a generalized conviction of the need for independent judgement
based on conscience and bible reading'. This has not
prevented historians right down to the present day from
portraying Puritanism as a force directed to constitutional
and even economic revolution, and one of overwhelming
power. But such a view of events fails entirely to answer
two key questions. If the motor of the Great Rebellion was
Puritanism, why were the 'Puritans' in the Long Parliament entirely unable from first to last to agree on the
nature of the religious reform supposedly central to their
programme? Secondly, if Puritanism was such an overwhelming manifestation, why did it collapse so ignomini-
ously, and to the astonishment of its enemies, in 1660, and
devolve into an apolitical, almost quietist minority? *The
Oxford Dictionary of the Christian Church* puts it in a nutshell,
thus: 'The term ''Puritan'', which never had a precise
use, ceased to be applicable after 1660.'

To my mind, the word 'Puritanism' should be used
with the utmost caution, and to describe the undeniable
religious disputes which bedevilled this period I prefer the

term 'The Church Question'. Because really the problem boiled down to a dispute over the nature of the English Church, its teaching, its ministry and its government, and once this was settled by compromise in 1661, the Church Question disappeared – at least for the next two generations. We also need to remember that despite the abusive employment of terms like 'Puritan', 'Arminian' or 'Anglican', until 1640 or 1642 all three held themselves to be members of 'one holy catholic and apostolick church'. This was a dispute within the Church, not with it; and at its height, in 1628, Charles I was gratified to note 'that even in those curious points in which the present differences lie, men of all sorts take the Articles of the Church of England to be for *them*'.

Today, when Anglican episcopalianism has spread over the world and is one of the dominant forms of Protestantism, it is difficult to appreciate what a bizarre appearance the English Church of the sixteenth and seventeenth centuries presented. It was unique among reformed churches in retaining an episcopate claiming descent, like the Pope, from St Peter himself, and retaining almost intact the pre-Reformation structure of church government. Large parts of its liturgy were a direct translation of the Roman mass, it laid no particular emphasis on preaching, and it retained at the heart of the communion service a dangerously ambivalent position on the key question of the transubstantiation of the elements arrived at simply by conflating the wording of the two prayer books of 1549 and 1552, whose authors had supposed they were saying precisely opposite things. It did not even have an agreed translation of the Bible. It is not surprising that many members of the Church thought it presented too little contrast with the Church of Rome, and too much contrast with the indubitably reformed churches of the West, in Germany, Switzerland, Scotland and France.

A vigorous movement for church reform was mounted in Elizabeth's reign, and on one front it was successful. Bishops and clergy alike willingly embraced the extreme theological positions of Calvin, and their belief in predestination and election was affirmed in the Lambeth Articles of 1595, promulgated by Archbishop Whitgift, the hammer of the Puritans. This was confirmed in 1618 by England's official adhesion to the edicts of the Synod of Dort. Purists continued to demand the adoption of the even more stringent articles drawn up for the Church of Ireland in 1615, but the distinctions being drawn here are very fine; to all intents and purposes, the theological standpoint of the Church of England was rigidly Calvinistic.

The question of liturgy and ceremonial was more difficult. There had been attempts under Elizabeth to float a revised prayer book, but these were abandoned after the failure of Cope's 'bill and book' in 1587, and there is no evidence that they were anything more than minority fads, brewed in the universities. In any case, the isolation of many rural parishes permitted a wide degree of latitude, and it must be assumed that many clergymen used what portions of the existing book they approved of, subject always to the control of the patron. The obligation on the minister to wear a surplice was an issue which roused the most intense emotion in certain clergymen, but was not calculated to interest many laymen. As for the physical surroundings of worship, these had been drastically altered under Edward VI, to an extent we now find it difficult to visualize after the further round of alterations initiated by the Cambridge Movement in the nineteenth century. The glory of candles, coloured vestments, stained glass, statues and ornaments, the music of choirs and organs, were reserved for cathedral and collegiate churches; elsewhere the faithful worshipped in a bleak, whitewashed barn dominated not by the altar but by the pulpit, with a wooden table in the nave for the celebration of communion. The royal arms and the tables of commandments installed under Charles II were almost glamorous.

Preaching and the ministry of the word was another aspect of the Church Question. The pre-Reformation clergy had for the most part conformed to the new ways, but the sudden emphasis on preaching took them unawares; previously their function had revolved round the mystery of the mass, and many of them were unfamiliar with the greater part of the Bible. Yet the laity now insisted that salvation lay through scripture alone, and it was the duty of the clergyman to interpret scripture to them. This demand the Church in general could not meet, and complaints of non-preachers and illiterate preachers continued into James I's reign. But successive archbishops, Parker, Grindal, Whitgift and Bancroft (through to 1611), were as deeply concerned with this problem as any 'Puritan'; heroic efforts were made to expand the intake of the universities and even found new colleges there, and by the end of James I's reign the aim of a graduate clergy was substantially achieved. In fact, as James I's 'Directions to Preachers' show, by 1622 the problem was not to encourage preaching but to curtail it. Indeed, some have hypothesized that the expansion of the universities created an unemployed intelligentsia of activist clergy, but in the absence of any firm statistics on the number of benefices available and their value, and the number of clergymen available to take them, this must remain speculative. (Again, if this was indeed a problem, we have to ask why no more is heard of it after 1660.) However, it is true that many borough corporations, trading corporations and professional bodies, their thirst unassuaged by one sermon a week, took on ordained 'lecturers' to preach on Sunday afternoons, and as early as 1604 the problem merited the attention of Convocation.

There was, of course, an economic aspect to all this. The income in kind from most benefices had been commuted at the end of the Middle Ages to a fixed money payment, whose real value had declined with the prevailing inflation. Many benefices, formerly controlled by the monasteries, had passed altogether into the hands of local landowners. In any case, an income appropriate for a celibate, comparatively uneducated priesthood was insufficient for the needs of married graduates with families, conscious of their professional status. To meet the problem, benefices were doubled up, even trebled up, under one clergyman, or curates were appointed at starvation salaries. Here the remedy lay in the hands of the patrons; the middle classes would only get the standard of pastoral care they required if they were willing to pay for it. No solution was ever found, and it was left for Queen Anne (not Parliament) to step forward with a scheme to supplement clerical salaries. Again, we notice that this is a problem which was not so much of a problem after 1660.

The main stumbling-block remained the bishops. Their authority was felt to be basically popish, and in the 1570s and 1580s there was a concerted drive in Parliament and the universities to replace them by some form of Presbyterian church government, whether the title of bishop was retained or not. But Elizabeth's systematic pillage of episcopal lands had reduced their financial power, and with it their authority, and the Marprelate Tracts of the 1580s were generally felt to go much too far in public ridicule of a class who were, after all, peers of the realm. Many of Elizabeth's earlier ministers, like Leicester, Walsingham and Burleigh, had been anti-episcopal and even Puritan in their attitude, though they had more sense than to support the Puritan opposition in Parliament, to which the Queen was implacably opposed. The succeeding generation, whether at Court or outside it, was much more conformist, and they were encouraged in this attitude by the emergence in the 1590s of 'Independency' or 'Brownism', the growth of separatist congregations owing no allegiance to any central body. This was a movement disliked by all, and it encouraged men to rally to the side of law and order; in the 1590s, Archbishop Whitgift was able to impose a satisfactory degree of conformity and obedience on the clergy, with the cooperation of the council, the judges and the local magistrates. The bishops now seemed a harmless body of men, and the rather laodicean appointments made by James I confirmed this trend.

The difficulty is that the history of 'Puritanism' in this period has been charted by reference to sermons and treatises put out by clergymen. The attitude of the laymen remains ambivalent. Certain it is that they were consistently anti-clerical; the clergy were a lower social order, and their duties essentially auxiliary in nature. There was never the least suggestion that they should be allowed into the House of Commons, and not until half-way through the reign of James I were any of them appointed to the Commission of the Peace – and then not in any significant numbers until after 1660. Even at the universities a distinction existed between gentlemen, who tended not to take a degree, and clergymen, who did, their education being essentially vocational. The laity wanted a strong and wealthy church, for sure, but not one that was too strong or too wealthy. When they had their way, in the Long Parliament, all the many schemes put forward had this in common: that they assumed the dominance of the laity over the clergy, whether through Parliament or through the elected elders of local congregations.

The other face of religion was Roman Catholicism. Successive Popes had refused to cancel the Bull *Regnans in excelsis* of 1570, declaring Elizabeth and her successors deposed. So the English Catholics remained a treasonable element, subject to a battery of penal laws designed to ruin their finances, inhibit Catholic worship, destroy their priesthood and arrest proselytization. This last aim seems to have been substantially achieved, but it is apparent that even under Elizabeth the legislation designed to dispossess the Catholic landed classes was never efficiently and consistently enforced. On the contrary, the fines for non-attendance at church seem to have eliminated the Catholic lower classes, leaving the surviving minority of Catholic gentry and nobility as it were marooned. The wave of Jesuit missionaries, who in the 1580s had seemed to pose the most urgent menace to State and Church, had been broken, and the Jesuits were now at odds with the secular priests as to whether they should attempt to extend the Catholic mission at all. In 1601, Elizabeth and Cecil were fishing in these troubled waters, and on James I's accession there was some hope of limited toleration, destroyed, of course, by the Gunpowder Plot of 1605.

However, though the gentry as local magistrates seemed curiously reluctant to enforce the laws against Catholics, as members of parliament they remained vociferously anti-Roman, viewing with suspicion any overtures towards toleration, and even demanding the promulgation of new penal statutes to reinforce those already in existence. Abroad, they declined to acknowledge the *détente* which succeeded Philip II's death, and persisted in maintaining a 'cold war' situation. James's attempts at an alliance with Spain were greeted with suspicion, his proposal to marry his son to a Habsburg princess with incredulity. Charles's eventual marriage to Henrietta Maria of France did more than any other single factor to undermine his position. Sincere and even aggressive Protestants as they were, the first two Stuarts could never convince their subjects that they did not have a strong leaning towards, or at least a weakness for, Rome.

## The Ancient Constitution

The fact that seventeenth-century Englishmen could not make a distinction between domestic and foreign policy testifies to the success of Elizabethan propaganda against Rome; it also testifies to the deficiencies in English education. There is plenty of evidence to show that the English upper classes from 1540 onwards were obtaining more education than ever before; more of them were attending the universities and the Inns of Court, though few of them stayed the course to the end. But it is not the quantity but the quality of education which is in some doubt. Teaching was focused, naturally, on the classics, on Rome, and to a less extent on Greece; the study of more recent history, of modern languages or geography, was a spare-time occupation; teaching at the Inns of Court was devoted to an extremely idiosyncratic legal system having no European parallel. Study of Roman history allied with study of the Common Law, combined with a reading of the medieval chronicles so fashionable in the sixteenth century (and perpetuated in Shakespeare's history plays), produced the theory of 'The Ancient Constitution'.

This was slow to emerge in a strictly definable form

because it was so very much taken for granted; also it received its final impetus from the account of medieval English history offered by the great jurist, Sir Edward Coke, which was not published until 1642. It was, like the Common Law itself, a manifestation of English chauvinism. According to this theory, representative institutions, whether on a local level, as with the jury, or a national level, as with Parliament, were part of the Teutonic inheritance of Britain, conveyed to these islands by the Saxons, and uncorrupted by the slavish tendencies of the Mediterranean. (It was sometimes known as 'The Gothic Constitution'.) As far back into the misty Saxon past as men could delve, the rights of the English people had been known, ascertained and respected, kings had been elected (even William the Conqueror), and the people's will had been expressed in popular assemblies; in the Anglo-Saxon Witan, in fabled mass gatherings called by the Norman kings (for instance, by Henry I at Salisbury in 1116), and finally in Parliament. The rights of free-born subjects before the law and the King had been confirmed by the Normans, extended by the Angevins, and reaffirmed most resplendently in Magna Carta. Magna Carta, in fact, became something of a cult in the sixteenth and seventeenth centuries.

Belief in the gentry's role in central government was confirmed by their obvious and substantial participation in local government, as justices of the peace, commissioners of sewers, sheriffs, coroners, jurors and electors. Though much of this system was the creation of medieval kings, much of it also stemmed from the self-help customs of the Anglo-Saxons and the Teutonic tribes, and was known to do so. The counties kept contact with the central government by the election of Members of Parliament – such election, particularly for the shire, being the ultimate affirmation of class status. The reverse contact, of the central government with the provinces, was less certain, and depended very much on the twice-yearly perambulation of the assize judges, covering regions rather than counties. The government's right to appoint justices and sheriffs, given its almost total ignorance of the localities, was unimportant and, even at the height of the conflict between King and Parliament, went unquestioned. Thus the fury roused by James II's and Lord Somers's attempts to appoint to these offices on a national plan. The Corporation Act of 1661 failed, as did any subsequent attempt to regulate the boroughs. In the Lord Lieutenant, established under Elizabeth, but only appointed to each county in the Civil Wars, the government acquired a potential *intendant*, but local independence ensured that he remained an umpire rather than a captain, and the emergent convention that he should only be replaced for treason lessened the usefulness of the office. Again, James II's attempts to appoint and dismiss Lord Lieutenants as if they were government officials was decisively resented.

But naturally the most sought-after distinction for a gentleman was membership of Parliament, and by the end of the sixteenth century the landed classes had absorbed a majority of the borough seats properly reserved for townsmen. A House of Commons which ought to have contained 90 country gentlemen, elected by the shires, and 372 burgesses, contained in 1584 and 1593 only 53 resident townsmen; the rest of the seats had been appropriated by the landed classes, plus a smattering of courtiers, lawyers and other London-based members of the professional classes. Arguably the main motive for securing such representation on the part of an individual was status confirmation, but once at Westminster, a corporate sense of grievance often made itself felt.

## Parliament

Of course, the role of Parliament is central to any discussion of seventeenth-century English politics; on the other hand, our awareness of its later development, or even of its exploits during the Great Rebellion, sometimes leads us to read into it qualities and powers it did not possess, nor want to possess, in 1603.

Elizabeth's financial needs, and perhaps a desire to present a united national front against a foreign enemy, had caused her to meet Parliament with increasing frequency during the closing years of her reign, in 1589, 1593, 1597 and 1601. But these were all separate parliaments, and their sessions were brief; men still spoke of 'this parliament' or 'the parliaments', not of 'Parliament' in general. Apart from the granting of taxation, its main function was to reinterpret or add to the law by statute (whether it could change the law or not was still a moot point), and to set a seal on important Acts of state – as when it formally vested the Crown in James I by the Act of Succession in 1604.

Whether it could proceed further than this, and take a share in policy-making, was a question which generated considerable friction. Under Elizabeth it had claimed a right to amend the Church Settlement by statute, on the grounds that it had been established by statute in 1559; this dispute was substantially unsettled, and rumbled on into the next reign. It had also presumed to advise Elizabeth on the succession; first it pressed her to marry, then to eliminate the heir-presumptive, Mary Queen of Scots, then to recognize Mary's son James. Elizabeth refused these demands with varying degrees of asperity, but arguably it was only on such general matters, where public opinion was strong and on the whole informed, that

32

Parliament was in a position to tender advice; it lacked the detailed knowledge to intervene effectively in foreign policy, and Elizabeth went to the assistance of the Huguenots and the Dutch, for instance, in her own good time and in the manner which suited her best.

Not that parliamentary pressure was always ineffectual The draconian anti-Catholic legislation of the 1580s owed much to the House of Commons, and it is inconceivable that Elizabeth, left to her own devices, would have executed her cousin Mary, an anointed queen. In almost every parliament of the reign she was kept hard at work resisting the Commons' claim to initiate discussion on any subject and draft legislation of their own devising. Yet they continued to do both with comparative impunity, despite an unequivocal denial of their rights in the matter by Lord Keeper Puckering in 1593. Precedents were being established, though of an arguable nature.

On the other hand, there is no doubt that the work of Sir John Neale on Elizabeth and her parliaments has, perhaps unintentionally, placed an undue emphasis on conflict and confrontation, ignoring the wide areas of agreement and cooperation between her and Parliament. It was the breakdown of this general cooperation which worried James I and irritated Charles I. In the same way, Wallace Notestein's famous paper on 'The Winning of the Initiative by the House of Commons', by its very title, gives an impression of combative and progressive development which is deceptive (if not entirely false). Neale himself has shown that parliamentary opposition was stronger in the first half of Elizabeth's reign than it was in the second; under James I it was stronger in 1604 and again in 1610 than it was in 1606 and 1607; it could even vary from session to session in one year, as in 1610 and 1621.

Nor should we overlook the intense conservatism of this

33

age, a conservatism which lasted well into a major rebellion in the 1640s, and eventually produced an exaggeratedly conservative reaction, which swept away as if it had never been the so-called 'English Revolution' of the 1640s. Reverence for monarchy was an instinctive element in the political culture. Passive obedience to the ruler was one of the basic teachings of the Church of England, enforced from the catechism upwards. It was originally conceived as a counter to papal claims, and the more exaggerated one's fears of popery, the more exaggerated one's devotion to the monarchy. Nor was this necessarily inhibited by Puritanism; Calvin, just as much as Luther, acknowledged the authority of the Christian Prince, and his supremacy over all other magistrates. In England the authority of the King, within reasonable limits, was also upheld by the theory of the Ancient Constitution.

Nevertheless, in the 1920s and 1930s there arose a flourishing school of historians, led by the American Charles McIlwain, who believed that there was a continuous struggle for sovereignty between the early Stuart kings and their parliaments. There is no support for this in fact, unless one distorts the record by taking every random disagreement over details of policy or procedure as part of some 'master plan'. Basic issues were seriously debated only once under James I, in 1610, when the Commons decided that sovereignty was embodied in the joint entity King-in-Parliament. James did not seriously contest this, and though Charles I made it clear in the 1620s that he regarded Parliament as much the less important element in the combination, it is not clear that this was controversial. Whatever Charles's plans or dreams in the 1630s – and they are much more likely to have been dreams – in his Answer to the Nineteen Propositions in the summer of

1642 he came down firmly in favour of a balanced constitution, with power shared between King, Lords and
Commons.

Nor did either side accept the idea that constitutional
relationships, which they believed had existed time out of
mind, might change; the structure of politics and society
was governed by laws as immutable as those which controlled the revolution of the sun and the stars round the
earth; the most that could be envisaged were adjustments,
which would enable the machine to run more smoothly.
In the past, such 'adjustments' had involved the deposition of Edward II and Richard II, and their subsequent
deaths 'by natural causes'; they had involved the coercion
of King John; but, by the seventeenth century, any further
adjustments were much more likely to be made at the
expense of Parliament. We have been brainwashed into
accepting the Gardiner–Notestein–Neale theory of inevitable, predestined, almost effortless parliamentary advance.
But, to contemporaries, the opposite seemed the case: all
over Europe princely power was waxing, and the powers
of diets, estates and corteses were waning, or disappearing
altogether. Nor was the English House of Commons, on
the face of it, well equipped to meet this situation. Its
representative nature was a polite fiction, subscribed to by
the Crown when it wished to secure 'national' approval
for important Acts of state; but everyone knew that in
most boroughs the franchise was exercised by an élite, and
that the distribution of seats across the country was quite
irrational – thus the redistribution schemes persistently
floated during the Civil Wars and Interregnum. The only
answer was a plea of 'virtual representation', put by Sir
Edward Coke in 1624, when he said, 'The Commons are
the representative body of the realm, for all the people are
present in Parliament by person representative.' But when

the Commons of 1604 claimed to speak for the people, King James told them, 'This House doth not so represent the whole commons of the realm as the shadow doth the body, but only representatively' – that is, figuratively. In fact, the Lords were more representative than the Commons, though they only represented themselves. As we have seen, the landed classes were grossly over-represented in the Commons at the expense of the mercantile or manufacturing community; thus there were only sixty-four merchants in the Long Parliament of 1640 (12½ per cent of the whole). This imbalance became particularly bizarre after 1660, when English trade underwent a notable expansion. It is customary to talk of 'the rise of the lawyers' in the Commons, and indeed eighty-eight were elected to the Long Parliament, but this still amounted to only 15 per cent of the whole, and only Edward Hyde and Oliver St John made a significant contribution as political leaders. We tend to forget, too, that the arbitrary medieval exclusion of the clergy from the Commons involved the exclusion of the teaching profession and virtually all the intelligentsia as such.

Moreover, it was difficult to see how an assembly of this size could play an effective or constructive role in government. It had reached 478 by 1603, by 1625 it numbered 505, and though under Charles II it was frozen at a total of 513, this was increased yet again in 1707, by the Union with Scotland. The Long Parliament contrived to fight two civil wars to a successful conclusion, conquer Scotland and Ireland and defy the world, but only after its numbers had been drastically reduced by desertion or expulsion. In normal circumstances, 500 men, recruited by random and often inscrutable methods of selection from a country still highly provincialized, where counties were still divided one from another by dialect, relative wealth, inherited customs and difficulties of communication, could neither impose unity on themselves nor bear to have unity imposed upon them. Members with constructive ideas were few, and because of the profound inertia in favour of royal government, the presence of a handful of privy councillors in the House of Commons could often outweigh a more numerous opposition; on the other hand a few determined men, well versed in the unaccustomed art of public speaking – the seventeenth-century electorate did not expect speeches from its candidates – could exercise a disruptive influence out of all proportion to their numbers. In Elizabeth's closing years, problems of control were becoming acute, and it was clear that if the government relaxed its grip, as it did under James I, there was nothing to take its place. In 1601, the House was disorderly to a degree: members 'hemmed and laughed and talked' during speeches, they ignored rebukes from the Speaker, and they were told by Sir Robert Cecil that their behaviour was 'more fit for a grammar school than a Court of Parliament'. There is much sense in James I's comment to the Spanish ambassador after the failure of the Addled Parliament in 1614: 'The House of Commons is a body without a head. The members give their opinion in a disorderly manner; at their meetings nothing is heard but cries, shouts and confusion. I am surprised that my ancestors should ever have permitted such an institution to come into existence.'

*The Money Question*

And if Parliament survived, it was not because of its innate goodness or political utility, still less because of its constructive statesmanship, of which there is no evidence, but because of the unusually firm control it had secured on over taxation, a control the Crown never seriously challenged.

Since the fourteenth century, the Crown had enjoyed the 'Great Customs' on the import of wine and the export of wool, known as 'tunnage and poundage'. From 1485 these were granted to each monarch for life, as they were to James I in 1603. This, plus the income from the Crown Lands, from fines and forfeitures, and the incidents of feudal overlordship, provided a regular income for the Crown; in theory, direct taxation was exceptional, though under Elizabeth, with inflation biting, it tended to become the rule. Direct taxation was limited to the Subsidy and Fifteenths and Tenths. Fifteenths and Tenths were a rudimentary income tax levied on personal property, 15 per cent for country-dwellers, 10 per cent for townsmen, but the assessments had never been properly revised, and by 1603 they brought in a mere £30,000, derisory even by the standards of the day. The Subsidy was more substantial: 4s. in the £ on land and 2s. 8d. in the £ on personal property. But the subsidy rolls had not been revised since 1547, and took no account of the subsequent growth in the size of estates or the general rise in the value of land. The nobility, separately assessed by the Lord Chancellor, were even more leniently treated; in 1601, for instance, the Earl of Derby was taxed on £400, though his rent roll was valued at £4,035 a year. If we include the clergy, who taxed themselves separately through Convocation, a subsidy is usually reckoned at £80,000, though this round sum conceals a fluctuation as high as £90,000 and as low as £72,000. But one subsidy a year was regarded as the maximum, so that multi-subsidies were spread over the following years; when James I ascended the throne the four subsidies voted in 1601 were still coming in.

These are almost despicably low figures, but the money seems to have been paid willingly enough, and during the

Spanish War of Queen Elizabeth, direct taxation became regular and annual. In 1589 Parliament voted a double subsidy, in 1593 and 1597 treble subsidies, and in 1601 a quadruple subsidy. But it is a myth to suppose that such taxation was only voted in time of war; Elizabeth demanded direct taxation from every parliament she met, and only once, in 1566, was she challenged. Parliament's insistence that James I and Charles I should 'live of their own' in time of peace was not a return to previous conditions, though Parliament may have thought it was.

If we are asked could they afford to pay more, the answer would have to be yes. True, the period 1614 to 1629 was one of economic depression, but so were the 1640s, when the Long Parliament, without apparent effort, managed to relieve the landowning classes – or that proportion which was within its jurisdiction – of £80,000 a month, not £80,000 a year! The money was there, given the right kind of compulsion, plus a belief in national leadership; if that belief was not there, then even the output of such taxation as there was could not be maintained. In 1621, a subsidy produced £72,500; in 1624, £67,000; in 1625, £63,000; and in 1628, £55,000.

Nevertheless, the increasing unwillingness of Parliament to vote taxes and the reluctance of the public to pay them threatened Parliament's future, not the monarchy's. The Stuarts have always been denounced for their absolutist theories, but historians have turned a blind eye to the implications of such theories, and their possible success. Strafford in 1640, urging Charles I to do 'all that power might admit', is not an isolated example; he stands at the end of a long line of royal councillors, usually anonymous, who after every break with parliament were willing to urge the collection of taxes by force. Under James I, occasional attempts at 'benevolences' and forced loans met with little success, but the advent to power of Buckingham and Prince Charles put a new complexion on things, and the Benevolence of 1622, backed by the full weight of the Privy Council, brought in £116,000. The writing was on the wall. In 1624, Sir Benjamin Rudyard warned the Commons, 'I am afraid if this parliament fails it will be the last of parliaments.' Two years later, Sir Dudley Carleton, speaking for King Charles, spelled it out. 'In all Christian kingdoms,' he said, 'you know that parliaments were in use anciently, until the monarchs began to know their own strength, and, seeing the turbulent nature of their parliaments, at length they by little and little began to stand upon their prerogatives, and at last overthrew the parliaments throughout Christendom, except here only with us.' In fact, in 1627 Charles backed up a new forced loan with extreme pressure, using imprisonment as a means of coercion, and he squeezed nearly £250,000 out of the nation in twelve months; more than three subsidies. But for his commitments abroad, this might have been the decisive breakthrough.

The Crown's ultimate failure, inevitable in retrospect, was not so easy to predict at the time. Unfortunately the Elizabethans, surviving until 1621 in the person of Francis Bacon, were blindly committed to Parliament: to them its regular summons was a reflex action as natural as breathing. Nor was Bacon's successor, John Williams, any less conservative; he denounced the advocates of direct taxation as 'Rehoboam's ear-wigs', and in 1622, with Buckingham at the height of his power, successfully blocked his demand for a second benevolence in one year. King James himself, much as he resented and loathed Parliament, regarded it as a natural and inevitable part of government, and even one which conferred splendour on himself, as he showed in two notable speeches in 1606 and 1610. He was as much an

Elizabethan as anybody. The Common Law judges were
another staunchly conservative element. The verdict in
the Five Knights' Case in 1627 was exceptional; it was
based on the King's need to imprison suspects for security
reasons, yet it caused the judges who gave it manifest
uneasiness. Even the judges who endorsed ship money in
1638 explicitly denied the King's right to 'impose charges
upon his subjects in general, without common consent in
parliament'. 'The people of the kingdom,' added Sir
Robert Berkeley, 'are subjects, not slaves; freemen, not
villeins to be taxed *de alto et basso*.'

## The Civil War Question

It is an unfortunate fact that any discussion of the state of
England in 1603 ends in an examination of the causes of
the Great Rebellion. The event casts its shadow before;
indeed, long before. Almost every English historian from
Gardiner down to Lawrence Stone traces the causes of this
event back to 1603, to 1558, even to 1529. They are, in
fact, devotees of the theory of historical inevitability,
which has been called, in less reverent terms, 'the rolling
stone' theory. According to this hypothesis, a stone
dropped on the mountain heights (say, in 1558), rolls
irresistibly down the slopes, gathering weight as it goes,
dislodging larger boulders, scree and snow, creating a
cumulative movement which bursts on the unsuspecting
villages below as an avalanche.

However, this is a theory which is now viewed with
some scepticism; by Conrad Russell and G. R. Elton, to
name only two. Elton points out that 'in that century
people lived and agreed and quarrelled with one another,
fighting for power and favour and rights and religion (and
many of them doing none of these things) without ever

undermining their conviction that they lived in a cohesive society and under a working government'. He goes on, 'It is only by directing all developments towards the distant end of 1640 that the debates and the dissatisfactions which are the experience of any live society assume the guise of necessary causes.' Gardiner and his successors tried to elevate the Commons' Apology of 1604 and their Protestation of 1621 into critical confrontations, when they were merely tactical manoeuvres. The first real confrontation, the first time when men began to fear for the stability and cohesion of government, was in 1628 or 1629. Yet John Pym's speech at Manwaring's impeachment in 1628 is a defensive gesture, a rejection of revolution and a call for gradual reform and adjustment. Charles I's Answer to the Nineteen Propositions, on the very eve of the Civil War, still called for similar adjustments and accused his opponents of social disruption.

It is impossible not to turn more and more towards a tactical or political explanation, and find the causes of the Civil War in the state of the monarchy; first, its general weakness, which unbalanced the working constitution – as many contemporaries realized – and secondly, the perverse ineptitude of Charles I and some of his advisers, which triggered off a series of crises, beginning with the Scottish National Covenant of 1638, which made civil war inevitable. The 'rolling stone' in fact started rolling when that celebrated maidservant threw her stool at a bishop in St Giles's, Edinburgh, on 23 July 1637.

## The Monarchy Question

An anonymous Machiavellian, writing in the 1590s, said that a prince could only achieve 'power or strength' if he had 'money, arms, counsel, friends and fortune'. The

Stuarts certainly lacked *counsel*, in that those who advised them to extreme courses were always in a minority, and the majority of their ministers were infected by a kind of liberal constitutionalism which offered no solution to their current predicament. They lacked *friends*, in the sense that they never had a powerful foreign ally (in this connection the French alliance of 1624 was a decisive disappointment), and also in the sense that until 1641 they could never split the upper classes and call to their aid an unscrupulous loyalist faction. In *money* they were most notably deficient, and here their extravagance accentuated the effects of inflation, and the problem was compounded by their abysmal relations with Parliament. Moreover, the need to sell more and more crown lands, dispose of more and more local privileges, in order to balance income and expenditure, contributed to the steady decay of the demesne, and the erosion of the power base necessary to mount a *coup d'état*. The ever-mounting crown debt undermined their credit, making it difficult to borrow more money except at enhanced rates of interest, and here the narrow, housewifely traditions of Elizabeth militated against them. One of the mysteries of the seventeenth century is why the Stuarts never followed the obvious precedents set by the kings of France and Spain, and simply repudiated their debts. As it was, they waited for Charles II to take the first tentative step in this direction, with the Stop of the Exchequer in 1672. Above all, the Stuarts lacked *arms*. The Tudors had neglected to form a standing army, and by 1603 it was too late; in fact, the slender and sickly military traditions of the sixteenth century were further eroded by the pacifist policy of James I. There was no lack of English military volunteers in the armies of the continental nations, but even after they returned they remained curiously detached from English life; arguably the most influential of these professionals, and certainly the most famous, was a Yorkshire recruit to the army of the Archdukes in Flanders, Guy Fawkes. A century of internal peace had its technical drawbacks, too. In 1630 the Venetian envoy remarked that the government had considered imposing an excise, but 'the king has not the support he would require in an open country without fortresses, exposed to the fury of a very fierce people'. Finally, the Stuarts obviously lacked *fortune*, in the sense of good luck.

For all these reasons, Stuart absolutism was a plan which stayed on the drawing-board. But this does not mean to say that it was unreal or visionary. What is unreal is the belief that the political struggles of the seventeenth century revolved around nineteenth-century notions like personal liberty, freedom of speech or constitutional government, or that they were concerned at all with abstractions like sovereignty, which existed only in the minds of advanced philosophers like Thomas Hobbes. The issue was one of power, of physical authority, the ability to command men's obedience, and though both sides exercised considerable restraint, and tried to discuss issues in a civilized and constructive way – indeed, they had no choice, because neither could call on great resources – brute force was always latent in the situation.

Nor – it is important to realize – was this aggression all on one side. The level of violence in ordinary Elizabethan and Jacobean society was shocking. As Stone reminds us, 'The behaviour of the propertied classes, like that of the poor, was characterized by the ferocity, childishness and lack of self control of the Homeric age.' Stone attributes this to chronic dyspepsia, occasioned by an unbalanced diet, but to the psychologist it is evidence of 'the emergence of a new psycho-social climate leading to the formation of a new type of personality', and the Elizabethans' intense concern with what we would call 'the ultimate meaning of life' betrayed a need to find a new and stable frame of reference for their behaviour. Before we laugh at such theorizing, we should remember the literature of the time. Shakespeare's tragedies, and particularly *Hamlet*, deal with the sick mind, and they fail to resolve its problems. The monarchs in his history plays, with the exception of Henry V (and even he had severe teenage problems), are disorientated and drifting, their personalities fragmented. With the advent of Webster and Tourneur, the sickness turned inward, as their world turned inward: 'the earlier balance of court and country, civilization and nature, art and feeling begin to break up', and the scene narrows to the Italian ducal palace, 'whose corridors lead man to the extremes of his own being where he finds and loses himself in murder, madness, dream, violent sexuality, terror, death, torture and mirrors of his own self'. This neurosis was not confined to the drama; neither the poems nor the sermons of John Donne can be read with any comfort by the sensitive, and Chapman summed up the Jacobean view of the world in the words:

> A heap it is of undigested villainy,
> Virtue in labour with eternal chaos.

'Virtue in labour with eternal chaos' is an apt motto for the early seventeenth-century House of Commons. Even historians who would reject the appellation 'Whig' with horror, treat Parliament's excesses with the fond indulgence of a psychotherapist towards a schizoid juvenile delinquent. James I and Charles I had no doubt of what they were up against. James found the Parliament of 1621 full of 'fiery and popular spirits', 'ill-tempered spirits', 'evil-affected and discontented persons'. Charles was more specific: 'passionate brains', he called his opponents in 1629, 'empirics and artists', 'distempered persons', full of 'boldness and insolency of speech'. He used the word 'distemper' three times in one proclamation, and its unequivocal meaning was 'insanity'.

Sir John Eliot's excesses in 1629, which so provoked King Charles, are well known. Yet every parliament in this period, without exception, was swept from time to time by dizzying changes of mood and outbursts of violent emotion, against the King, against the Church, against its own members, or against fictional or semi-fictional bogey-men such as 'undertakers', 'monopolists', 'papists' or 'Arminians'. The Addled Parliament of 1614 was the nadir, and no unbiased observer can regard its conduct as anything but childish, hysterical and downright vicious; but in the next parliament, in 1621, the Commons again flew without warning into what even Gardiner calls 'a whirlwind of passion' over a miserable old Catholic, Floyd, who had uttered a very mild slander against the King's daughter, the Electress Palatine. Member after member leaped to his feet and yelled that Floyd should be pilloried (twice), whipped at the cart's tail (twice), have a hole burnt through his tongue, have his nose lopped off, then his ears. Reason eventually prevailed, but it was a very modified reason; Floyd was still pilloried three times, paraded bareback on a horse facing backwards, and fined £1,000, which he could never pay.

But the most frightening thing was the total absence of any sense of humour. In the same session (in 1621) a young lawyer from Lincoln's Inn made a 'malapert' speech against a Bill for the better observance of the Sabbath; he pointed out that the 'Sabbath' was not Sunday but Saturday, and that even then King David danced before the Ark of the Lord. The House took this with awful seriousness. An adjournment gave them the chance to calm down, but they still expelled young Mr Shepherd, and John Pym, who ought surely to have known better, ponderously observed: 'The peace of this kingdom consists in the peace of this House.'

This instability reached a climax in 1641, and during the debate on the Grand Remonstrance Members of Parliament 'took their swords in their scabbards out of their belts and held them by their pommels in their hands'. One of them, Sir Philip Warwick, 'thought we had all sat in the valley of death, for we, like Joab's and Abner's young men, had catched at each other's locks, and sheathed our swords in each other's bowels'. Contemporary foreigners clearly regarded the English as an exceptionally excitable and bloodthirsty race – an opinion confirmed by the treatment they meted out to Charles I. Typical were the words of one Dutchman, who admitted that the English were 'bold, courageous, ardent and cruel in war', but added that they were also 'very inconstant, rash, vainglorious, light and deceiving'. No interpretation of the early seventeenth century is complete which does not take account of such facts, nor of the fact that James I and Charles I were both foreigners, that James did not see England until he was thirty-seven, and Charles was raised in a protected environment until the age of nineteen or twenty. It is a truism that they did not understand the English; it is not always acknowledged that their subjects took some understanding.

47

# JAMES I AND PEACE, 1603–18

A great deal has been written about King James I, without any conclusive elucidation of his character, which was complex, extensive and shallow.

His advent was welcome. Queen Elizabeth had long outlived men's affection, if not their fear and respect, and after fifty years of petticoat government (since Mary I's accession in 1553), they welcomed a male ruler, and the end of female tantrums, sulks and irrationality. James was a highly intelligent man who had found time in the hurly-burly of Scottish politics to publish several volumes of quite creditable poetry and biblical exegesis, as well as his more notorious political treatises, the *Basilikon Doron* (1603) and *The Trew Law of Free Monarchies* (1598). The two last were published in England on his accession, and his forthright insistence on the Divine Right of Kings did not at this stage frighten his new subjects as much as it did the Whig historians. They were happy to have a learned and literary ruler. More to the point, James had already shown himself a seasoned and eminently successful ruler. Beginning with every possible disadvantage, and without any firmly structured system of government such as existed in England, he had reduced to order a nation which for the past half-century had been one of the most turbulent and undisciplined in Europe. When he succeeded to the English throne at the fairly advanced age of thirty-seven, he was already a man with great achievements behind him, and he knew it.

The fact that he knew it, and often said it, contributed to his undoing. He was over-confident. And though his apprenticeship in Scotland was of obvious value it also had disadvantages, which were perhaps less obvious. He had acquired habits of rule which he found it impossible to break, supposing he ever wanted to; yet they were habits not suited to English conditions. Scottish government was loosely structured and informal, not to say primitive. The unicameral Scots legislature, the 'Estates', was small, dependent and easily managed or bullied; everything really hinged on the King's capacity to handle individuals, whether they were high noblemen or Presbyterian leaders comparable to bishops. In fact, his rule in Scotland was based on a system of aristocratic clientage common enough in Western Europe, but inappropriate to English conditions. In 1621, with his finances at rock bottom, he was still paying annual pensions of £5,000 to the Duke of Lennox and the Earls of Arundel and Montgomery, £4,000 to the Earl of Suffolk (though he had been forced out of the Treasury in 1618, convicted in Star Chamber of rampant peculation and fined), and £3,000 each to Lord Wallingford and the Earls of Salisbury and South-ampton (though Southampton was to lead the opposition in the Lords in the next parliament) – and all this at a time when a total landed income of £3,000 was considered ample to support the dignity of a peer. He had nothing comparable to offer the middle classes, whether in Scotland or England.

James had emerged from his Scots experience a crafty, patient, voluble man, who was almost undefeatable in face-to-face negotiation. He had an early chance to display this skill at the Hampton Court Conference of 1604. He

49

had the boldness to meet Puritan demands for minor church reform by bringing their leaders together with the bishops for a debate under his own chairmanship, and he was triumphantly successful. He took the sting out of the Church Question, he pacified the reformers if he did not satisfy them, and at the same time he cracked the whip over the bishops, who were made to put their own house in order by the Canons of 1604, and were notified that they now had a master prepared to interest himself in the minutiae of church discipline, worship and administration, and to approach matters of religion with a much more open mind than Elizabeth's.

However, his tactic of buying time by promising all things to all men misfired badly with the Roman Catholics, who deluded themselves into believing the King's vague and expansive promises of toleration, and were disillusioned when he bowed to pressure from his ministers and Parliament for persecution. The result was the Gunpowder Plot of 1605. With regard to Parliament, his failure was obvious, and almost inevitable. He could not delegate management, and was frustrated by a body which was too large for him to negotiate with face to face, and which he could not even personally approach, except through the medium of public speeches.

Undoubtedly too much has been made of his public persona, his undistinguished and faintly vacuous features, straggling reddish hair, small nose, watery eyes; his weak, spindly legs, his Scots accent, his dribbling mouth, his obvious homosexuality. Not more than one out of a thousand Englishmen ever saw him. His son Charles I was handsome, dignified and chaste, but much good it did him. Nevertheless, James was not the king men were looking for in the early seventeenth century. He was lazy, never realizing that the wealthier the kingdom the more complex it was, and the more time was required to govern it. He spent far too much time reading and talking instead of doing; he had no time for the day-to-day chores of government – he even retreated to Royston or Newmarket at the height of the parliamentary session. He remained a foreigner – being Scots, he just might as well have been a German, or a Portuguese – and a foreign king polarized the already existing tension between 'Court' and 'Country'. Naturally, he brought with him many Scotsmen, and naturally he favoured them; this is how he was able to control that ungovernable country from afar. But the patronage, perquisites and gifts lavished on Scotsmen, however much their amount was exaggerated, still represented a diminution of favour to Englishmen. Since he had not grown up in England, it was difficult for him to establish firm social links with the upper classes, and this was accentuated by his lack of mobility; apart from his journeys to and from Scotland in 1603 and 1617, he rarely strayed outside Hertfordshire and Suffolk.

This produced a sharp division between those who knew him and those who did not. Those who knew him found his laziness, his inattention to business and his sheer incompetence trying. Most of his ministers would have liked a less intelligent, more active man like his son Prince Henry, whose death in 1612 was to many Englishmen the real beginning of disillusion. James was an old man who dreamed dreams. Some of his dreams – the toleration of Roman Catholics, the union of the kingdoms, the plantation of Ulster – have appealed to posterity as statesmanlike and enlightened, but to contemporaries they seemed treacherous. His love of compromise was jarring in a world of violent extremes, and his motto, 'Blessed are the peacemakers', was inappropriate to a nation which had been in a state of emergency for half a century, and to an era in which the potentiality of military command was still one of the most important attributes of a ruler. One of his contemporaries said of him that 'he loved not a soldier, nor any fighting man', and the remark was not intended as a compliment.

Those who knew him only at a distance, or not at all, found him menacing. A king might be expected to push the royal prerogatives further than a queen regnant, whose main aim must be survival. James's record in Scotland was at once a guarantee, but at the same time a threat, and his published writings on authoritarian, divine monarchy constituted a programme. We are so accustomed to regard James I as a ninny, we are so conscious of his ultimate failure, that we tend to discount him. At the time he was regarded with profound suspicion, and as the House of Commons tersely put it, in 1604, 'The prerogatives of princes may easily, and do daily grow; the privileges of the subject are for the most part at an everlasting stand.' The Commons' attitude towards the King's cherished union with Scotland is significant. Here was no desire that England should absorb Scotland, rather a fear lest Scotland absorb England – a tribute to their confidence in the ability of an anointed ruler to overcome economic and demographic fact. They even refused to allow him the title 'King of Great Britain', though he assumed it none the less.

James's first decision was perhaps the most important, though the least noticed. It is accepted as inevitable that he should appoint as his chief minister (Secretary of State and Master of the Court of Wards) Elizabeth's chief minister, Sir Robert Cecil. Cecil had corresponded with him latterly, and may be said to have eased his accession, but gratitude is not exacted from princes, though it may be expected. A much more natural choice would have been one of the Howard cousins, Lord Henry Howard and Lord Howard de Walden, newly created Earls of Northampton and Suffolk respectively, who were descended from Thomas Howard, Duke of Norfolk, executed in 1572 for plotting on behalf of Mary Queen of Scots. (Though he had not attempted to succour her in life, James was deeply solicitous of his mother in death, and had her body transferred from Peterborough to Westminster Abbey.) The Howards were crypto-Catholics, much more likely than Cecil to pander to his project for a grand rapprochement with Spain. Nevertheless, Cecil, made Lord Cecil in 1603, Earl of Salisbury 1605, enjoyed a monopoly of power such as Elizabeth never allowed him, shared only with his friend Thomas Sackville, Earl of Dorset, whom he succeeded as Lord Treasurer on his death in 1608.

Whatever one's view of Salisbury's competence – and after his death in 1612, James, for one, was very free with his criticism – his paramount authority bred complacency in his friends and frustration in his opponents. The Cecilian appetite for dominance led to the disgrace of Sir Walter Raleigh in the first months of the reign; a mysterious episode which was to have unforeseen implications. Salisbury's lack of self-confidence made him unable to brook even the least likely rival, still less train his successor; on his death, chaos supervened in the scramble for power. For the time being his survival meant that the tone of government remained firmly Elizabethan, and it was the same with the Church; Richard Bancroft, who succeeded Whitgift at Canterbury in 1604 and lived until 1611, was a man of the last reign; so, obviously, was Lord Chancellor Ellesmere, who was appointed in 1596 and lived until 1617, when he was succeeded by Bacon, another Elizabethan whose thinking had not shifted since the great Queen's death. (Bacon's successor in 1621, the pragmatic, talkative

53

and worldly-wise Bishop of Lincoln, John Williams, was in complete contrast; in fact, of all James I's servants he is the one who most resembles his master.)

The Crown's most pressing problem in 1603 was one of finance; not only did it lack the means to take the initiative, it was questionable whether the new monarch would be able to maintain the standard of living appropriate to an anointed king. The cost of the Spanish war had forced Elizabeth to sell off a considerable part of the Crown lands, reducing her income from about £150,000 to about £110,000 in fifteen years, and the real value of this income was being constantly eroded by inflation. When James came to the throne he found a debt of nearly £430,000, and as a married man with three children, each entitled to their own household and household staff, his legitimate expenses would far exceed those of the spinster Elizabeth. Parliament had granted four subsidies in 1601, which would continue to be collected into 1605; since the war was now ending, it could not be asked to give more, and the question was not even raised in the session of 1604.

Salisbury was a true Elizabethan, and his only remedy was strict accounting and unbending economy. Unfortunately, the monarch was not of his mind – or, if he was of his mind, he was not of his temper. James was an open-hearted and extravagant man, and his training in financial matters was notably deficient. In Scotland his minuscule income (£58,771 in 1599, and only £39,759 of that collected) had for the most part come before him physically and had been disbursed in the same way; credit was virtually unknown. His fiscal operations were not so much feudal as neolithic. He always had difficulty in visualizing money in the abstract, and one of his new subjects was quick to note that, 'He was very liberal with what he had not in his own grip, and would rather part

54

with £100 he never had in his keeping than one twenty-shilling piece within his own custody.' Add to this the fact that he was pre-eminently a man who liked to be liked, who liked giving, and it is not surprising that by 1608 the Crown debt stood at £597,337, and expenditure exceeded income by £80,000 a year. Much of this was sheer extravagance; up to August 1607 his outright gifts to courtiers amounted to nearly £100,000; in one year (1604) he spent £47,000 on jewels alone, and in 1608 over £30,000; as early as 1605, his giddy, spendthrift queen, Anne of Denmark, had accumulated a debt of £40,500, mainly on personal items like clothes.

The elaborate masques of Inigo Jones, which were a feature of the reign, could not be ignored by the public – in fact, their function was to be noticed; as was the lavish scale of Court entertainment, reaching new heights in 1604 for the Spanish peace delegation, and in 1606 for the state visit of James's brother-in-law, the King of Denmark. His courtiers, gladly throwing off the restrictions imposed by Elizabeth, emulated his example; they built houses, it was said, 'like Nebuchadnezzar's', they threw away fortunes on gambling, on such vulgar displays as the 'double supper' or at the tilts. One of his chaplains later wrote:

> To what an immense riches in his time did the merchandise of England rise to above former ages! What buildings! What sumptuousness! What feastings! What gorgeous attire! What massy plate and jewels! What prodigal marriage portions were grown in fashion among the nobility and gentry, as if the skies had rained plenty.

To a certain degree this was acceptable; the King's prestige was the nation's prestige, and the nation could not afford to seem a pauper. On the other hand, there was a growing body of opinion, puritan in tone if not 'Puritan' in religion, which argued that if kings were indeed God's vice-gerents they should model their lives on His, and keep in mind the Christian virtues of abstemiousness, sobriety and charity. Moreover, though it was accepted that great ministers of state must be suitably rewarded – thus the great and manifest wealth accumulated by Lord Salisbury caused very little murmuring – too many of James's courtiers were handsomely rewarded without offering any apparent service in return. The most notorious example was his Scots favourite James Hay, whose motto was, 'Spend and God will send'. Clarendon calculates that Hay received more than £400,000 from the Crown (at least £4 million in modern currency), 'but on his death he left not a house or acre of land to be remembered by'. So there was never very much likelihood that James would be treated by Parliament with the same generosity as Elizabeth, especially since he needed larger sums than she did without the excuse of a war emergency. Even in 1604 his prospects were not good; the subsidies voted in 1601 were still coming in, and if the economy was not as unhealthy as some Members of Parliament thought, it is their opinion which counts not ours.

As it was, James's first encounter with Parliament was a disaster. However, this is a matter we must get into proportion. The problem of parliamentary 'management' assumed increasing importance as the century progressed, and it has loomed large in the minds of historians, who, since they are most of them teachers as well, have tended to allot 'marks' to rulers for their conduct of Parliament in a distinctly pedagogic way: six out of twenty to James I, sixteen to Queen Elizabeth, minus two to Charles I, and so on. But this assumes that the top mark of twenty was attainable, and this is, in fact, difficult to demonstrate. It was not only the first two Stuarts who failed to manage Parliament competently; so did Oliver Cromwell in the 1650s, and so did Charles II. It was a problem which largely defeated William III and Anne, despite the much greater patronage resources at their disposal. Elizabeth's management of Parliament has probably been over-praised; it was certainly a hazardous exercise in acrobatics, and almost certainly she did not always achieve her aims – though it is difficult always to be sure what those aims were. We now know that even the aggressive and auto-cratic Henry VIII had his difficulties.

James himself was theoretically well adapted to Elizabeth's role; he told Parliament in 1624, 'A skilful horseman doth not always use the spur, but must some-times use the bridle and sometimes the spur. So a king that governs evenly is not bound to carry a rigorous hand over his subjects upon all occasions, but may sometimes slacken the bridle, yet so as his hands be not off the reins.' The theory was unexceptionable, but the practice was not so simple. He was denied the personal contact he wanted, and was good at, and instead he bored the Commons with long, didactic speeches. He lacked the concentration, the minute attention to detail, which was the foundation of Elizabeth's techniques, and there is no doubt, as he him-self said later, that he was misled by the ministers he had inherited, particularly Salisbury.

For a start, there was no obvious reason why Parliament should be summoned at all in 1604. There was no immediate grant of taxation to be expected; and Salisbury's hope that they might make a spontaneous 'gift' was unrealistic. Their opinion on peace with Spain was not solicited, and the Act confirming James's accession was not an urgent political necessity, as was the similar Act of 1485 confirm-ing Henry VII's accession; the rival candidates had fallen away. Parliament was left with a proclamation of summons which invited them to redress 'abuses . . . either in consti-tution or administration' of the law, which, it could be argued, led straight to the 'Form of Apology and Satis-faction'.

Problems of control were intensified by James's decision to promote Elizabeth's leading ministers to the Lords, and by Salisbury's failure, once in the Lords himself, to ensure adequate government representation in the Commons. He was unreasonably suspicious of the brilliant Francis Bacon; he denied him a seat on the Privy Council while he lived, and blocked his appointment as Solicitor-General until 1607. A belated attempt to seat the Chancellor of the Duchy of Lancaster, Sir John Fortescue, as member for Buckinghamshire by voiding the election of his opponent, Sir Francis Goodwin, led to a furious dispute which clouded the relations between government and Commons from the beginning.

In this instance the government had a very strong case, and if it was never coherently put, Salisbury and Lord Chancellor Ellesmere must bear the blame. James's proclamation of summons had barred outlaws, but this merely repeated similar prohibitions by Elizabeth; and Goodwin was undoubtedly an outlaw, though only in a technical sense. More to the point, Chancery had moni-tored election returns time out of mind, though it had not voided a return for fifty years, and the Commons' claim to the contrary was palpably false. But these points were never properly put; and instead James's sudden and intemperate intervention, denying the Commons' right even to discuss the matter, transferred the issue from a specific legal point to one of general constitutional import. This was to prove a recurrent pattern, as was James's eventual climb-down after a display of unnecessary force; for the final compromise, by which both candidates resigned, was a defeat for the government, because the Commons did not particularly want Goodwin, whereas the government badly wanted Fortescue. Moreover, the Commons had now established their sole right to scrutinize returns, and they used it thereafter to award representation to boroughs which had enjoyed the right at any time since 1265, never mind how long it had been allowed to lapse. As a result they added 'new' boroughs, while the Crown neglected its own powers, used often by Elizabeth, to create genuine new parliamentary boroughs by letters patent. (When Charles II tried to revive the practice he found that he had left it too late.)

James's apparent aggression in the Buckinghamshire Election Case confirmed members' worst fears, and they lectured him on his rights and theirs in 'A Form of Apology and Satisfaction', a document drawn up at the end of the session but never presented; it is not even clear that it passed the House. It was once seen as a milestone along the road to Revolution, but no one today would attach that degree of importance or forward significance to any document prior to the Grand Remonstrance of 1641. But it is not always recognized that its main purpose was financial, and it was concerned with the reduction of the King's feudal rights as lord of land. It developed from a petition on wardship, the right of the King to take into custody estates whose heirs were ineffectual, being either minors, widows or lunatics; and the further right of 'marriage', which allowed him to arrange their marriages where appropriate. It also called for the abolition of 'respite of homage', a fine levied on all heirs succeeding to their estates, and 'distraint of knighthood', which obliged men owning land worth more than £40 to assume this honour. The King's right to levy food and transport for the Court at advantageous prices, largely commuted to a general tax on all counties, and known as 'purveyance', also came in for strong criticism. The Apology also asked that the limit of legal memory be brought forward from 1189 to 1553, so as to prevent the vexatious investigation of long-forgotten debts to the Crown, and that established 'assarts' (encroachments by landowners on the royal forests) be legalized. Above all, members wanted a relaxation of the rule that the King's agents could in no circumstances be prosecuted at law.

This may seem small beer compared with such grand conceptions as personal liberty and freedom of speech. But a parliament of landowners gave more attention to such things than is always appreciated, and opposition to the King's rights as lord of land was growing as a desperate Treasury struggled to maximize the permanent income of the Crown. It was an important, sometimes a central issue in the sessions of 1604, 1607 and 1610, and in the parliaments of 1614, 1621 and 1624, and it long outlived the better-known issue of Impositions, first raised in 1607.

In addition, there were wrangles over church reform, James's proposals for the union of the two kingdoms met with a chilly reception, and there was bad temper on both sides over small incidents – as when most of the Commons were prevented from hearing the King's opening speech by an over-officious guard. When he prorogued them in July, he lectured them on their conduct and gave a clear enough warning of reprisals: 'The parliament not sitting; the liberties are not sitting; my justice shall sit always in the same seat. Justice I will give to all, and favour to such as deserve it . . ., in cases of equity, if I should show favour, except there be obedience, I were no wise man.' They were pursued down to the shires by two inauspicious documents, a proclamation dated 16 July 'enjoining conformity to the form of the service of God now established', and writs under the privy seal for a forced loan. This was a practice well established under Elizabeth, but far from popular, especially since latterly hers had not been repaid. It brought in £112,000, but the Lord Treasurer kept a list of those who refused, with an ominous note against many names, 'to be sent for'. It is eloquent of the strained atmosphere that a group of Northamptonshire gentlemen who petitioned the following winter against the removal of Puritan ministers were in fact 'sent for', and accused of treason.

In fact, the new king's handling of the religious question was fair and sensible, and his conduct of the Hampton Court Conference has been made to appear clownish by undue emphasis on one or two remarks taken out of context. Long experience with the Presbyterian Church of Scotland had made him a virtuoso in theological debate, and, as we have seen, he was at his best in face-to-face bargaining. He was a good chairman, and for the most part his demeanour was 'most grave and princely' and his contributions to the debate 'pithy and sweet'. He ordered new Canons to regulate church ceremonial and administration, as well as a new translation of the Bible: the Authorized Version of 1611, which was to prove the glory of his reign. His refusal to countenance the moderate reforms demanded by the 'Puritans', and his decision to enforce conformity on the clergy, were justified in the event. Very few ministers chose to suffer deprivation – not more than a hundred, perhaps as few as sixty, and none of them of much repute – and in 1605 conformity was extended to university graduands, thus striking at the root of the matter. The decision excited a storm of protest from a group of Puritan gentry in Parliament, and grumbling continued in 1606 and 1607, reaching a climax with the

Commons' Petition on Religion in 1610. But after that it died away until 1628, and those who see the rise of Puritanism as a continuous process gain scant comfort from James I's reign. On the other hand, James made it clear to the bishops that they must put their own house in order; they must eliminate the holding of livings in plurality and discountenance incompetent and uneducated ministers. In fact, the expansion of the universities, encouraged by Archbishops Whitgift and Bancroft, ensured a steady supply – in fact, an over-supply – of graduates in holy orders. The Church, which had suffered under the unscrupulous management of the great Queen, began in King James's reign to pull itself together. Under his son it was ready to take the offensive.

His handling of the Catholic problem was, in contrast, inept. His own genuine desire for toleration, and for a *détente* between the Catholic and Protestant powers, which was encouraged by the Howards, was offset by Salisbury's determination to achieve absolute security and by his own fear of assassination, for which the Catholics had been notorious since William the Silent's death in 1584. The result was a stop-go policy on the enforcement of the penal laws which enraged the Catholic ultras and brought on their plot for the mass destruction of the King, the council and House of Lords by gunpowder on 5 November 1605. The serpentine manoeuvrings of Salisbury in an attempt to implicate the Society of Jesus in this endeavour have roused suspicions – particularly in some Catholic apologists whose approach to the evidence is somewhat mystical – that the whole affair was a government fabrication. This is to attribute to seventeenth-century governments a degree of sophistication, competence and authority only attainable (and that rarely) by omnicompetent modern agencies like the K.G.B. and the C.I.A., but the long-term motives of the lay conspirators are admittedly somewhat obscure. Their leaders had already been implicated in the very Protestant rising of the Earl of Essex in 1601, and some historians see them not as religious fanatics at all, but gentry poor whites, or 'hobereaux', who found in Catholic activism a rationalization of their economic and social grievances; 'Robin Hoods', Salisbury called them, with a flick of contempt.

The whole wretched affair weakened the long-term prospects of Catholicism; the annual church service commemorating it continued well into Queen Victoria's reign, and it was still being thrown in the faces of the English Catholics under Edward VII. But in the short term the repercussions were surprisingly mild; Parliament put another two penal laws on the statute book in 1606, and a third in 1610, but they were no easier to enforce than the existing mass of legislation they were intended to supplement. Nor did James abandon his aim of toleration; in fact, fear may have spurred on his efforts. He drafted a new oath of allegiance in 1606 which he expected that Catholics would be allowed to take, though his efforts were frustrated by the obstinacy of successive Popes. Even then, once parliamentary pressure was removed after 1610, persecution died down, a tendency encouraged by James's long-drawn-out negotiations with Madrid. The number of Catholics executed in these years is suggestive: between 1607 and 1610, eight; 1611–18, nine; 1619–25, none.

Temporarily the plot also worked to James's political advantage. Faced with the fact that they had nearly lost him altogether, as well as his promising son Henry, Prince of Wales, the Commons in 1606 took a kinder view of his failings. They were not pleased to find that the annual deficit was now £52,000, nor that the debt was £550,000 (inflated by Salisbury, in fact, to £735,000, an act of doubtful wisdom), but they voted three subsidies and three fifteenths, which would bring in £390,000 over three years. However, when they were recalled the following winter (1606–7) for a third session, which was arguably unnecessary, and certainly unnecessarily long, the situation deteriorated again. To James's great displeasure they finally rejected his proposal for union with Scotland, and they took the opportunity to launch a strong attack on purveyance and to criticize the King's new import duties, or 'impositions'. It is now apparent that Salisbury had virtually abandoned the direct management of the Commons, and was trying to direct Parliament as a whole by the use of conferences between the two Houses. But this was a slow and clumsy device, and in this session and the next it began to prove counter-productive. The Commons proved increasingly reluctant to allow their delegations to these conferences any freedom of manoeuvre, and in the meanwhile, left very much to themselves (during most of the 1606–7 session there was only one privy councillor in the House), they fell into bad ways. It is no accident that 1606 sees the first appearance of the Committee of the Whole House, a fiction which allowed them to dethrone the Speaker, still a crown official, and indulge in free-ranging, informal discussion. Nor, in general, was Salisbury's position so robust. The Earl of Dorset's death, though it gave Salisbury the Treasury, removed an entirely reliable ally, and it made way for the appointment of Henry Howard, Earl of Northampton, as Lord Privy Seal. Criticism was heard in high places, Northampton was emerging as a possible replacement and had already taken under his wing the unsophisticated new favourite the King had picked up the year before, the Scotsman Sir Robert Ker.

A thorough assessment of the Treasury's resources now convinced Salisbury that the only solution was to drive a bargain with Parliament for a permanent income. This had best be postponed until the current subsidies had all been collected, at the end of 1609, and in the meanwhile the customary rights of the Crown, in wardship, marriage and the administration of the land law in general, were pressed with renewed vigour; new investigating commissions uncovered old debts, concealed assarts and entails, and unauthorized enclosures of common land, and Salisbury boasted of imposing fines of £730 in a day for enclosures, and £300 the next. The more money he had in hand the better, and it was as well that the Commons should be reminded that the Crown still had privileges it was worth buying out. However, it is doubtful if James could afford to give up his right to impose taxes on trade, which had recently been extended beyond the ancient customs on wine and wool. In 1606 a merchant called Thomas Bate appealed against an import duty on currants imposed by Elizabeth. The Court of Exchequer not only dismissed the appeal, but laid it down that the King was the supreme economic comptroller of the nation, with the power to regulate trade by the imposition of whatever duties he saw fit. Though Parliament grumbled prodigiously in 1607, the generality of merchants did not, and in 1608 Salisbury issued a new Book of Rates, extending the scope of the new duties, or 'impositions'.

So, when he met Parliament again in February 1610, he had increased his bargaining power, and he had also reduced the King's debt to £280,000 (nearly half of which was in respect of forced loans from the previous reign, and need not be taken too seriously). To him it seemed the time was ripe to put forward his radical scheme for a 'Great Contract', by which Parliament would vote the monarchy a regular income of £200,000 a year in perpetuity in return for the abandonment of its rights of wardship, marriage and purveyance.

Unfortunately, Parliament was not ready for such a scheme, and neither was the King. The financial pressure of the Treasury over the previous two years had irritated the Commons, who were already irritated enough, and Salisbury's tactics in recalling this crabbed and disputatious Parliament, which in 1607 had shown ominous signs of cohesion in opposition, are questionable. Nor were they usual. None of Elizabeth's last six parliaments had sat for more than six months in all, some for much less, and none of them for more than two sessions. In 1614 and 1621 James himself speedily cashiered recalcitrant parliaments, and his example was followed by his son in 1625, 1626, 1629 and 1640. The result in 1610 could have been foreseen; a seasoned House of Commons got the bit between its teeth from the beginning. It took up all the old financial grievances from previous sessions, great and small, and put them into a Petition of Grievances submitted at the end of the session, in July. It revived all the old criticisms of the existing church settlement, and embodied these in a further petition. It welcomed the principle of the Great Contract, but it was unable to conceive how the necessary money could be raised by taxation; at the same time it demanded further concessions in return, particularly the abandonment of impositions, which were denounced as unconstitutional. For the first time it voiced its apprehension, real or feigned, at James's theories of monarchy, and made him suppress a new textbook of civil law, Cowell's *Interpreter*, which awarded the King an independent legislative power. Several members, in fact, doubted the wisdom of granting the King a revenue which would make him independent of Parliament.

On his side, James doubted from the beginning the wisdom and propriety of bargaining with Parliament in this way, and in the event he was more than justified. He could not help but associate the new willingness of the Commons to criticize his concept of monarchy with Salisbury's willingness to dispose of specific elements of the royal prerogative. On the general point, he was willing to make substantial concessions, and in an important speech on 21 March 1610, which has been persistently misunderstood, he admitted that the absolute power of kings applied only in primitive or uncivilized societies, and in an advanced political society like England it was regulated by the laws, and even by implied contract, or 'paction', with the people – words which were to be used by the Whigs to justify the Revolution of 1688. Nor need his sincerity be doubted; after all, the full title of his most famous book is, *The Trew Law of Free Monarchies, or the Reciprock and Mutuall Dutie betwixt a Free King and his Naturall Subjects.* Nevertheless, he was not prepared to allow the Commons to debate his right to levy impositions. Unfortunately – or perhaps fortunately – he climbed down, probably on Salisbury's advice, and after an exhausting debate stretching from 23 June to 2 July, the House decided that impositions were taxes, and that taxes could only be imposed by the King in Parliament, that is, by statute. It was an affirmation which had no immediate effect.

As it was, by July 'outline' agreement was reached on the Great Contract, but then Salisbury adopted the unusual plan of allowing the members a recess to consult their constituents as to the best means of raising £200,000 a year. As a result they returned in October much less cooperative than before. In the meanwhile James, perhaps dimly aware of the danger of continued inflation, but unable to encompass the notion of taxation on a sliding scale, raised his demands to £500,000 a year. At this stage Salisbury's pet device of managing the Commons by conferences with the Lords – never very robust – cracked completely. The Commons, who had already criticized James's lavish expenditure pretty freely during the previous session, now openly attributed it to his Scots favourites. James, frustrated at his inability to get into personal contact with his subjects, summoned twenty members to meet him at Royston, only to find himself denounced for attempting to exercise his influence in an unconstitutional way. After further mutual acrimonies, they were prorogued early in December, and, despite Salisbury's protests, dissolved in February 1611.

From 1611 to 1621, with only the briefest interval, James ruled without Parliament and substantially without purpose. What general popularity he had once enjoyed had now evaporated, and the country seemed to be drifting. Nostalgic annual celebrations of Queen Elizabeth's birthday, 17 November, had already begun, and James's prestige slumped further with the sudden death of the eighteen-year-old Prince of Wales in 1612. Henry's virtues were much exaggerated, but he was certainly the antithesis to his father, and while he lived much could be forgiven James in the knowledge that his death would bring a new dispensation. Prince Charles, a reserved boy of twelve and little known, was no substitute.

At the same time there was a serious relaxation in executive authority. No paramount minister ever arose to replace Salisbury (for Buckingham, even at the height of his power, was not a 'working' minister), and the rivalry between various contenders made for instability. In fact James did not fill Salisbury's offices when he died in 1612, taking over the direction of government himself instead;

given his disinclination for hard work, this could not last, but there was no obvious alternative. He increasingly took advice from Francis Bacon, but Bacon (Attorney-General, 1613) was a second-rank minister who lacked nerve. The ambitious Henry Howard, Earl of Northampton, and his cousin the Earl of Suffolk, were favoured but not trusted. All the same, James inclined more and more towards their scheme for an alliance with Spain, capped by a marriage treaty, with religious toleration at home and the indefinite postponement of Parliament. Their hopes were dashed in 1613, when James married off his daughter Elizabeth to Frederick V, Elector Palatine, the leading Calvinist prince in Germany, but they rose later in the year with the marriage of Suffolk's daughter to the court favourite Robert Ker, now Earl of Somerset, and the arrival of a new Spanish ambassador, Don Diego Sarmiento de Acuña (later Count Gondomar), who at once established an extraordinarily close friendship with the King.

But no one could solve James's financial problems. His debt was still about half a million, his annual deficit £50,000. A desperate Salisbury had created a new hereditary order of knighthood, the baronetcy, in 1611, and at £1,095 apiece they had produced £90,000; a forced loan in the winter of 1611–12 brought in £116,000 (though this, of course, only added to the existing debt). Another feudal aid, this time for Elizabeth's marriage, was a fiasco, and in 1613 the embargo Salisbury had imposed on the sale of Crown lands was broken. Though Northampton bitterly opposed it, the only answer was another parliament.

But the Addled Parliament of 1614 was a particularly spectacular fiasco. Northampton was not only uncooperative, but did his best to foment trouble. James aroused expectations he was not in the end prepared to

69

satisfy by negotiating some months beforehand with a group of country gentry, led by Sir Henry Neville, for a kind of mini-Great Contract; they would drop the question of impositions and vote more subsidies if he would relax the administration of his rights as a landlord. (This has been viewed with scepticism by a succession of historians from Gardiner downwards, but the attitude of the 1604–10 Commons makes it clear that this was one of the gentry's most pressing grievances.) Unfortunately, as soon as the news leaked out James threw Neville over and appointed as Secretary of State Sir Ralph Winwood, a hispanophobe odious to the Howard family. Also he had never sat in Parliament before. The mischief was compounded when James ordered all his ministers and courtiers to make the best use of their influence and patronage at the elections.

This, plus the new ascendency of Sarmiento and Northampton, and the rumour that James had been negotiating directly with backbenchers, gave the new Commons the idea that they had been packed by government 'undertakers'. Winwood was entirely unable to contain the explosion of fear and rage which followed, which was quite disproportionate to the 'evidence', let alone the true situation. After eight weeks of singularly ugly and fruitless contestation, in which every aspect of royal policy was viciously, intemperately and confusedly attacked, they were dissolved, on 7 June. So abortive had the meeting been that in 1620 the judges were called upon to decide whether the proceedings had constituted a true and legal meeting of Parliament at all.

James was quite rightly furious, and his celebrated remark to Sarmiento afterwards (p. 37 above) cannot be dismissed as senile spleen. Parliament's irresponsibility was underlined by the fact that it was manifestly unable to

secure public support for its grievances, not even impositions – which were, in fact, not so much as mentioned in
the next two parliaments. Would Parliament meet again?
The question was far from unreal. The States-General of
France was dissolved in 1614 and did not meet again until
1789. Fortunately, the only minister with the necessary
resolution and drive for unconstitutional measures,
Northampton, died a few days after the dissolution; his
cousin Suffolk got the Treasury at last, but he was weak
and lazy. A 'benevolence' was ordered in July 1614, which
quickly raised £23,000 in London; but Lord Chief
Justice Coke ruled that it could not be backed by the privy
seal and the provinces responded with little more than
£500. To advisers like Bacon parliaments were an in-
grained habit, and as early as November 1615 the Council
was advising another. This was too much, but the King's
finances were now so weak that tradesmen were beginning
to refuse further credit; in the years 1615–17 he only kept
afloat by getting a small loan from the City of London and
selling back to the Dutch government the 'cautionary
towns' handed over to Elizabeth as a security against their
debt to her. (The debt was £618,000, and James only
received £210,000. On the other hand, the towns cost him
£25,000 a year to administer.)

The Overbury Case, which broke in October 1615, now
dragged his prestige even further down. A belated inquiry
into Sir Thomas Overbury's death in the Tower two years
before revealed that he had been poisoned by hirelings of
Lady Somerset, the Lord Treasurer's daughter, with the
connivance of the royal governor of the fortress. And he
was poisoned because he knew, and threatened to reveal,
that the countess had obtained an annulment of her first
marriage, to the Earl of Essex, by witchcraft and illicit
drugs, and that she had been Somerset's mistress long

71

before their wedding. The King had taken a personal interest in these annulment proceedings, brushing off the doubts of the Archbishop of Canterbury, and had virtually presided over the wedding celebrations. His honour was irremediably damaged, even though Somerset and his countess were tried, found guilty and sentenced to life imprisonment.

But the death of Raleigh, an episode positively cluttered with symbolism and reeking of appeasement, was yet to come. In January 1616, James opened serious negotiations with Madrid for a marriage treaty on his son's behalf, hoping for a fat Spanish dowry as much as anything. But this was a proposition that split the Spanish as well as the English Court, and despite the virtuosity of Sarmiento and the dogged hard work of Sir John Digby at Madrid, negotiations moved slowly. Nor were they helped by James's quixotic decision to release Sir Walter Raleigh to seek gold up the Orinoco river (in modern Venezuela). Raleigh had been in the Tower since 1603, under suspended sentence of death on a trumped-up charge of treason, but he knew as well as anybody else that Spain had now colonized the Orinoco area. Immediate protests from Madrid rose to a crescendo when Raleigh returned in 1618, with no gold, of course, but having sacked a Spanish settlement. James dare not surrender him to the Spanish authorities, nor dare he put him on trial for an offence he himself had countenanced, so he had him executed for his supposed crime of 1603. Unfortunately, Raleigh, who in his hey-day had been the most hated man in England, was now a popular idol: the only surviving symbol of mythic Elizabethan values now increasingly cherished. His uncompleted *History of the World* had an unexpectedly wide appeal, and it was later reputed to be Cromwell's favourite book, the Bible apart. Riots broke out in

London, the Spanish embassy was sacked, but Raleigh went to the scaffold on 29 October 1618 amid scenes of studied and well-publicized pathos. In the crowd around the scaffold, we are told, stood John Eliot, John Pym and Edward Hyde, the future Earl of Clarendon.

The execution of Raleigh seemed the inevitable culmination of tendencies evident since James's accession: a total collapse of dignity, honour and moral values, a truckling to foreigners and Catholics, and above all an aimlessness and lack of purpose. Raleigh's death might have been accepted, in time, if it had led to an immediate treaty with Spain with solid advantages for England – just as the judicial murder of the unlucky Captain Green in 1705 was eventually accepted as the price of Union with Scotland in 1707. As it was, it promoted that dangerous dichotomy between 'Court' and 'Country' which was becoming an evident feature of politics, but had less to do with politics than with moral attitudes. In the words of Lawrence Stone:

> The Country was virtuous, the Court wicked; the Country was thrifty, the Court extravagant; the Country was honest, the Court corrupt; the Country was chaste and heterosexual, the Court promiscuous and homosexual; the Country was sober, the Court drunken; the Country was nationalist, the Court xenophile; the Country was healthy, the Court diseased; the Country was outspoken, the Court sycophantic; the Country was the defender of old ways and liberties, the Court the promoter of administrative novelties and new tyrannical practices; the Country was solidly Protestant, the Court more than half Popish . . .

And so on. It is suggestive that, in October 1614, in the wake of the Addled Parliament, James issued a proclamation ordering the nobility and gentry then in London to depart to their residences in the country; another followed in December 1615, threatening to put offenders out of the commission of the peace in their counties, and yet another in April 1617.

# BUCKINGHAM AND WAR, 1618-29

Only one man emerged unscathed from the chaos and disgrace of James's middle years, and that was George Villiers, his last and greatest favourite. Knighted on his first appearance at Court in 1614, Villiers was strategically placed to succeed the fallen Somerset; in 1616 he was made a viscount, a Knight of the Garter and Master of the Horse. An earldom (of Buckingham) followed in 1617, a marquessate in 1618. James brushed aside envious protests with the celebrated words, 'Jesus Christ did the same, and therefore I cannot be blamed; Christ had his John, and I have my George.'

The nature of the relationship between Buckingham and his master is a matter for speculation. Many things, obviously, suggest that it was homosexual, but they are outweighed by other considerations, and particularly the attitude of Prince Charles, who was at first extremely jealous of the new favourite, but by 1620 had become his firm friend and most loyal supporter. From all we know of the future Charles I it is unthinkable that he should have made a friend of a man who was his father's lover. There is little doubt that some if not all of James's previous relationships with men friends had been homosexual, but Buckingham was that much younger, and James that much older now. He was only just fifty, but he was ill and prematurely old; he may have had the royal disease of porphyria. When he visited Scotland again in 1617 he

announced that it was to see again for the last time the
scenes of his youth; and much as he had neglected his queen,
her death in 1619 snapped another link with the past. He
was lonely; Buckingham was young and lively, and his
extensive family gave the King the kind of domestic society
he needed. He may also have been a son-substitute – a
proper son, not one like Henry or 'Baby' Charles.

But much of this is irrelevant. The enormous hostility
which built up against Buckingham had nothing to do with
his personal relations with the King. Men like Somerset
had enjoyed a similar relationship, without the same unpopularity. The difference was that Somerset never competed for political power whereas Buckingham not only
competed for it but acquired it; by 1620 his hold over the
King was so absolute that he could almost be regarded as
wielding the power of a regent, or deputy king. His control
of patronage was particularly resented, 'in dispensing
whereof', says Clarendon, 'he was guided more by the
rules of appetite than of judgment'/ His family was large
and their needs in proportion. And from those who
enjoyed his patronage, of whatever rank, he demanded a
slavish submission and obedience profoundly alien to
English contemporary thinking. He was a man of over-
mastering charm, but he was also a man of aggression and
violence (as his foreign policy showed), and his anger with
those who opposed him or even disagreed with him was
unassuageable.] With reason he was called 'The English
Alcibiades'

Such men do not attract first-class historians, and he
has not received his full due. Certainly his influence in the
field of government policy was at first entirely beneficial.
He appreciated his own ignorance, and was willing to take
the best advice; from Francis Bacon and from Lionel
Cranfield, Surveyor-General of the Customs, whom he

insisted on appointing as a 'trouble-shooter' to investigate government expenditure. The result was startling. Cranfield, backed to the hilt by the young Buckingham, forced Lord Treasurer Suffolk to resign, followed by the Lord High Admiral, the Earl of Nottingham (better known as the Armada veteran Lord Howard of Effingham); Suffolk was put on trial for gross peculation. Buckingham himself took over the Admiralty, and Cranfield edged Viscount Hay, one of James's oldest personal friends, out of the key household post of Master of the Wardrobe. The result was a dramatic fall in expenditure, and a sharp rise in government income following the appointment of a muck-raking treasury commission headed by George Abbott, Archbishop of Canterbury. Cranfield negotiated a new and much more profitable farm of the customs duties in 1619, and took over the Mastership of the Court of Wards. It was a more intelligent application of Salisbury's technique as Lord Treasurer, 1608–12. The death of Queen Anne led to great savings (even if her embalmed corpse did have to lie in state for ten weeks while the Treasury hunted out enough money to bury her), and in 1620, for the first time in the reign, government income matched expenditure.

It was, of course, a qualified triumph. The Crown still had a substantial debt, now £900,000. Cranfield's economies alienated James's courtiers at a time when he could look for little support from anyone else. The economic crisis and the war emergency in Europe (of which more later) were beginning to bite, and some of Buckingham's economic devices alienated large sections of the community, not just the comparatively narrow circle of the Court. The sale of honours is a notable example. James I had always been lavish in his award of honours, compared with Elizabeth, and by 1620 he was selling them on a large scale. Knighthoods had been sold from way back in 1606, and in the years 1616–20 an unprecedented 563 new knights were dubbed, as against 501 in 1606–16. Worse still, forty-eight English peerages were created between 1603 and 1620, as against eighteen for the whole of Elizabeth's reign; not all of them were sold, but at least twenty-one of them were. Irish peerages were peddled with even less restraint. Baronetcies had always been legitimately sold, but ironically, with the extension of their numbers (the original limit of 100 was soon stretched to 144), their market value fell from £1,095 to as low as £600. This 'inflation of honours' was taken with the greater seriousness because, as we have seen, there was no other objective test of social standing; it was to be one of the chief counts in Buckingham's impeachment in 1626, and an important factor in the 'revolt' of the upper house in 1621. Even more ominous was the use made by Buckingham and his cronies of monopolies, which had provoked a startling and unexpected revolt against Elizabeth in the Parliament of 1601, quelled only by complete surrender. Whether in trade or manufacture (as with the monopolies on gold and silver thread), or in administration (as with the patents for inns and alehouses), monopolies were regarded as economic parasitism, particularly to be deplored during a period of recession. Cranfield warned against them, but his reward was to be by-passed for the Lord Treasureship, which went instead to a docile Buckingham man, Viscount Mandeville, in 1620.

By this time James was deeply involved, much against his will, in Germany. In 1619, Bohemia rejected its Habsburg king-elect, the new Emperor Ferdinand II, and offered the crown to James's son-in-law, the Elector Palatine. Against James's advice Frederick accepted. Ferdinand called in the Spanish Army of Flanders under

Ambrogio Spinola and offered Maximilian of Bavaria the Palatine and the electoral title. The Bavarians duly routed Frederick at the Battle of the White Mountain, outside Prague, in September 1620, and Spinola invaded the Palatinate. James believed he could impose a compromise by diplomatic means, and he may have been right. With the truce with the Dutch about to expire Spain did not want to tie up her best army and her best general in Germany, and the English navy had considerable potential nuisance value, as James reminded Philip III when he dispatched a small fleet to the Mediterranean in September 1620. He also hoped that an alliance with England, and a royal marriage, would bring Spain round even further, and oblige her to bring crucial pressure on Ferdinand, which was within her power. Unfortunately, Frederick could not be brought to realize that the game was lost, and he must accept a compromise which would leave him in an inferior position; nor was Ferdinand any more cooperative. What was seen as Catholic aggression caused a sharp reaction in England, and a demand for intervention in Germany, however unrealistic this might be. (In fact, a token force under Sir Horace Vere was sent to the Palatinate; the beginning of an ineffectual but highly expensive English commitment in Europe which continued until 1628.) Buckingham and Prince Charles, scenting an opportunity for glory, backed the war party, and James was jockeyed into pledging war unless Frederick was restored to the Palatinate by the spring of 1621, than which nothing seemed less likely. Buckingham experimented with another benevolence, this time raising the militia contribution of those who refused, and appointing some of them sheriffs, but despite this pressure it only raised £6,000 in the provinces (as against £28,000 in London). A new parliament was the only answer, and one was summoned for January 1621; but by then England was in the depths of a major economic slump.

This slump was blamed on the King, for his use of monopolies, and more plausibly for his interference with the wool trade. His interference was undoubtedly maladroit, but it was well-intentioned, and not devoid of good economic sense. Woollen cloth was England's staple export, yet it was shipped out in an intermediate state, to be cleaned, dyed and finished in the Netherlands. Alderman Cockayne argued that this was robbing English businessmen of cash profit and English workmen of employment, and he was confident that the Flemish and Dutch refugees who had settled in East Anglia in the previous generation provided a sufficient reservoir of skilled craftmanship. In 1614 he persuaded the King to cancel the Merchant Adventurers' charter and prohibit the export of the unfinished cloth. Unfortunately, the Dutch reacted with an embargo, and in any case, the embryo dyeing and finishing industry could not cope; James reversed his policy in 1617, but in three years the whole industry had been seriously damaged from top to bottom, and it was allowed no time to recover. The outbreak of war in Germany in 1620 and in Flanders in 1621 ravaged the export market, which suffered from the reckless manipulation of their currencies by the North German states, the notorious *kipper-und-wipperzeit*. The recession in the wool market was accompanied by a drastic run on English coin, which was sucked into Northern Europe, while a succession of wet summers and savagely cold winters from 1618 to 1621 forced up the price of food and added to the miseries of the unemployed; wages fell, and so, because of the shortage of coin, did rents. The crisis wrecked the economy of the Cotswolds for good, and caused a ten-year recession in East Anglia.

Few contemporaries could diagnose the trouble correctly, and none could offer a cure. Even Cranfield, equally experienced in commerce and government, put much of the blame on the increased imports of luxury goods to cater for the tastes of the Crown and the nobility. Together with the slump in the export trade, this had caused England to infringe the basic principle by which exports must always exceed imports, so that bullion flowed into the country, not out. Dignified by the term 'mercantilism', this is not something peculiar to the seventeenth century, of course; it is a preoccupation of modern governments. Where the seventeenth century went wrong was in failing to allow for 'invisible exports', in the form of services, and in attaching too much importance to gold and silver as such.

In 1620 the basic cause of the depression was not James's lumbering interference or his extravagance, but an irresistible swing in fashion away from the 'Old Draperies', the heavy, blanket-like woollens which were England's speciality, towards the 'New Draperies', a lighter, more easily tailored and cheaper cloth which had caught on, understandably, in the Mediterranean countries and was now spreading north. The refugee weavers of East Anglia could cope in the long run, but the adjustment took time; a centuries-old industry had to be phased out and its workers reabsorbed into the working population while a new industry was built up in another area. Moreover, the 'New Draperies' called not only for new techniques but for a new, shorter wool, produced by different sheep, or sheep differently reared. The cloth industry remained in a convalescent state for the next twenty years, its recovery punctuated by frequent relapses, in 1625, 1629, 1636 and 1649. An outbreak of bubonic plague, as in 1625, or a quarrel between the King and the merchants, as in 1629 and 1630, was enough to send prices tumbling.

A class of landowning legislators, ill-acquainted with economic theory, or for that matter economic fact, may be forgiven for supposing that the King had blundered horribly, though it was perverse of them to blame the shortage of bullion on the monopoly of gold and silver thread held by Buckingham's brothers. All the same, the new parliament, when it met, was prepared to be co-operative; in many ways, it was anxious to redeem the fiasco of 1614. On his side James made a handsome speech, admitting his past errors and blaming them on Salisbury. Initial proceedings were rather unreal; public opinion undoubtedly demanded armed assistance for Prince Frederick, but it was difficult to see how this could be done; there was no army and only a tiny fleet, and very little money for either. Parliament tacitly endorsed James's resort to diplomacy rather than arms, and in the circumstances the two subsidies they voted him must be considered generous. When it was objected that this would not provide an army for Europe, the opposition spokesman, Sir Edwin Sandys, riposted, 'If we go to the Palatinate, a million will not discharge the army.' The Commons then turned to a four-month investigation of monopolies and other administrative abuses, under the leadership of Sir Edward Coke.

Coke's greatness was acknowledged by all his contemporaries; his posthumous prestige as a jurist was even greater, and his writings were the basis of Anglo-American legal education for the next two centuries. He was also a uniquely difficult man. Sir John Eliot said of him in 1628, 'I cannot think of flattery, but we may here thank him whom posterity will hereafter commend.' His widow remarked in 1634, 'We will never see his like again, thank

God.' His distinguished career as a law officer of the Crown began under Elizabeth and culminated in the Chief Justiceship of Common Pleas in 1606, and of King's Bench in 1613. But his abrasive temperament and his almost religious devotion to the common law soon brought him into conflict with King James.

In Coke's campaign to restrict the activities of the church courts, and particularly High Commission, James's concern was peripheral, and Coke enjoyed the support of most of his colleagues, if only because their income was threatened by High Commission's encroachment on the field of wills and marriage settlements. Here the death of the combative Archbishop Bancroft in 1611 brought a truce. But in his attempt to restrict the King's personal interference with the judiciary – lobbying judges before-hand, consulting them during cases, even (theoretically) taking cases himself – Coke enjoyed no support from his colleagues and had few precedents to back him. The result was a number of personal confrontations with the King which have been overblown by those who wish to see him as a prophet of constitutional liberty. He was, in fact, putting the case for the independency of the judiciary from the executive, and though he was far in advance of his time, his teaching was to have important repercussions on American constitutional thinking. On the other hand, he had no sympathy with encroachment by the legislature on either the executive or the judiciary, and his thinking on impositions, for instance, was entirely orthodox; it may well be because of him that they did not reappear as an issue in the 1620s. In 1616, after a particularly furious quarrel with James over Peacham's Case, he was dismissed, and his passing was not noticeably mourned by his colleagues or by a wider public; to most it was inevitable, if not overdue. But he was not regarded as indelibly disgraced, nor did he think of himself as being in opposition; he was readmitted to the Privy Council in 1617, paid assiduous court to Buckingham, to the extent of marrying his only daughter and heiress to the favourite's half-witted brother, and became a member of the reformist Treasury Commission 1618–20. He sat in 1621 as a government spokesman in the Commons.

Once the myth of Coke, the scourge of the Crown, is swept away, however, it becomes that much more difficult to explain his role in opposition. He may have had a genuine loathing for monopolies, but it is more likely that he recognized that this House of Commons was frenetically excited (p. 46), that it was committed to an attack on impositions, and that it would overreach itself unless he assumed control. As it was, the Commons spent most of its fury on two comparatively minor entrepreneurs, the notorious Sir Francis Mitchell and Sir Giles Mompesson, without directly touching Buckingham, their master, and it would be interesting to know if this was simply a result of their usual lack of exact aim or of Coke's restraining hand. In marked contrast was the conduct of the House of Lords, where the Earl of Southampton led an immediate assault on Buckingham direct, blaming him for the 'inflation of honours' in recent years. When Coke advised the Commons to bring Mitchell and Mompesson to the Lords for judgement, the Lords gladly complied, but from then on the attacks on both Buckingham and monopolies went astray. Attention was diverted from the holders of monopolies to the 'referees' who had authorized them, usually the Lord Chancellor or the Lord Treasurer, who were grudgingly absolved of blame and had indeed taken no direct profit. Lavish promises from James to cancel existing monopolies and scrutinize future applications more carefully averted a threatened Monopolies Bill, and though Buckingham was subject to countless minor humiliations in the Lords, Prince Charles's strong support – it was an unheard-of novelty in itself to have a prince of the blood in Parliament at all – saved him from worse. The opposition were still far from clear precisely what they were attacking and why, or who their leaders were, and their most resplendent success was accidental, arising from a random accusation of corruption against Lord Chancellor Bacon (now, in fact, Viscount St Albans). Whether the charge could have been substantiated or not is difficult to say, but when the case was brought before the Lords, Bacon's nerve broke and he pleaded guilty. He had a powerful enemy in Coke and another in Cranfield, and to a hard-pressed Buckingham he was eminently expendable. Only James tried to cushion his epic fall as best he could.

By now it was mid May, and foreign relations had not been discussed for weeks, but the Commons were preparing two swingeing new laws against Catholics which would not look well in Madrid, and on 3 June James asked them to adjourn into the new year. After some initial hysteria they agreed, but not before their patriotic and Protestant zeal had led them to pass a rash declaration that if the King's diplomacy was unsuccessful, they 'would be ready to adventure the lives and estates of all that belong to us, or wherein we have interest, for the maintenance of the cause of God, and of his Majesty's royal issue'. Unfortunately, James's diplomacy was ineffectual; Maximilian of Bavaria seized the Upper Palatinate, Spain withdrew her army into Flanders, and with it went her coercive influence at Vienna; England must help defend the Lower Palatinate herself or abdicate her already precarious position in the councils of Europe, and Charles and Buckingham pressed James to recall Parliament in November. They had meanwhile put their house in order; since the end of the previous session all existing patents of monopoly had been cancelled or disowned, and the incompetent Lord Treasurer Mandeville, a convenient scapegoat, was forced to resign in favour of Cranfield.

So, when Parliament reassembled in November and was asked to validate the resolution it had passed in June, its bluff was called. It could not stomach the taxation needed for an all-out war, yet a limited commitment in the Rhineland would leave James free to continue his manoeuvres at Madrid. It was strongly suspected that the two subsidies already voted that year were underpinning James's free spending at home, specifically on the new Whitehall Banqueting House, designed by Inigo Jones as a fit setting for the Habsburg nuptials, and now nearing completion. After a long debate they voted one further subsidy, and in return demanded the enforcement of the penal laws against Catholics, who were increasingly becoming a pawn in foreign policy. The suggestion that they include in the petition a request that James break off relations with Spain unless she would bring effective pressure to bear on the Emperor, originated with Buckingham and was probably intended to bring this dangerous parliament to an end.

The manoeuvre certainly succeeded. James refused even to receive the petition, lest he should appear – even if he subsequently rejected it – to allow the Commons a right to advise him on foreign policy. He angrily accused them of encroaching on 'matters far beyond their reach and capacity', criticizing his prospective allies and even interfering with his son's marriage, and he reminded them that he had the right to imprison members during a session, though he had not exercised it so far. The Commons replied, reflexively, that freedom of speech was their 'ancient and undoubted right'; James made the book answer that it was theirs only by his grace. A face-saving formula was needed, as in 1604 (over elections) or 1610 (over impositions), but James was now aware that in both cases issues of principle had been compromised, and this time he would not budge; the most he would offer was to renounce the third subsidy and give them a free hand with domestic reform. But the Commons instead drew up a short, categorical protestation of their rights (18 December). James responded with a snap prorogation, came down in person to the House of Commons to tear the protestation out of the Journal with his own hands, then ordered a dissolution.

James had shown astonishing violence, but, perhaps because such violence was not typical of the man, it had no marked long-term effects, and to regard any of these events as tending towards revolution is teleological. In the next parliament they were forgotten. Honours were even, and Buckingham was much more dissatisfied with the outcome than James. Parliament had done good reformist work on monopolies and had voted taxation; the stalemate that had persisted since 1610 was broken and impositions were apparently a dead letter. The Commons' protestation had been strictly defensive; they had not even claimed the right to advise the king on foreign policy, only to discuss it. If anything, James was the aggressor; in tampering with the sacrosanct journals, threatening to imprison Members of Parliament during the session, and actually imprisoning several (including Coke) afterwards. (In fact, he had done this after the Addled Parliament, and again in June 1621.) In the momentum of James's anger, some of his advisers (headed, no doubt, by Buckingham) advised him to extreme courses; but they were denounced by John Williams, bishop of Lincoln, Bacon's successor as Lord Keeper, and one of the few ministers not terrified of

Buckingham. The impositions on wines were doubled and a benevolence was ordered; this time lists were drawn up, men were assessed beforehand, and the recalcitrant were summoned before the Council and threatened with service in Ireland or Germany. The result was over £116,000, or nearly one and a half parliamentary subsidies. But when Buckingham pressed for another benevolence in October 1622, it was blocked by Council.

Meanwhile James's diplomatic offensive, launched by Digby (now Earl of Bristol) at Madrid, ran out of steam. While Philip IV havered over the marriage treaty, Bavarian troops were steadily conquering the Lower Palatinate, and in February 1623, despite Spanish protests, Maximilian was granted the electoral title. Buckingham was alternating in the roles of hawk and dove; having lost ground with James, he was conscious of his increasing dependance on Charles, who had now wished himself into a total and absolute commitment to the 'Spanish match'. As a result, they both departed incognito for Madrid in March 1623 to conclude the match personally. Bristol was shocked, the Spanish Court astounded, the English public terrified; but the days when sovereign princes were terrorized or personally blackmailed were long gone by (and perhaps existed more in Scottish history than English), and this madcap expedition did have the effect of telescoping the current diplomatic manoeuvres, which otherwise could have gone on for another ten years. Philip IV was forced to put his terms on the table: complete toleration for Roman Catholics, ratified by Parliament, any child of the marriage to be raised a Catholic. James had probably always known that this would be the outcome, but he had not expected the denouement so suddenly or so soon; his tenuous liaison with Spain, gently revolving round a series of long-drawn-out negotiations never likely to come to a conclusion in his lifetime, was his contribution to European peace. Charles was astounded, Buckingham was willing to buy time; James's decision to make him a duke, the first created outside the royal family since 1485, showed that he was on the up and up again. Charles took the necessary oaths – he even agreed to receive preliminary instruction from a priest, something he could never entirely explain away – then he left for Santander as precipitately as he had come.

Behind all these negotiations lay the idea, once favoured by the Howards, that the restoration of a Catholic dynasty in England was practical politics. At least, this was the logical end of James's whole Spanish policy; the Earl of Bristol realized this, and so probably did Buckingham, an ever-ready opportunist whose mother had already turned Catholic; this is why they both found it so difficult to explain away their conduct later. The majority of the nation, it was assumed, would swallow any religious policy firmly and confidently presented – the sixteenth century had shown this – and at worst a Catholic underground opposition would be exchanged for a Puritan underground opposition. As a bonus, this would probably mean the final parting of the ways for King and Parliament. It is ironic that Charles, who was to be destroyed by a militant parliament with extreme Protestant leanings, should apparently be unaware of any such solution. He landed in England in October 1623 in a perfect fury at what he considered his 'betrayal', and was bolstered up by the wave of public relief and joy which greeted his return. Buckingham, trailing behind, was ready once more to exchange the role of dove for hawk. Bristol was nominated the scapegoat; he was recalled from Madrid and at once banished to his country estates, while a new parliament was summoned for February 1624.

The air of unreality persisted. We know that Buckingham and Charles did a deal with the Commons beforehand, and its scope is indicated by the passing of a Monopolies Act, followed towards the end of the session by a whole series of unnoticed statutes regulating trade and manufacture and settling complaints about the administration of the land law which had been voiced since 1604. (The parliament of 1624 passed thirty-five statutes, as against nil in 1614, one in 1621, nil in 1626, and seven in 1628–9. The protracted parliament of 1604–10 only passed seventy-three.) However, what the Commons had pledged in return is uncertain. Buckingham enjoyed a glamorous prominence. All thought of proceedings against him was dropped, he strutted high and free, and his doctored account of the Madrid fiasco was credulously received at an unprecedented joint session of both Houses; war it was to be, and here was England's war leader.

But from the first there was confusion between James, Charles and Buckingham as to how the war should be waged and at what cost. The Commons took it for granted that the Lord Admiral meditated a sea war against the traditional enemy, and, drunk with imagined Elizabethan splendours, they believed that this could be self-financing, if not profitable. According to Sir Edward Coke, 'England was never richer than when at war with Spain. If Ireland is secured, the Navy furnished, the Low Countries assisted, we will not care for Pope, Turk, Spain nor all the devils in hell.' Sir John Eliot yelled, 'Are we poor? Spain is rich. There are our Indies. Break with them; we shall break our necessities together.' To Sir Edward Cecil it was all too easy: 'Ten thousand men,' he said, 'will go through Spain.' Charles and Buckingham did not subscribe to these beliefs, but they did not gainsay them; they simply moved behind Parliament's back to raise a hired army for the Continent under the notorious German condottiere Ernst von Mansfeld, and sought French help at the cost of yet another marriage alliance with a Catholic power. James, advised by Cranfield, refused even to break off negotiations with Spain unless Parliament would vote five subsidies at once and promise a further subsidy annually until his debts were paid – an unusual venture into realism.

But Parliament offered only three subsidies (though they were to be levied in one year), and they wrote into the subsidy Bill a clause breaking off negotiations with Spain, and another which appropriated the proceeds to the Irish establishment, the navy and aid for the Dutch. James refused to curtail his diplomatic manoeuvres in return for a financial settlement which did not even allow him to intervene in the Palatinate – the ostensible purpose of the whole exercise – and he even threatened to amend the Subsidy Act before he gave his assent; but he was borne down. Cranfield, who had his own axes to grind, launched an intrigue against Buckingham, but he was outflanked by charges of peculation which led to his impeachment and fall in May. This was another sacrifice to Parliament, and James defended his finance minister as best he could. In a famous confrontation he told Buckingham that he was making a rod for his own back, and he told Charles 'he would live to have his belly full of parliaments, and when he should be dead he would have too much cause to remember how much he had contributed to the weakening of the crown'.

At the end of the session (29 May) James put a brave face on things. He thanked the Commons for their 'obedience and good respect', which bid fair to make this 'the happiest parliament that ever was', and promised to meet them again 'towards the winter'. Right at the end of the proceedings he made a few extempore remarks, calling to mind 'the breaking up of three former parliaments together', and comparing this with 'the happy conclusion of this session'. In fact he dared not meet them again. Buckingham proceeded to spend £720,000 on war preparations, not including the navy, against expected receipts of £253,000, and he simply ignored the terms of the Subsidy Act. True, £96,000 was appropriated to the Dutch, and £24,000 to Ireland, but, in addition, £240,000 was consigned to Mansfeld's army and an incredible £360,000 to Denmark, to finance her intervention in North Germany. Of course, these were just ledger entries; something had to give, and it was Mansfeld. His ragamuffin conscript army, starved of pay and provisions, set off for the Palatinate in the winter of 1624–5, but got no further than Flushing, where it simply melted away through sickness, starvation and desertion. Meanwhile, the alliance with France signed in November was another failure; Cardinal Richelieu was not interested in the Palatinate, but he was interested in the Valtelline, 500 miles south, which he promptly seized. Charles, having to the relief of the nation escaped one Catholic princess, was now saddled with another – Louis XIII's sister, Henrietta Maria – and again had to make embarrassing promises on behalf of her co-religionists; in fact, the penal laws were covertly suspended in December 1624. England had deliberately sacrificed her influence at Madrid, her only real means of intervening in Germany; and though when James died on 27 March 1625 she was at war with Spain, because of financial destitution, administrative ineptitude and military unpreparedness she had yet to strike the first blow.

James I was a strange medley of opposites; he was a fool in some sense, but in others a great man. He spoke and wrote like a tyrant, but he acted like a circumspect constitutional monarch, and he had much more to put up with from Parliament than they from him. It is difficult not to sympathize with his occasional petulance, nor to applaud his intellectual virtuosity; at the end of it all he emerges as one of the most *likeable* of English monarchs, and this is something no one can take away from him. In the words of his harshest contemporary critic, Sir Anthony Weldon: 'He was (take him altogether, and not in pieces) such a king, I wish this kingdom have never any worse – on the condition, not any better.' And Weldon, writing in the 1640s, was obviously thinking of Charles I.

Charles Stuart is also a man of contradictions and controversy. The philippics of the Whig historians, notably Gardiner, portray him as sick in mind and essentially stupid, beneath a veneer of intellectualism and culture. But the prince who took the lead in the Parliaments of 1621 and 1624 was quick-witted enough, and the man who composed the *Eikon Basiliké* was very far from being stupid. His political conduct in the 1620s was active enough, even precipitate; if he went into slow motion in the 1640s it was because all the alternatives open to him then were equally unattractive and there was some wisdom in playing for time. Similarly, he is portrayed as shy, uncouth in his personal relationships, and unable to command allegiance on his own terms; absolutely unforgiving. Yet he could forgive the Earl of Bristol, and win his allegiance in 1641; he could admit in later years that his blind allegiance to Buckingham had been misplaced. He won the respect and devotion even of his last gaoler, the Cromwellian Colonel Thomlinson.

Certainly as a young man he was everything his father was not, being clean, sober, dignified, handsome, courteous and chaste. It was said of him at the end of his life that he had 'never violated a woman, struck a man, or spoken an evil word'. His court was regal and magnificent, without the vulgar inanities and insobrieties of his father's. For the last five years of James's reign, the prince had been an imposing and prominent public figure. He came to the throne with considerable reserves of good will, and it is astonishing how quickly he squandered them.

His devotion to Buckingham, now almost universally disliked and distrusted, did not help, of course. But there were other reasons, directly personal to Charles himself. He was greeted with the same wariness as his father had been in 1604, and for similar reasons; here was a young, vital, energetic man succeeding a senile dotard; it was to be expected that he would use his prerogative to the full, and men must look to their liberties – the enforcement of the benevolence of 1622 had been a pointer to the future, so was the nine-month imprisonment of Sir Edward Coke in the same year. Charles had an aggressive, unsubtle self-confidence which had been encouraged, if anything, by his dealings with the last two parliaments. His were the politics of confrontation, not discussion; in the second session of 1621 he had sought the authority of James, absent in Newmarket, to imprison the opposition leaders while Parliament was sitting; James had refused. He was not as vocal as his father about the Divine Right of Kings, but he believed in it more firmly, and was not prepared to compromise as James had been. James's beliefs, in fact, were largely a reaction to Scots conditions, and, as we have seen, he was willing to qualify them. Charles took them over unaltered as a blueprint for the English constitution.

And he began under severe handicaps. He and Buckingham had tacitly accepted the conditions imposed on them by the previous parliament, that the war should be waged principally against Spain, and principally at sea. It would have been difficult to reconcile this with

Mansfeld's expedition, even if this had proved a resounding success, and it was difficult to explain the fiasco of the
French Alliance, the arrival of a popish queen, and its
concomitant undertakings. Buckingham as Lord High
Admiral scented opportunities of glory in a maritime war,
and was already preparing a pseudo-Elizabethan expedition against Cádiz; he was willing enough to accept the
bargain made with parliament, even if it meant abandon-
ing the Palatinate, or drastically demoting it on the list of
war priorities. To Charles, however, the recovery of the
Palatinate was still the main aim; his honour was involved,
and he was devoted to his sister, the exiled 'Winter
Queen'. But the cost of decisive action in Germany was far
beyond anything the Commons was likely to vote, especially to a bankrupt and incompetent government.

His first parliament met in the most difficult circumstances; in June, the high summer, with a severe outbreak
of bubonic plague raging in London. Their predecessors
the year before had voted a triple subsidy to be collected in
one year – an unprecedented step – and they were unlikely
to improve on it. Henrietta Maria arrived a few days
before Parliament met, and at once involved Charles in
personal difficulties which sharpened his temper. She
detested Buckingham, she declined to attend a Protestant
coronation, and she clearly did not take to her new
husband (they had been married by proxy in May). For
the next three years he was a frustrated man and a hen-
pecked husband. Parliament received no guidance from
the Crown, but they voted two subsidies, which, in view of
all that had been done and all that had not been done, was
generous. They then accepted an adjournment, after
three weeks, to escape from plague-stricken London, and
when they reassembled at Oxford they were given something like a full view of the situation. But the King was not

very communicative (as was his wont), and his ministers were vague. To equip the fleet for Cádiz no more was needed than the two subsidies already voted, perhaps less; to re-equip Mansfeld's expedition and subsidize a Danish invasion of North Germany would cost no man knew what. The government was so inexperienced in such matters that there was real difficulty in naming a figure; they thought £600,000 would be enough, but perhaps even this was insufficient. Worse still, it was not entirely clear what the King's objectives were, nor even who his enemies were going to be (apart from Spain). The news that under the terms of the French treaty English ships had now joined Richelieu in the siege of the Huguenot citadel of La Rochelle did not please, nor were the Commons mollified – indeed just the opposite – by a spectacular and over-bearing visitation from Buckingham. Opposition to Buckingham in the Lords, quiescent since 1621, was rising swiftly, and both Houses asked the King to seek the advice of 'a grave, religious and worthy council'. He replied that he would govern as he wished, 'through one or many or nobody'. Still only two subsidies had been voted, and the Commons had delayed the grant of the ancient customs (tunnage and poundage), which since 1485 had been granted to each monarch for life, on the plea that it was time to revise and consolidate the whole system of import and export duties; but at this stage Charles took the sudden and highly questionable decision to dissolve Parliament altogether (12 August).

He and Buckingham gambled everything on the great expedition to Cádiz, which sailed in October. The looting of the Spanish bullion fleet would replenish an exhausted Treasury, and a signal victory over the traditional enemy would renew the glories of Elizabeth's reign, pacify any future House of Commons, and loosen the public's purse strings. When the expedition ended instead in an expensive fiasco, which exposed serious deficiencies in the sphere of military and naval organization, for which Buckingham had assumed full responsibility, they had nowhere to go. They had to summon another parliament for February 1626, to try and get supplies for another campaigning season, and this in itself was a confession of failure. In fact the Commons, despite the Cádiz fiasco, was ready to pursue the war, and vote money for it – their objection was solely to Buckingham; but Charles mulishly refused to distinguish between himself and the duke. He was already convinced that the Commons was engaged in a campaign against him personally, or even against the monarchy in general; ordering members of his Council of War not to give evidence before the Commons as requested, he said, 'It is not you that they aim at, but it is me upon whom they make inquisition.'

Unfortunately, Charles had excluded from the new Commons the steadier opposition leaders – notably Sir Edward Coke and Sir Thomas Wentworth, a rising Yorkshire squire whose natural bent in favour of constituted authority had been distorted by aversion to Buckingham – and this left the field open for the unbalanced Sir John Eliot, who shared the King's liking for direct confrontation. It was he who hit upon the device of impeaching Buckingham for high treason, on a strange *mélange* of charges ranging from the engrossing of offices to the murder of James I. Buckingham was confident of his ability to answer his accusers, but the situation in the House of Lords was threatening. Here the 'constitutional opposition' of 1621, led by Puritans like Wharton, Spencer, and Saye and Sele, was now supplemented by John Williams (already dismissed the Lord Keepership), the Archbishop of Canterbury and the powerful Earl of Pembroke. They

97

insisted on hearing the Earl of Bristol, who was still exiled in the country. When Bristol came at their summons Charles charged him with high treason for conspiring to effect his conversion to Catholicism in 1623; Bristol riposted by accusing Buckingham of planning the whole Madrid expedition to that end. They could not both be telling the truth, and it was decidedly unwise for Charles to match his word against a subject's. It is eloquent of his diminished standing, with his reign scarcely twelve months old, that the Lords decided to hear Bristol first.

Meanwhile, these disputes were given a sharper cutting edge by the emergence of a new religious movement directly sponsored by the King. There had been stirrings as early as 1621, provoked as much as anything by the out-break of what could plausibly be represented as a war of religion in Germany. James's *Directions to Preachers* in 1622 was aimed at suppressing all contentious preaching, but especially Puritan preaching on the fundamentals of election, reprobation and grace. But the Parliament of 1624 complained to the King of the writings of the lively Richard Montague, which seemed to impugn the standing of the continental reformed churches, to associate the English Church too closely with the Roman, and to partake of the theological doctrines of the great Calvinist heresiarch, Arminius. James dismissed the matter, but the Parliament of 1625 took it up with renewed vigour, provoked by Montague's restatement of his views in a pamphlet dedicated to the King, *Appello Caesarem*. Charles's reply, typically, was to make him one of his royal chaplains.

There were, of course, much deeper implications. Charles and Buckingham, as befitted young, vigorous men, had extended their patronage from time to time to various reformers at opposite extremes of the Church; for a time, Charles's principal chaplain had been John Preston,

Master of Queens' College, Cambridge, and an extreme Puritan. But finally his favour had rested on a reform group led by William Laud, bishop of St David's, who now emerged as his chief ecclesiastical adviser, displacing George Abbott, Archbishop of Canterbury, whose authority was weakened by his accidental manslaughter of a gamekeeper in 1621. The rise of Laud had, in fact, displaced Williams, though as Bishop of Lincoln he continued his most formidable opponent to the end.

It is important to realize that 'Laudianism' was not reactionary but revolutionary; quite as revolutionary as Puritanism, which it threw on to the defensive, where it remained. Laud and his followers argued that the Church of England was the only true Catholic Church, preserved from the blasphemous and superstitious errors of Rome by its comparative isolation in the Middle Ages. The reformed churches on the Continent were denounced as heterodox, the slow drift of the Anglican Church towards some form of presbyterianism was abruptly arrested, and the authority of the bishops, as something derived directly from God, was vigorously reaffirmed. Whether, as his opponents insisted, Laud embraced the heresy of Arminius, which posited free will as against predestination, is remarkably obscure, and is still the subject of learned debate. It is not entirely clear that this is relevant, anyway; though strict predestination remained the official doctrine of the Church of England, the heirs of Calvin had already of their own volition taken steps to modify his awful proposition that each man, even before his birth (some said before Adam's Fall), was *elected* to salvation or *reprobated* to damnation, and the doctrine of the Covenant of Grace, which short-circuited this verdict by the exercise of mind-bending casuistry, had been framed by the leading English Calvinist divine of the previous generation, William

Perkins. But since the condemnation of Arminius by the Synod of Doort, and particularly his doctrine that man could accept or reject God's saving grace by the exercise of free will, 'Arminian' had become a catch-all term of abuse in Puritan circles.

What is true is that, in the church services, Laud took the emphasis off the sermon, and thus off such theological complexities as predestination and free will, and placed it on the communion; the church service was not designed to perfect one's understanding of God, which was a presumptuous aim anyway, but to renew one's faith in Him and permit one to worship Him in blind gratitude, with the officiating clergyman in his old role of mediator or intercessor with Jesus Christ the Saviour, not an interpreter of God's ways to man. This is what lay behind the Laudians' campaign to rebeautify church buildings, to enforce the use of vestments, and to replace the wooden communion table by an altar set apart in the chancel – an emphasis on physical realities which brought down on them the accusation that they were cryptopapists, but at the same time gained them the support of those Protestants who still craved an element of mystery or ritual in their religion. Charles's own personal preference for the Laudian way was reinforced by his belief in his ultimate power as Supreme Governor, which was in turn enhanced by the Laudians' belief in the autocratic nature of ecclesiastical authority. His attitude was that the nature of the English Church and its doctrines were open to several interpretations, all of them covered by the accommodating imprecision of the Thirty-Nine Articles, and as Supreme Governor he had the right to enforce that which he found good. To Puritans like Eliot and the Earl of Warwick, who had been happily imposing their own interpretation on Anglicanism for years, this savoured of anti-Christ.

Meanwhile, confrontation reached a climax on 11 May, when Charles ordered Eliot and Sir Dudley Digges to the Tower for personally insulting him. (They were accused of likening Buckingham to Sejanus, which implied that the King was Tiberius.) The words were explained away, and the two martyrs were released, but the session was wrecked. When Charles belatedly requested supply, and the regularization of the customs, the Commons demanded Buckingham's dismissal. Charles's reply, on 15 June, was another snap dissolution, followed by his first attempt at prerogative government. The charges against Buckingham were referred to Star Chamber, which promptly acquitted him, and the King issued a proclamation 'for the establishing of the peace and quiet of the Church of England' which demanded total conformity to the present establishment of the Church and threatened its critics with condign punishment. Worse still, he began to finance his continuing war policy by extra-parliamentary means, first by a request for a 'free gift', then by the slightly more respectable machinery of a forced loan.

This policy was premeditated, in the spirit if not in the letter, and Charles was psychologically prepared for it. In his first two parliaments he had been as provocative as the Commons – in fact, in 1625, much more so – and he had made it clear that he was far from regarding them as indispensable. He told them in March 1626, 'Remember that parliaments are altogether in my power for their calling, sitting and dissolution; therefore as I find the fruits of them good or evil, they are to continue or not to be.' In May, in what was clearly an 'inspired' speech, Sir Dudley Carleton warned them that the King, if frustrated, would turn to 'new counsels', and there was little doubt what they would be (see p. 40 above). Now, in September 1626 and on through the winter, 'new counsels' were taken and their advice pushed through with the utmost vigour. When he jibbed at authorizing the forced loan, the Lord Chief Justice, Sir Randolph Crew, was dismissed, and immediate pressure was applied to prominent gentry spokesmen, and sustained; some were dismissed the magistrates' bench, others were conscripted as officers in the new fleet, and a few, to make an example, were consigned to what seemed likely to prove indefinite imprisonment, outside their own counties. The ghostly authority of the Church was invoked in support, and in celebrated sermons the Laudian divines Robert Sibthorpe and Roger Manwaring argued that it was man's Christian duty to obey the King, provided his commands were not against the laws of God; Manwaring went so far as to say that to refuse royal taxation was a sin. Even more effective was the support of the law. In November 1627 the celebrated 'Five Knights' of Middlesex, imprisoned for refusing the loan, sued out writs of habeas corpus in King's Bench; but the court, after pondering the precedents, rather reluctantly agreed that the King did have the right to imprison any of his subjects without due process of law, on a plea of national security which was not subject to their assessment.

The result was encouraging. So much emphasis has been placed on resistance to this loan that its success has been overlooked; but by Michaelmas 1627 it had brought in £233,261 (or more than three subsidies), and there was another £113,730 to come. With prize goods of £146,492, the total receipts at the Exchequer for this year were £850,000, and Charles had sloughed off considerable war expense by leaving it to the inland counties to clothe new levies and transport them to the Coast ('coat and conduct money'), then forcibly billetting them free, on the local population. If the King's war policy had been less active and ambitious, or if it had achieved even a moderate success, or if Buckingham's diplomacy had been less maladroit, then personal, authoritarian government might have come to stay. As it was, Charles was still maintaining a presence in Germany by funding Christian IV of Denmark to the tune of £12,000 a month, despite his defeat by the Imperialists at Lutter in 1626, while Buckingham had now succeeded in embroiling himself with France, formerly billed as England's premier ally, and had committed himself to raising the siege of La Rochelle. But his first attempt, in September 1627, was a ruinous fiasco. 'Since England was England,' wrote one Member of Parliament, 'it received not so dishonourable a blow.' Peace by capitulation was unthinkable to Charles, though it might have saved him; instead he summoned his third parliament in three years for March 1628.

Both sides had learned a lesson. Charles dropped his tactics of provocation and confrontation; Wentworth and Coke in the Commons, Pembroke in the Lords, dropped their attack on Buckingham; Eliot was for the moment suppressed. Wentworth persuaded the House to vote five subsidies, but the Bill was not sent up to the Lords; instead Coke brought forward, after one or two false starts, a Petition of Right, which obliged Charles to admit that he could not imprison men without cause shown, levy any tax or benevolence without parliamentary consent, impose martial law on civilians, nor compel them to billet troops. The Lords were won over, and the King's face saved, by the pretence that this was a restatement of existing law, hitherto misunderstood by the judges, but Charles put up a dogged, step-by-step resistance which was only ended by news from abroad. In April the last English garrison in North Germany surrendered, at Stade, on the Elbe, and in May the second expedition to La Rochelle returned without firing a shot, unable to penetrate the besiegers' defences.

To mount another expedition, and retrieve his and Buckingham's honour, he needed the five subsidies, and on 7 June he gave his assent to the Petition of Right amid general rejoicing.

Unfortunately, the Commons' very success brought deterioration and disintegration. Wentworth relaxed his grip, and Eliot resumed control of a House thinned by summer absenteeism. He drew up a provocative remonstrance on the growth of Arminianism, and completed the impeachment of Manwaring for his divine right sermons the previous year. (Charles, still moderately conciliatory, pardoned Manwaring but suppressed his writings.) The crunch came when the Commons began to prepare a Bill to legalize the collection of customs duties over the past three years; scenting the possibility of blackmail, and insisting that he needed no such authorization, Charles announced a prorogation for 26 June. The Commons at once drafted a remonstrance declaring that the collection of customs duties without their consent was an infraction of the Petition of Right. This raised the slumbering issue of impositions and provoked a minor revolt among the merchants, whose ringleader, Richard Chambers, was imprisoned, bailed by King's Bench, then referred to Star Chamber. The Court of Exchequer ordered the confiscation of the merchandise in question until the issue could be referred to Parliament.

In the meanwhile the whole structure of the political scene was changed by the assassination of Buckingham at Portsmouth on 23 August. The expedition he was on the point of leading against La Rochelle was abandoned, and the city surrendered in October. The war effort could be wound up, and a new Lord Treasurer, Richard Weston, later Earl of Portland, could begin to rationalize the Crown's finances. Sir Thomas Wentworth, alienated by

Eliot's intransigence, had already returned to Court; in July he was raised to the peerage, and in December he was appointed Lord President of the Council of the North. Former enemies of Buckingham's – Bristol, the Earl of Arundel, Archbishop Abbott, Lord Cottington – returned to their allegiance too, and were well received. Charles was deeply wounded by the public rejoicing at the favourite's death, but gone was the urge to provocation; it was replaced by a deep, cautious resolve to get the better of those he held responsible. His new stability was probably enhanced by a complete reconciliation with the Queen, which thenceforward made his one of the happiest of English royal marriages. (She was pregnant in 1629, but miscarried; the future Charles II was born in 1630.) On one issue he was not prepared to compromise. A fortunate wave of deaths on the episcopal bench in the second half of 1628 enabled him to promote Laud to London and fill eight more sees with his nominees; one of them the controversial Richard Montague, now Bishop of Chichester. In November 1628 he re-issued the Thirty-Nine Articles, with a proclamation stating that any disagreement as to their interpretation must be settled by Convocation, and then only with his permission – which was unlikely to be given, since he would not 'endure any varying or departing in the least degree' from 'the settled continuance of the doctrine and discipline of the Church of England now established'

In January 1629, he met Parliament again with a moderate speech, pointing out that he had levied customs duties not as a right but as a necessity, and another Bill was brought in to legitimize the practice, when all of a sudden Eliot raised a question of privilege, in that one of the merchants in dispute with the government was a Member of Parliament, John Rolle. John Pym, who had been rising to prominence since 1621, warned him, 'The liberties of this House are inferior to the liberties of the kingdom; to determine the privilege of this House is but a mean matter, and the main end is to establish [the] possession[s] of the subjects.' Charles helped the matter along by assuming personal responsibility for Rolle's treatment, and on 24 February a committee appointed earlier, on Eliot's insistence, brought in a report deeply critical of Laud's policy for the Church. On 2 March, with rumours of prorogation and dissolution in the air, the House refused to acknowledge Black Rod's summons to the House of Lords; Denzil Holles and Benjamin Valentine held the Speaker down in his chair while Eliot launched an intemperate attack on Lord Treasurer Weston. He then pushed through three resolutions; to the effect that those advising popish or Arminian innovations in religion were 'capital enemies to this kingdom and commonwealth', as were those in any way participating in the collection of customs duties. These last were also 'innovators in the government' and those who paid the duties were 'betrayers of the liberty of England, and enemies to the same'. Not surprisingly, that same day Parliament was dissolved.

## CHARLES I ALONE, 1629–40

The session of 1629 confirmed Charles in the belief that, since his accession, he had been faced by a deliberate conspiracy to suborn his authority. 'Their drift,' he said in a proclamation drawn up just after the dissolution, 'was to break through all respects and ligaments of government, and to erect a universal, oversMaying power to themselves, which belongs only to us, and not to them.' A week or two later he announced that another parliament would not be summoned until 'our people shall see more clearly into our intentions and actions', and so should have 'come to a better understanding of us and themselves'.

Nor was this generally unacceptable. Eliot's conduct was indefensible; it had not been supported by responsible opposition leaders like Pym, nor by the Lords. Charles's policy and actions up to 1628 had roused understandable misgivings, but the Petition of Right, the death of Buckingham and England's impending withdrawal from the war, now seen as inevitable, defused the tension. Moreover, though Charles's general treatment of Parliament had been offensively offhand, he had made much less effort than his father to control or limit debate – apart from the isolated case of Eliot and Digges in 1626 – and in 1629 he had shown himself to be moderate and constructive. In these circumstances, Eliot's conduct seemed deliberately calculated to destroy that regal power which even Charles's

harshest critics recognized as essential to ordered government. Wentworth expressed the majority sentiment in a
classic statement to the Council of the North in December
1628. 'The authority of the king,' he said, 'is the keystone
which closeth up the arch of order and government, which
containeth each part in relation to the whole, and which,
once shaken, infirmed, all the frame falls together in a
confused heap of foundation and battlement.'

Naturally the lawyers took this view, and many who had
been spokesmen of opposition in the 1620s – William Noy,
Dudley Digges, Edward Littleton, John Selden – made
their careers at Court in the 1630s, as much out of conviction as ambition. Similarly the judges. Charles arrested
nine members immediately after the dissolution; five were
soon released, but he hung on to Eliot, Denzil Holles and
Benjamin Valentine, moving them from prison to prison to
evade writs of habeas corpus. Not until January 1630 did
he bring them before King's Bench, but then the charge of
conspiring in Parliament to overthrow the King's government was accepted. They were sentenced to imprisonment
until they acknowledged their fault, and Eliot died
unrepentant in the Tower in 1632, more serviceable to the
cause of Parliament as a dead martyr than a live leader.
Sir Edward Coke died in 1634, aged eighty-two, having
lived to see the Petition of Right reduced to a nullity; the
attempt to bind the King by general charters or mani-
festoes rather than direct statutes died with him. Charles
confiscated his papers, and as a result the second part of
his *Institutes*, so influential in the development of constitutional thought, and containing ammunition even for
the Levellers, was not published until 1642.

The merchants' revolt, being so obviously prompted by
a desire to evade customs duties, roused little public
support. The boycott spread through 1629 even to the

conservative Merchant Adventurers, and the port of London came to a standstill, but Charles held firm. Richard Chambers was fined and imprisoned by Star Chamber, the stop in trade aggravated an existing crisis in the cloth industry, and before the end of the year resistance cracked and the recalcitrant merchants fell over one another to avoid being the last to come in. The Court of Exchequer duly confirmed Chambers's sentence. The slump in trade and industry, accentuated by serious outbreaks of plague, continued into 1631, and could conveniently be blamed on the Commons' unilateral action in 1628 and 1629.

The merchants' revolt is out of character, because, despite weighted Marxist interpretations of 'The Eleven Years Tyranny', Charles's new government, with its emphasis on trade expansion,, its encouragement of new developments in industry, its commitment to peace and its attempts to put down piracy and privateering, was in many respects a merchants' government, and despite some friction over the Ulster Plantation, its good relations with the larger magnates of the City were maintained up to 1640 and beyond.

There were exceptions, of course. It was probably unwise of the government Commission on Clothing to try to maintain the level of wages in the textile industry – the idea was too advanced, and infringed the generally accepted law of a free market. Monopolies crept back in 1631, this time on a new soap-making process (the Act of 1624 had excepted new inventions); extended in 1635 to salt-refining and starch- and brick-making. But the merits and demerits of these schemes are befogged by contemporary propaganda, which was naturally partisan; abuse of monopolies did not feature on the reform agenda of the Long Parliament. Similarly with the steady increase in customs duties and impositions levied by Portland after 1630; the Long Parliament finally authorized impositions. The legalization of Sir William Courten's association of East India traders can be regarded either as a blatant encroachment on chartered rights, or an attempt to open up an underdeveloped area of trade unduly monopolized by the East India Company. Similarly, the King's part in the great fen drainage scheme can be seen as an unscrupulous encroachment on the activities of independent entrepreneurs, or the lending of indispensable backing to one of the most ambitious land-improvement schemes of the century.

It was, of course, the landed classes that bore the brunt of the Crown's policy in the 1630s – though it is still not clear whether this was consciously intended. In 1631, with the endorsement of the Court of Exchequer, men worth £40 a year in land or above were fined for not assuming the honour of knighthood. In the same year the Book of Orders, 'for the better administration of justice and more perfect information of his Majesty', laid down a new code of conduct for magistrates, and attempted to bring them more firmly under the control of the Council. In 1634 began the strict enforcement of the antiquated Forest Laws, and neighbouring landowners were heavily mulcted for encroachments made on the Forest of Dean since the death of Richard I; the same principle was applied to Waltham Forest and the New Forest, and in 1637 to the Forest of Rockingham. (Rockingham's circumference was extended from six miles to a notional sixty, and fines totalling £51,000 imposed, though these were eventually wittled down to £23,000.) The Commission on Depopulation fined other landlords for enclosure of common lands; perhaps the most debatable of these measures, for no effort was made to rectify the 'wrong' done, if any.

Finally, in 1635 and with the full backing of the judges, ship money – levied in 1634 on the coastal counties – was extended inland, and to encourage realistic assessment it operated in reverse order to the parliamentary subsidy; that is, each county was assessed by the central government for a lump sum, which it was left for the high sheriff to find. This was to be the pattern for all future direct taxation, beginning with Pym's assessment in 1642.

We are assured by the Whig historians, beginning with Gardiner, that this roused the most furious opposition in the provinces, and this 'fact' is generally accepted. In fact, there is scarcely any hard evidence for it, and what there is is associated with predictable individuals like the Earl of Warwick and Lord Saye and Sele. Much too much has also been made of the association of certain leaders of parliamentary opposition with the Providence Company for the exploitation of New England. The Pilgrim Fathers left long before the 1630s, and it is unwise to associate the exodus to Massachusetts with persecution at home, especially when much of it took place before Laud's drive for conformity gathered momentum.

The only hard fact about ship money is that it was one of the most efficient taxes of the century, in terms of percentage proceeds and economy of administration. In 1635 £199,000 was demanded, the equivalent of three subsidies, and all but £5,000 collected: in 1636 the government was £7,000 short on £196,000, in 1637 £18,000. The yield declined slightly year by year, but it was still amazingly high; which is not really surprising, since it was a tax with the announced purpose of building a fleet to put down privateering in the Channel, an acknowledged problem, and such a fleet was equipped and set out to do the job, however ineffectually. These were years of prosperity, too. There was a slight trade recession in 1636, but in 1633 began a cycle of good harvests which held until the end of the decade; from the 1640s men looked back nostalgically on the scorching summers of 1637 and 1638.

The turning point came in 1638, when the government lowered the ship money assessment to a mere £70,000, and collected less than a third. Whig hagiography associates this with the notorious case of *Rex* v. *Hampden*, which was decided in February 1638. This is possible, but not a shred of direct evidence can be adduced for it, and it seems strange that a verdict firmly in favour of a practice established for three years should suddenly provoke resistance, especially when the judges went out of their way to state that this did not confer on the King any general right of extra-parliamentary taxation. They decided 7:5 that Hampden's refusal to pay ship money could not be sustained, but three of the five who voted for him did so merely on technical grounds. It is surely more logical to associate the 'strike' against ship money with the Scottish Rebellion of 1638. (The Scots National Covenant was also drawn up in February 1638, a fortnight after the verdict was handed down in *Rex* v. *Hampden*.) If the judges would authorize a special tax for the navy, then the next step, especially in view of the Scots revolt, would be a special tax for the army. If the King then thrashed the Scots – and to the chauvinistic English there seemed no reason why he should not – then he would be left with an army in being. It was power, not right, that was at stake.

Similarly, the vexed religious problems of the 1630s boiled down in the end to a question of political or social power. Laud's persecution of the 'Puritans' was directed principally against independent, lower-class sectaries and congregationalists who were viewed with equal loathing by the church authorities and the reforming clergy; indeed,

credit should be given to Laud for recognizing the danger
from this quarter much earlier than his critics. Similarly,
Prynne, Bastwick and Lilburne, who had their ears
cropped by order of Star Chamber in 1637 for libelling the
bishops, made unlikely heroes for the parliamentary
classes, who cared little for freedom of speech (outside
Parliament) and a great deal for social stability. We notice
the same ambivalence here as with the Marprelate Tracts
in the 1580s; no one liked the bishops, but that did not
mean that any dirty Tom, Dick or Harry was free to abuse
them in print. The controversy over the position of the
altar in churches, and lesser matters like music, stained
glass and vestments, is even more difficult to evaluate; but
in 1641 a majority of the Lords and a large minority of the
Commons voted for the *status quo*. Those who think that by
confining preachers to a consideration of the Thirty-Nine
Articles Laud was limiting freedom of theological debate
have clearly never looked at the articles. In recent years
we have been driven to revaluate the appeal of Laudian
ism to contemporaries. Laud found the nation in a trough
of disillusion, deeply worried by the eclipse of Protestantism in Europe, and in place of the Puritan concept of
England as God's elect nation, belied by recent events, he
offered a concept equally chauvinistic and equally
satisfying; the *ecclesia anglicana*, that perfect reflection of
the Church of Christ and the Apostles, resistant equally to
the superstitions of Rome and the errors of Wittenberg and
Geneva. His idea that worship should be dignified, uncontentious, evocative and emotive appealed to all those
bored and repelled by the argumentative austerity of
sermon-dominated Puritan services. His appeal to free will
was a relief to those whose consciences were tormented by
the awful dilemma of election or reprobation. His belief in
the corporate nature of the Church, and the intercessory

role of the clergy, comforted those who flinched from that direct relationship with God and His Son which was central to the Puritan view of life. The fact that the median age of the royalists in the Long Parliament was ten years below that of their opponents suggests a conflict between generations, and it is not far-fetched to associate this with religion. Certainly this was the one question on which the Long Parliament could achieve no consensus, and in 1660 Laud's theological and liturgical concept of the Church was triumphant.

But his social and political encroachments were a serious issue, perhaps the only one. With his belated promotion to Canterbury on Abbott's death in 1633, he inaugurated a campaign to restrict lay influence in the Church. The right of corporations to employ 'lecturers', or preachers without cure of souls, was drastically restricted; noblemen were allowed only one domestic chaplain, gentlemen none at all. The 'Foeffees for Impropriations', a group of Puritan laymen who had been buying impropriations on the open market and using the income to subsidize lecturers, were compulsorily wound up (but this was a minor phenomenon, which has received more publicity than it merits). More serious were the plans laid for modifying the lay patron's right of presentation to benefices, and relaxing his control over the incumbent's stipend. Moreover, the Court of High Commission, which had hitherto been primarily an engine for enforcing clerical conformity, now turned to consider the moral iniquities of laymen whose social status put them beyond the reach of the lower church courts. Gentlemen and noblemen suddenly found themselves haled before High Commission and forced to pay maintenance to their estranged wives, or heavy fines for adultery or incest, and (what was worse) to do public penance like any lubricious ploughboy or carted whore.

Laud's obsessive belief, voiced as early as 1625, that Puritan church reform masked a lay conspiracy against the state as well as the Church, made him impatient to suppress nonconformity in all its aspects, and led to a confusion between the lay and ecclesiastical courts. Thus, when High Commission proved an insufficient weapon, he was ready to turn to Star Chamber, as in the Prynne–Bastwick–Lilburne case. Up to the 1630s, Star Chamber was a respected court, supported by the common lawyers and the judges, and as useful to the subject as the sovereign. It was its association with ecclesiastical government in the 1630s which tainted its reputation irremediably, led to its abolition in 1641, and gave it in common parlance an association with repression and injustice which has persisted to the present day.

And the prospect of complete ecclesiastical government was never far away, given Laud's commanding energy and his exalted view of episcopal authority, answerable not even to the King but only to God. The example of Cardinal Richelieu in contemporary France was obvious enough. By 1633, Laud had emerged as chief minister of state, overshadowing Lord Treasurer Portland entirely. Solidly backed by Archbishop Neile of York, he dominated the Privy Council and Star Chamber, and in 1635 his triumph was consummated by the appointment to the Treasureship, vacated by Portland's death, of William Juxon, Bishop of London, the first ecclesiastic to hold this office since Wolsey. The irritation of the lay nobility at their displacement from high office was exacerbated by class resentment; all the Laudian bishops had risen from the lower middle class, or even the working class. (This was to hold good until the eighteenth century, and it encouraged the anticlericalism which was already a marked feature of English upper class thinking; Henry Compton, Bishop of London (1675–1713), and Sir Jonathan Trelawney, Bt (Bristol 1685–9, Exeter 1689–1707, Winchester 1707–21) were the first men of noble or gentle blood to rise to the episcopate.) Indeed, as late as 1641 the church question was essentially social or even personal; the Long Parliament was at one in its desire to get rid of the present bishops, but it could not even agree to abolish the office of bishop.

Over and above all this was a continuing fear of Rome, keyed in with events in Germany. Gustavus Adolphus's lightning invasion in 1630 rescued the cause of European Protestantism at its last gasp, but his death at Lützen in 1632 threw all in the melting-pot again. Both Charles and Laud's contempt for popery was absolute, but it was easy to see Laud's innovations in ceremonial as tending towards Catholicism, and Charles's devotion to his aggressively Catholic queen cast a shadow across his motives which persisted to the end, despite the fact that persecution of lay Catholics was as severe in the 1630s as at any time in the seventeenth century. Under Henrietta Maria's influence, the Caroline Court undoubtedly acquired a decidedly Catholic aura, and there was a drizzle of spectacular conversions – Lord Treasurer Portland, Secretary of State Windebank, Sir Francis Cottington, Chancellor of the Exchequer (widely suspected), and a large number of noblewomen. Bishop Goodman of Gloucester's public avowal in 1640 naturally confirmed the popular assumption that the whole episcopal bench were crypto-Catholics; Laud was rightly furious. There was a similar trend in foreign policy. Ironically, left to himself, Charles tended to drift back on to the pro-Spanish policy favoured by his father; at one time he even contemplated an alliance with Spain to suppress the Dutch, England's chief mercantile rivals, a mirage pursued by his son in 1665 and 1672. He settled for a less adventurous course, but by the end of the 1630s Spain would have been hard put to it to maintain her Flanders army but for the bullion shipments landed at Plymouth and shipped out through Dover. It is not surprising that the leaders of the Long Parliament saw in all this 'a design to alter the kingdom both in religion and government'.

Suspicion was nourished by ignorance. Apeing his father, Charles issued a proclamation in 1632 banishing the gentry and nobility to their country homes – and unlike James he made a serious effort to enforce it through Council and Star Chamber. The isolation of the Court at Whitehall fostered a sense of exclusiveness; Charles I ventured outside London even less than his father had, and he was content to fall back on a life-style increasingly un-English. His highly developed taste in art was symptomatic of the gulf between him and his subjects.

The philistinism of the upper classes in this period is difficult to explain. It can perhaps be attributed to the fact that England had been isolated by the Wars of Religion from the mainstream of European culture; certainly the great collectors and cognoscenti of the age, like Endymion Porter, the 2nd Earl of Arundel, and Sir Kenelm Digby, were mostly Catholics. Charles's own tastes had been developed by his mother, Anne of Denmark, who performed a similar office for her elder son, Prince Henry. Charles inherited both his mother's and his brother's collections, his father being supremely uninterested, and built upon them. His visit to Spain in 1623 was seminal, and on his departure Philip IV gave him 'the greatest consolation prize in all history', Titian's *Venus of the Pardo*. In 1627 he bought the great collection of the Gonzaga Dukes of Mantua, giving himself at one stroke the lead in

this field, though his critics denounced it as nothing but a
heap of 'old rotten pictures and broken-nosed marbles'.
As they had no taste for art, so the English produced no
worthwhile practitioners, and Charles had to call on the
services of Peter Paul Rubens and Anthony van Dyck,
both of whom he knighted (see p. 342 below).

It was Rubens who painted the magnificent ceilings of
the Banqueting House at Whitehall, in 1637, depicting the
blessings of monarchical government and the apotheosis of
James I. Rubens described his patron as 'the greatest
amateur of painting amongst the princes of the world'.
Van Dyck took up permanent residence in England, and
painted a series of portraits of Charles I, regal, melancholy
and aloof, which have fixed our image of him for ever. The
climax of this *oeuvre* is his *Charles I on Horseback*, echoing the
imperial grandeur of Titian's *Charles V at Mühlberg* a
century before. The court masques of the 1630s, ever more
luxurious and stylized, embodied the same imperial
themes, portraying a monarchy almost Byzantine in its
theocratic paternalism.

It is extraordinarily difficult to assess this régime. It was
unsuccessful, of course, in the end, but we cannot assume
that failure was inevitable. When the Earl of Portland died
in 1635, he had balanced crown income and expenditure
at £618,000 a year, the debt stood at more than one and a
half million pounds (£1,163,000), but this was something
everyone was getting used to living with. The sale of
crown lands continued, but it was offset by increasing
impositions, particularly on colonial tobacco reshipped to
Europe. If Charles still lacked the money and the troops to
enforce direct rule, his subjects still lacked the means, and
above all the will, to oppose him by force. The 'personal
rule' of Charles I seems to us impermanent because we
know that it did not last; but short of a foreign invasion,

whether from Scotland or the Continent, it is difficult to
see what could have toppled it. Charles was a healthy man
in the prime of life; it is easy to imagine him dying in his
bed about 1660 (say), leaving the throne to a thirty-year-
old Charles II, moulded in his father's image, and long
married to a suitable Catholic princess chosen by his
mother, having grown up without even the memory of
Parliament.

It is too easy to blame the Scottish fiasco on the narrow
dogmatism of Laud. In fact, Scotland had been slipping
through Charles's fingers ever since his accession, and his
visit to Edinburgh in 1633 had only consolidated the
opposition to him. To govern Scotland from London was
just possible for a king like James, practised in the idiom of
Scots society and politics; it was impossible for a man who
was to all intents and purposes a complete foreigner. His
decision in 1637 to impose the Book of Common Prayer,
only slightly amended, on the Presbyterian Kirk was only
the spark which ignited the explosion.

The reaction was immediate and sustained. Outbreaks
in Edinburgh spread across the whole country, and the
General Assembly of the Church of Scotland assumed the
leadership of a national revolt against colonial domination,
which found a focus in the Covenant of 1638. Charles
promptly mobilized an army for the reconquest of Scotland the following year.

His failure was abysmal, though it is not clear that this
resulted from lack of money. The almost universal refusal
of ship money in this year was a symptom of defeat, not the
cause. Public confidence was lacking; indeed, there was
widespread apprehension of what a king victorious abroad
might turn to at home. The tactless presence of a number
of Catholic officers in the new army encouraged the belief
that some sort of coup was planned; the nickname

'Bishops' War' confirmed the deep lack of public sympathy or commitment. The war of 1625–9 had exposed crippling deficiencies in English military training and experience, particularly in the commissariat department, which had too easily been blamed on Buckingham. The English forces, ill-organized and ill-supplied, were thrown back by a fierce and fanatical Scots army, drilled and led by a veteran of the German War, Alexander Leslie. In desperation, Charles called upon his tenants-in-chief, but their assistance was largely confined to advice. In June 1639 he called a truce, began negotiating with the Scots, and sent for Wentworth from Dublin.

Wentworth's name has often been associated with Laud's in the implementation of a policy of 'Thorough'; but this is a posthumous label, based on a casual phrase in one of his admonitory letters to the archbishop. In these letters he certainly advocated a more aggressive and repressive policy than even Laud contemplated – he urged, for instance, that John Hampden be whipped – but his influence was indirect. Had he been appointed Lord Treasurer in 1635, as some suggested, it would have been different, but the Queen was hostile to him, and Charles shared her doubts. Nevertheless, he was now a notorious figure. He was the Lost Leader, the great apostate; the man who had ruled like a despot in the north and like a tyrant in Ireland. His rule in Ireland was brutally effective, but his methods would not stand up to detailed examination, and they proved one of the most serious counts against him at his impeachment. He roused antagonisms that only he could handle, and within two years of his departure Ireland rose in bloody revolt. However, he was now on the flood-tide of success, widely feared as the one man who might drive King Charles away from Parliament altogether, along the path to military dictatorship. His pattern of rule and his cast of mind are epitomized in a letter to Charles in 1637, urging him to eschew experiment in Scotland in favour of consolidation in England. 'This foundation well and truly laid,' he said, 'what under the goodness of Almighty God could be able to shake this monarchy, or stay the wheel of your Majesty's triumph?' He was to be the most important single factor in the outbreak of the Great Rebellion.

He came too late, of course. Charles was too deeply embroiled. Made Earl of Strafford and Lieutenant-General, he initiated vast and energetic schemes, but he underestimated the military effectiveness of the Scots, and he overestimated his own ability to dominate the new parliament he at once advised the King to summon for April 1640 ('The Short Parliament'). Militant, and at the same time apprehensive, the Commons refused to vote the huge sum of twelve subsidies now demanded unless their multitudinous grievances were settled, and when it became apparent that their leaders were negotiating with the Scots they were incontinently dissolved on 5 May, after only three weeks.

Strafford had already warned that if this parliament failed the King must 'use extraordinary means rather than, by the peevishness of some few factious spirits, suffer his state and government to be lost'. He now told him he was 'loosed and absolved from all rules of government', and 'being reduced to extreme necessity, everything is to be done that power might admit'. In fact, very little *was* done. A few Members of Parliament were jailed, a few London apprentices hung for rioting, bloodthirsty threats were used against London aldermen when they refused a loan. All this did was to confirm Charles and Strafford's reputation for brutal authoritarianism without their deriving any immediate benefit from it. The imposition of illegal taxation, the raising of troops by commissions of array, the employment of the Irish army against Scotland, were all discussed but not attempted. Resistance to Strafford from within the government exerted a paralysing effect, and Charles's public credit and popularity were still further eroded by Laud's decision to keep Convocation in session after the dissolution – in defiance of long-standing convention – and not only vote clerical taxation, but put through a new series of Canons which in the circumstances were insanely provocative: one of them reasserted the dogma of the Divine Right of Kings in the most extreme terms; another added fuel to the existing controversy over the position and nature of the altar in churches; another imposed on the clergy the notorious 'Etcetera Oath', pledging them to accept the government of the Church as then established.

In the brief campaign of that summer, not even Strafford's demoniac energy could revitalize the English army. The Scots invaded England, routed the English at Newburn and on 29 August took Newcastle. Still clutching at medieval precedents, Charles summoned a Great Council of the peerage to York, but it flatly advised him to make peace and summon another parliament. The award to the Scots of a subsidy of £25,000 a month, and their occupation of Durham and Northumberland as security against further claims, effectively shackled Charles to the Long Parliament, which assembled on 3 November 1640, and was not dissolved until 16 March 1660.

V

# THE GREAT REBELLION, 1640-42

The Great Rebellion of 1642 was the result of a tense struggle for power in the first two sessions of the Long Parliament. Obviously the new House of Commons was overwhelmingly critical of the King; in fact, it is difficult to speak of an 'opposition' when there was no government party for them to oppose; but they had no thought of revolution or rebellion, no thought of deposing the King or even making serious inroads on his prerogative. Their aim was reform, and reform of abuses which had arisen for the most part over the past ten years. The King had disturbed the balance of a perfectly acceptable constitution: by levying money without parliamentary consent, by abusing the powers of the prerogative courts, and by pressurizing the common-law judges to ignore the restrictions on his powers of imprisonment and punishment affirmed in the Petition of Right. In addition, there was a deep aversion to the policies of the bishops, both in Church and State. So the Commons' aim was to reform the judiciary and the episcopate and remove most of the existing high-court judges and bishops, to restrict the King's powers of taxation by statute, to compel him to consult parliaments at regular intervals, and to punish his immediate political and religious advisers.

This programme got under way at once. Laud and Strafford were impeached and sent to the Tower, a case was prepared against Lord Keeper Finch and the other ship-money judges, and Sir Francis Windebank fled to France under a similar threat. Committees were appointed to draft legislation on fiscal abuses and to consider the future of Star Chamber and High Commission. The only radical measure stemmed from the need to ensure that Parliament met regularly in the future, and the Triennial Act was the first reform statute to pass, on 16 February 1641. Its elaborate provisions for the automatic election and assembly of a parliament after three years if the King failed to summon one were probably unworkable, and in any case, they only applied to the next and subsequent parliaments; so it alienated the King without allaying the worst fears of his opponents, and its introduction was a bad political blunder. In all other respects, Charles placed himself on the side of reform; he told Parliament on 25 January that he would surrender 'what parts of my revenue that shall be found illegal or grievous to the public', regulate the courts of justice, 'reform all innovations in Church and Commonwealth', and 'reduce all matters of religion and government to what they were in the purest time of Queen Elizabeth's days'.

But influences were now at work which militated against a programme of peaceful reform. The apocalyptic preaching of many Puritan divines identified royal government with Antichrist and the Devil and raised expectations of a new Heaven and a new Earth. Moreover, the events of the last two or three years had convinced John Pym and his associates in the parliamentary leadership that a conspiracy had been in motion to erect a despotism in England and return the nation to Rome. This was the theme of Pym's 'keynote' speech on 7 November 1640, and it led to the decision to impeach Strafford for high treason instead of lesser crimes. The Commons' determination to destroy Strafford, not just imprison him or force him into private life, jeopardized any hope of a lasting accommodation with Charles, who had specifically invited the earl to come up to Westminster and guaranteed his safety.

In fact, an element of physical confrontation was always present in the deliberations of the Long Parliament, or as a background to them. Strafford was found to be negotiating with Spain for military assistance, even in the Tower, and the Queen was soliciting help from her brother Louis XIII; and her intrigues with the discontented officers of the English army came to light as the 'First Army Plot' in May 1641. As early as February, negotiations with Holland resulted in the betrothal of Charles's elder daughter Mary to William, son of the Stadholder Frederick Henry (the future William II of Orange), with some expectation of military aid. Charles's refusal to disband the Irish army, and the rumours of its imminent embarkation for England, created further tension.

The citizens of London were another extraneous element which offered violent, physical solutions. Their pressure was evident from the beginning, in the Root and Branch Petition of 11 December 1640, with 15,000 signatures, calling for the complete abolition of episcopacy. The political crisis engendered an economic crisis, and chronic unemployment provided a reservoir of idle youths and men ripe for riot. They first erupted in late January, on the news that Charles had reprieved a Catholic priest under sentence of death, and thereafter they were rarely off the streets. Damage to persons and property was negligible, and to some extent the mobs were guided and controlled by Pym and the City 'boss', Alderman Isaac Pennington; but there was always a doubt how far this control could be maintained in face of royal intransigence, and this contributed to Charles's decision to pass the Triennial Act. The King could now maintain that he had been forced to surrender his just prerogative by unconstitutional force.

Thus the attitude both of Pym and Charles made it impossible for the opposition to offer an alternative government. Early in 1641, various schemes were floated for a 'reform government' headed by the 4th Earl of Bedford, as Lord Treasurer, with Denzil Holles as Secretary of State and Pym as Chancellor of Exchequer, but they foundered on Bedford's premature death in May, leaving as sole survivors Lord Saye and Sele, the new Master of the Court of Wards, and Oliver St John, Solicitor-General, two aggressive radicals incapable of bridging the gap between the King and Parliament. The impeachment of Strafford and the problem of church reform drove a wedge between the two Houses, yet a strong aristocratic presence was generally acknowledged to be essential to sound government. At this critical juncture, Charles found himself driven back for advice on unpopular and discredited men like Lord Keeper Finch and Bishop Juxon, who in any case resigned the Treasury in May, and on the Queen.

The drift towards crisis was accelerated by the difficulty of dealing with Strafford. The Commons could not draw up a formal case against him until the end of January, and his trial did not open until 22 March. When it did, the prosecution were soon floundering in the face of a brilliantly improvised defence; the Lords were reluctant to convict one of their number for policies undertaken on the King's orders, they doubted the Commons' assertion that it was treason to 'come between' the King and his people, and they were unwilling to accept the alternative theory of 'cumulative' treason (that a series of similar acts, not individually treasonable, could be construed as treason). When the Lords adjourned the trial on 10 April as a protest against mob violence at Westminster, Pym had to agree to a Bill of Attainder. This would declare Strafford's guilt proved, but like any other Bill it was subject to the King's assent.

There is little doubt that Pym saw the threat of attainder as a tactical weapon, and it succeeded; the Lords resumed the trial at once. But Pym could no longer control the situation. Charles's second refusal to disband the Irish army, on 14 April, stampeded the Commons, and Pym was overborne by the 'Merciless Party'. The attainder passed on 21 April, 204 votes to 59, and was sent to the Lords. The following week William of Orange arrived to claim his bride, a plot was discovered to rescue Strafford from the Tower, and Charles refused a third request to disband the Irish army. Armed volunteers were now assembling in London, ostensibly to join Portugal's war of liberation against Spain, and on 2 May Sir John Suckling led a premature attempt on the Tower. The build-up to a *coup d'état* had begun.

In response, the Commons took its first revolutionary step: a unilateral appeal to the country against King and Lords. The Protestation of 3 May alerted the nation to the fact that there had been and still was a design 'to subvert the fundamental laws of England and Ireland, and to introduce the exercise of an arbitrary and tyrannical government by most ... wicked counsels, practices, plots and conspiracies'; and those who signed it engaged themselves to defend 'the true reformed religion, expressed in the doctrine of the Church of England', 'the power and privilege of Parliament' and 'the lawful rights and liberties of the subjects', as well as 'his Majesty's royal person, honour and estate'. At the same time the House brought in a Bill making it illegal to adjourn, prorogue or dissolve Parliament without its own consent; another revolutionary step, and a decided invasion of the royal prerogative. Two days later, Pym rallied the waverers by revealing a plot by army officers near to the Queen to disperse Parliament by force (The First Army Plot).

The great majority of the Commons were now half out of their wits with fear, and so were the people of London; for the next four days Whitehall and Westminster were besieged by angry mobs, and under this pressure the Lords passed Strafford's attainder on 8 May, together with the Bill to perpetuate the present parliament. This transferred the pressure to the King, who did not hold out long. Fearful for the safety of his wife and family, believing that mass revolution was on the point of breaking out in London, he gave the royal assent to both Bills the following day. Strafford, who in the end had magnanimously released Charles from all his promises, was executed on the 12th.

With Strafford safely dead, the Commons' programme of statutory reform, which had been in abeyance nearly six months, could go ahead. In June, July and August a long series of statutes declared ship money illegal and reversed the judgement in *Rex* v. *Hampden*, prohibited knighthood fines, defined the limits of the royal forests, abolished the Courts of High Commission and Star Chamber and suppressed the Council of the North and the Council in the Marches of Wales. The King's levy of tunnage and poundage was legalized at long last, but only for two months; it was to be renewed on the same terms every two months up to July 1642. There were doubts about Star Chamber, and some attempt was made to revive it in 1661, but it perished, and for good, in the reaction against Laud and all his works. Wardship, not dealt with this session, had to wait until 1646, and purveyance was not mentioned – an indication that these great issues of James I's reign had lost much of their potency. Similarly, all impositions then in force were legalized by the Tunnage and Poundage Act.

But these legislative triumphs, which a year earlier would have had men dancing in the streets, were now largely meaningless. To Charles the death of Strafford was the rape of his personal honour, and he made no secret of his lasting resentment. Almost his last words on the scaffold, in 1649, were, 'An unjust sentence that I suffered for to take effect, is punished now by an unjust sentence upon me.' He assented to any legislation put before him, but he made no public statements, and surrendered himself to the advice of the Queen, who had now taken Strafford's place as the leader of counter-revolutionary royalism. In mid May he announced his intention of visiting Edinburgh, where the very success of the Covenanting cause had brought dissension and disagreement, and there was some prospect of a new royalist party emerging. Moreover, to reach Scotland he would have to pass through the ranks of the English army, still discontentedly encamped in Yorkshire.

At the same time Pym was conscious of the fact that his own support, united against Strafford, united behind the Protestation, was slipping. Church reform had scarcely begun, yet it was already dividing the Commons, and opening a gap between them and the Lords. When the Commons debated the Root and Branch Petition on 8 February, no one was prepared to defend the present bishops, but the supporters of a reformed episcopacy rallied strongly, and proposals to rewrite the Prayer Book roused considerable passion. Weight was given to conservative arguments by the confusion already evident in London, arising from the spontaneous and almost total breakdown of ecclesiastical authority since Laud's imprisonment the previous December. The pulpits were free, clergymen could adopt or reject what observances they liked, restrained only by the will of their congregations, and separatists or Independants, rejecting any authority or uniformity at all, had emerged in astonishing numbers. Laud's belief that separatism was a serious, if concealed, problem was handsomely justified. Nor were some Members of Parliament happy at the popular riots which were now almost a daily occurrence, useful though they were to coerce the King. George Digby told the Commons of the danger of raising such multitudes by 'true or pretended stimulation of conscience', and lending their countenance to 'irregular and tumultuous assemblies of people, be it for never so good an end'. Sir John Strangeways warned them, 'If we make a parity in the Church, we must at last come to a parity in the commonwealth.' A right wing was emerging to counter-balance the 'Root-and-Branchers' and the 'Merciless Men' on the left, with, between them, a middle party led by Pym and Hampden which was to survive into the Civil War.

In an attempt to heal these divisions, Pym took up the only church proposal which had general support, and on 1 May a Bill to exclude the bishops from all secular employments, including the House of Lords, passed the Commons *nem. con.* But the Lords, resentful of the mob pressure now being brought to bear on them, and concerned at the religious anarchy prevailing in London, were certainly not prepared to alter the immemorial composition of their own house. On 24 May they deleted the clause excluding the bishops from Parliament; the Commons riposted by bringing in a Bill to abolish episcopacy altogether; the Lords took up the challenge and threw out the Bill at present before them.

The Root and Branch Bill was no mere charter of destruction; it offered a comprehensive secularization and reorganization of the Church, comparable with the Civil Constitution of the Clergy imposed on France in 1790. Not only were bishops to go, but deans and chapters; episcopal lands were to revert to the Crown, and dean and chapter lands were to be administered by trustees and used to finance a better preaching ministry at parish level. The discipline and government of the Church was to be placed in the hands of commissioners named by Parliament. But it would clearly never pass the Lords, and its progress through the Commons was protracted into August. In the meanwhile further attempts to coerce the Lords failed; in July they rejected a Bill to impose the Protestation of 3 May on all adult males, and they refused to sequester thirteen bishops now impeached by the Commons for their compliance with Laud's policy.

By this time the parliamentary leaders realized that they could no longer afford the luxury of quarrelling about religion. Charles showed no intention of forming a new government, and the assumption could only be that he hoped to restore the old régime by force; his journey to Edinburgh had been postponed, but he and the Queen were still planning to bring the Army of the North into play again, intrigues which broke five months later as the 'Second Army Plot'. Just as alarming in its own way was the emergence of the Earl of Bristol as the spokesman of constitutional royalism in the Lords, aided by his son George Digby, one of Pym's principal opponents, who was raised to the peerage in his own right in June. Aristocratic participation in reform was still politically vital, and acknowledged as such by the Commons leaders themselves; they could still be isolated and destroyed by a firm alliance between King and Lords.

Pym's remedy was the Ten Propositions, which he persuaded both Houses to accept on 24 June – a remarkable political *coup*, and eloquent of the extent to which Charles was still mistrusted, even by his potential supporters. The Propositions asked Charles to postpone his departure for Edinburgh until the Scots and English armies could both be disbanded, to bar all Catholics from Court and particularly from the presence of the young Prince of Wales, and to ensure internal security by calling out the militia and placing it under Lord Lieutenants who were 'faithful and trusty, and careful of the peace of the kingdom'. But the crucial request was that he replace his present ministers by 'such officers and counsellors as his people and Parliament may have just cause to confide in', and on matters of policy he also take the advice of a joint committee of both Houses set up for this purpose.

Nothing was less likely than that Charles I would accept these proposals, and he was right not to. Together with the Act which had already removed his control over the sittings of this parliament, the Ten Propositions would have effected a decisive change in the nature of the monarchy, and one not envisaged when Parliament was elected. He affirmed his faith in his present advisers, and set out for Scotland on 10 August, leaving Parliament still sitting, though in high summer it was now reduced to about eighty members and a dozen peers.

This shrunken body now hastened to conclude a peace treaty with Scotland, but in fact Charles passed through both armies without incident on his way north. He had made no provision for the government in his absence, and Parliament felt obliged to issue ordinances for internal security (disarming recusants, securing the arsenal of Hull, forbidding recruitment for foreign armies) which were a further encroachment on his executive power and of dubious legality; they also sent a joint committee hotfoot after him to Edinburgh. They then decided to take a six-week recess beginning on 9 September, which unfortunately left time for further disagreements on liturgy and ceremonial. The first session ended with the Lords issuing an order for the maintenance of the *status quo* in all London churches and the Commons publishing a resolution condemning all Laudian innovations.

Indeed, it was fortunate for the parliamentarians that Charles did not secure the aid he hoped for in Edinburgh; instead, he was driven to further concessions. He even had to agree to employ ministers in Scotland approved by the Scots Estates, a point not lost on Pym. The notorious 'Incident', implicating him in an abortive attempt to kidnap the Earl of Argyll, the lay spokesman of the Kirk, enhanced his reputation for cunning and dissimulation and emphasized his tactical maladroitness. However, the retirement from England of the Scots army seriously reduced the Long Parliament's coercive power over him.

When Parliament reassembled on 19 October, Pym played up the 'Incident' for all it was worth, even to the extent of bringing in the London trained-bands (or militia) to guard the House. But many members absent in July had now returned, opposition to Pym's tactics of confrontation was mounting, and the church question was as divisive as ever. The revival of the Bill to exclude the bishops from secular employments, and renewed discussion of the Prayer Book, were counter-productive; in fact they elicited from Charles (still in Edinburgh) a pronouncement which marks his first attempt to form an Anglican party. He authorized Sir Edward Nicholas, Secretary of State, to let it be known that, 'I am constant to the discipline and doctrine of the Church of England established by Queen Elizabeth, and I resolve, by the Grace of God, to die in the maintenance of it.'

But now the Irish rebellion gave another, and this time decisive turn to the screw. Physical confrontation was inevitable from the moment news reached London on 1 November that the Ulster Catholics had risen and the revolt was spreading south. The inevitable, though largely mendacious, accounts of atrocities committed on the Protestant settlers whipped public feeling to a frenzy. The rebellion at once brought to the forefront all the doubts about Charles's trustworthiness, truthfulness and sense of responsibility which had been growing since the very beginning of the reign – or before, if we count, as we must, the circumstances of his visit to Madrid in 1623, and his conspiracy of lies about it afterwards. Yet, under the law, only the King could recruit and command the large army which must now be raised for an Irish campaign. The reduction of his executive authority was more important than ever.

On 5 November the Commons rejected a resolution from Pym that unless Charles accepted officers and ministers approved by them they could not assist him in the reconquest of Ireland, only to fall back three days later on the much more revolutionary proposition that if the King would not change his advisers, Parliament would take steps to crush the Irish rebellion itself. (This was an 'Additional Instruction' to the parliamentary joint committee in Edinburgh; it was rejected by the Lords and went no further.) Meanwhile, a committee which had been drawing up a public statement of their case against the King ever since the previous December, was asked to complete its labours, and the result was the Grand Remonstrance. It provoked a debate of unprecedented length and bitterness on 22 November, and only passed by eleven votes (159 to 148) in a full house.

The Church Question was still the main stumbling-block, as it always had been, and this is betrayed by the Grand Remonstrances' honeyed approach. 'It is far from our purpose,' it said, 'to let loose the golden reins of discipline and government in the Church, to leave private persons or particular congregations to take up what form of divine service they please, for we hold it requisite that there should be throughout the realm a conformity to that order which the laws enjoin according to the Word of God.' But the form of service and the structure of the Church were to be changed, and they were to be changed by an assembly stiffened by the importation of Scots, Dutch and Huguenot divines; a proposal no sane Anglican could accept.

Over and above all this was the general tone of the document, often lost sight of now in discussion of particular points. From first to last it was a rehearsal of the now familiar 'conspiracy' theory, but it associated the King with that conspiracy more closely than ever before, and to such an extent that it was difficult to see how the authors proposed to rebuild the 'bridge' between him and Parliament. Equally serious was the Grand Remonstrance's all-out assault on the House of Lords, which was blamed even more than the King for blocking the way of reform. Its tone and language implied that it was either an attempt to bully the Lords yet again, or a warning that the Commons were ready to take unilateral action, with the support of the people. This prospect alarmed many members. 'This is a Remonstrance to the People,' said Culpeper accusingly. 'Remonstrances ought to be to the King for redress; we are not sent (here) to please the People.' Sir Edward Dering thought the same. 'When I first heard of a Remonstrance,' he said, 'I did not dream that we should remonstrate downward, tell stories to the People, and talk of the King as a third person.' They could not defeat the Grand Remonstrance itself, but they frustrated its main aim by refusing leave for it to be printed.

As a result it went off at half cock. It was not presented to the King until 1 December, and it was useless to pretend that it represented a consensus view, even in the Commons. Charles returned from Scotland at last on 25 November, and received a truly royal welcome from the City of London. The Lord Mayor and aldermen pledged their support, and he repeated by proclamation his pledge to support the Church as by law established. He had now extended his patronage to Edward Hyde in the Commons and Bristol in the Lords, but not his confidence; and it was suspected that he was still intent on an armed confrontation; there were rumours that he planned to arrest the parliamentary leaders, and further unemployed officers were gathering in London, ostensibly for service in Ireland. There were several minor clashes between them and the apprentices, but the King – unwisely as it turned out – insisted on removing the guards Parliament had placed round the Palace of Westminster.

All Pym could do was to bring in an Impressment Bill, denying the King the right to recruit men for service outside their own county, and then a Militia Bill (eventually promulgated as the Militia Ordinance the following spring), to place control of the county militia in the hands of Lord Lieutenants approved by Parliament. But it was unlikely that either Bill would pass at this stage, and Pym could only hold on to his remaining supporters by a wholesale compromise on religion; on 18 December the Commons accepted a Lords' resolution to tolerate no form of worship in the United Kingdom except that established by law, thus throwing over much of their public support in the City.

In fact, the King still had a good chance of prevailing by constitutional means. The Lords were rock steady, and on 12 December he issued a proclamation calling upon absent Members of Parliament to return to their duties within a month, hoping to swamp Pym's precarious majority. But he was rattled by the result of the elections to the City of London Common Council on 21 December, at which the allies of the parliamentary opposition swept the board, leaving the Lord Mayor and aldermen marooned. The example of their social superiors encouraged the mobs, and on the 23rd Charles made the fatal error of putting the Tower under the command of Colonel Thomas Lunsford, a highly efficient career officer, but a man with an unsavoury reputation for sadism, brutality and violence. Even the Lords protested, and the Lord Mayor warned the King that he could not accept responsibility for public order if Lunsford remained. Three days later, Lunsford was replaced by Sir John Byron, a more douce and acceptable choice, but the damage was done. Charles's choice of a tool like Lunsford cast further doubts on his motives; conversely, a further challenge had been made to his freedom to choose his own servants, and this time it had been successful. He could not fail to respond.

Just after Christmas came his last chance of triumphing constitutionally. For some time attendance at the House of Lords had been a hazardous ordeal for the bishops; on 27 December they were badly rabbled by the mob, and the next day only two of them took their seats. (The frustrated rioters launched a violent attack on Westminster Abbey, narrowly beaten off.) Unfortunately, Digby chose that day to put a resolution before the Lords that, under present conditions, their deliberations were no longer free, and they should adjourn to another place. It only failed by four votes. Had it passed, the political situation would have been transformed; throughout the crisis the Lords had retained their constitutional ascendancy, and it is difficult to imagine a majority of the Commons continuing to sit without them – they were only just prepared to do so in 1648.

Charles now began to lose patience. On 29 December he proposed that the Lords raise 10,000 volunteers for Ireland under his own command, he provocatively held a public dinner at Whitehall for his leading officers, and he ordered all his courtiers to wear swords. But then he suffered a severe setback. On 30 December, Archbishop Williams handed in a protest subscribed by eleven of his colleagues, asking that the proceedings of the 28th be expunged and the vote for an adjournment retaken, on the grounds that they had been prevented from attending by unlawful threats. It was a strange role for John Williams, who as Bishop of Lincoln had remained Laud's chief opponent from within the Church; he had been translated to the Archbishopric of York only a few weeks before as a candidate acceptable to Parliament. As it was, he soon joined Laud in the Tower, for the Lords now lost patience with the bishops, whose previous policies were largely to blame for the present crisis, whose continued presence had divided them from the Commons, and who were now trying to maintain that the House could not reach a valid decision in their absence. They simply dispatched their protest to the Commons, who promptly impeached all twelve for high treason (for 'attempting to subvert the fundamental laws of the kingdom' – already a stereotyped formula). The Lords promptly sent them to the Tower.

This not only undermined the King's immediate position in the House of Lords, it threatened a serious slippage in the long-term situation. On 1 January 1642, he

rejected a last plea that he offer Pym the vacant Chancellorship of the Exchequer; it went to Sir John Culpeper
instead, and the Secretaryship of State to Lucius Cary,
Viscount Falkland, another Anglican loyalist. At the same
time, acting on a rumour that the Queen was to be impeached for complicity in the Irish rebellion, he moved
to impeach instead five of the Commons leaders, Pym,
Hampden, Denzil Holles, Sir Arthur Haslerigg and
William Strode, together with Viscount Mandeville
(later Earl of Manchester). Proceedings were also contemplated against the leaders of the upper house: the
Earls of Warwick, Essex and Holland, and Lords Wharton,
Saye and Sele, and Brooke. The Lords refused to order the
arrest of the 'Five Members', and so did the Commons;
both Houses voted the Attorney-General's indictment 'a
scandalous paper'. Charles at once accelerated his plan
for a military *coup d'état*. He replaced the normal, London-
based garrison of the Tower by artillerymen from the old
Army of the North, announced that henceforward
Parliament would be protected by his own guards, headed
by the Earl of Lindsey, and ordered the Lord Mayor to
mobilize the trained-bands and prevent further rioting, by
gunfire if necessary. On the afternoon of 4 January he rode
down to Westminster at the head of three or four hundred
armed men and entered the House of Commons himself to
arrest the 'Five Members'; only to find that they had fled
to the City.

The enormity of this assault on the privilege of Parliament swung public opinion decisively against the King –
Lords, Commons, Mayor and Aldermen, the Inns of
Court. The Commons as a body took refuge in the City, at
Grocers' Hall, where they made the momentous decision
to assume control of the City trained-bands and appoint
their own commander, Philip Skippon. On 10 January,

the King and Queen left London for Hampton Court, fearing for their own safety and hoping to raise support in the provinces or abroad.

In fact he found little support, and civil war seemed as unlikely as ever. The Protestation of May 1641 and the Grand Remonstrance, belatedly published in December, had obviously done their work, plus a steady stream of pamphlets and sermons from London; many were anxious to remain neutral, few would stand out against Parliament. For two months Charles stayed within reach of London, at Windsor, Hampton Court or Greenwich, while his position deteriorated. Plans to seize the arsenals at Hull, Portsmouth and Kingston were all frustrated; his entourage was riddled with informers. In February, Henrietta Maria left for the Continent in search of assistance, but it was soon apparent that neither Louis XIII nor the Prince of Orange was in a position to help, embroiled as they still were in the Thirty Years War. It is eloquent of the weakness of his cause that Charles even considered hiring mercenaries from Denmark.

In contrast, Parliament's authority was not in the least diminished by the King's departure, nor the numerous desertions which followed. Its omnicompetence and, in a sense, its right to speak for the nation were blindly accepted, and such disobedience as it experienced was entirely passive. A sense of emergency strengthened Pym's hand, and his control was extended to the House of Lords, which now passed the Militia Bill from the previous December and the Bill to exclude the bishops from Parliament, so long contested between the Houses. Desperate by now, Charles gave his assent to the bishops' Bill. He refused the Militia Bill, but he accepted the alternative Impressment Bill, by which he surrendered control of troops raised for Ireland, and he offered to refer the settlement of the Church to Parliament, reserving only a general right of veto.

This was a basis for negotiation, but Charles was still deeply mistrusted, and he was known to be seeking military aid abroad and planning to secure Hull as a port of embarkation – though it is difficult to see what else he could have done in the circumstances. As for the spokesmen of the Long Parliament, they had been overtaken now by 'the irresistible momentum of revolution', though the stalwart conservatives, or 'conservationists', who now comprised the Middle Party backing Pym, Holles and Hampden, would have rejected the label 'revolutionary' with disgust, assuming they even understood it. It was impossible for them to turn back, and almost as difficult for them to stand still. For one thing, the whole economy and the social order seemed on the point of breakdown. There were enclosure riots all over England: in Durham, Yorkshire, Huntingdonshire, Lincolnshire, Middlesex, Somerset, Dorset, Wiltshire and Cornwall. There were riots against the Forest Law in Northamptonshire, Essex, Surrey, Hampshire and Berkshire, and riots in the Fens against the drainage scheme. Working-class resentment found a religious focus in minor jacqueries against local Catholic gentry. On 31 January 'the poor artificers' of London and Westminster presented a petition to Parliament calling simply for bread; next day their wives picketed the Commons, pleading that their children were starving. Even Charles requested Parliament to look into 'the decay of trade'. War offered a way out, and a few already dimly perceived it. War would solve the unemployment problem, and at the same time discipline the lower classes, who seemed almost out of control. Accordingly, on 5 March both Houses voted to put the kingdom 'in a posture of defence', appointed new Lord Lieutenants in

counties amenable to their influence, placed the navy
under the command of the Earl of Warwick, and passed an
ordinance to levy £4 million in taxation by December.
Ironically, the new tax was modelled on ship money, in
that the central government assessed each county for a
lump sum, to be raised by local committees appointed in
the ordinance. This 'assessment' financed the ambitious
operations of the Long Parliament and Oliver Cromwell
right up to 1660, and was the model for subsequent land
taxes.

Parliament's actions were now so far in advance of its
ideas, and it was so difficult to justify its conduct by reference to any past tradition, that it merely invented arguments as it went along. In March, Charles pottered north,
vainly hoping to raise popular support in Yorkshire, and
still intent on seizing Hull. The refusal of the parliamentary
governor, Sir John Hotham, to admit him to the town on
23 April provoked him to a strong protest. In reply,
Parliament derided 'this erroneous maxim, being infused
into princes, that their kingdoms are their own, and that
they may do with them what they will'. On the contrary,
they said, his executive power was only 'entrusted to him
for the good and safety and best advantage [of the nation];
and as this trust is for the use of the kingdom, so ought it to
be managed by the advice of the Houses of Parliament'.
When he issued a proclamation on 27 May forbidding his
subjects to obey the Militia Ordinance, Parliament inched
forward another step, this time driving a distinction between the person and the office of a king, and envisaging
the latter as transferable elsewhere. They roundly declared
that their own decisions had 'the stamp of royal authority',
even though 'his Majesty, seduced by evil counsel, do in
his own person oppose or interrupt the same', and that
'the King's supreme and royal pleasure is exercised and

declared in this high court of law and counsel after a more
eminent and obligatory manner than it can be by personal
act or resolution of his own'.

Charles's resources were still so thin that on 1 June
Parliament sent him the 'Nineteen Propositions'; terms of
unconditional surrender which required him to give up all
his powers of command, appointment and policy-making
right across the board, even in the education, upbringing
and marriage of his own children. Terms as harsh as this
were enough to provoke a public reaction in themselves,
and they also produced a new-look Charles, preaching
moderation, public order and the preservation of the right
order of society, which made an appearance in the
'Answer to the Nineteen Propositions', on 18 June, and in
other royal pronouncements in the months that followed.
The new Charles I (so liberal that he was appropriated by
the Whigs of William III's reign) survived to the very
scaffold, but how far he was sincere is still a teasing problem. The 'Answer to the Nineteen Propositions' was composed by Culpeper and Falkland; it alarmed Edward
Hyde, who arrived at the King's headquarters at York too
late to change it. They argued that the English constitution was a mixed or balanced government, consisting
of monarchy, aristocracy and democracy, and that
the Commons were claiming powers which would tip the
balance fatally towards democracy. (Hyde objected to the
implication that the King was merely one of three estates –
not a supreme entity above the three estates of lords, clergy
and commons – and this proposition was in fact declared
treasonable in 1660.) But they came through strongly in
the end, with a prescient warning that, if Parliament held
to its present course, it would let in the common people,
who would 'call parity and independence liberty, destroy
all rights and proprieties, all distinctions of families and

merit, and by this means this splendid and excellently distinguished form of government [will] end in a dark, equal chaos of confusion, and the long line of our many noble ancestors in a Jack Cade or a Wat Tyler'.

In a time of mounting disorder, such appeals could not fail of their effect; already in May and June a trickle of peers and gentry, including many Members of Parliament, had begun to come in to the King at York, followed by Lord Keeper with the all-important Great Seal – and unlooked-for prize. On 15 June thirty-five peers subscribed to an engagement stating that neither they nor the King desired a war of aggression, conquest or revenge; their aim was 'the firm and constant settlement of the true Protestant religion, the just privileges of Parliament, the liberty of the subject, and the law, peace and prosperity of this kingdom'. Commissions of array were at once issued to raise troops, and loans were floated to pay them, though for the moment Charles was reliant on the generosity of two millionaire earls, Newcastle and Worcester. Newcastle seized the town of that name later that month, giving the royalists a port at last, and he secured Northumberland and Durham. Charles's following was still small, but early in July Herefordshire, Worcestershire and Warwickshire declared for him, and on the 9th Parliament began mobilizing an army of 10,000 men with the Earl of Essex as Lord General. It published a declaration accusing the King of starting the war, and on the 15th the first blood was shed, in a scuffle at Manchester.

With war now inevitable, opinion among the upper classes began to swing in the King's favour; whatever Charles's faults, he remained their liege lord. He was also assisted by a declaration of both Houses on 18 August that all who supported him were traitors. All the same, when he raised his standard at Nottingham three days later the

effect was disappointing, and it needed another intemperate pronouncement from Westminster to speed recruitment. On 6 September Parliament rejected the King's
latest peace overtures out of hand, and announced that the
war would be financed by mulcting those who had been or
were to be declared 'delinquents', as well as 'other
malignant and disaffected persons'. This vague and
arbitrary threat created a climate of uncertainty in which
no man could feel safe. Next day they went far beyond any
previous agreement on the ecclesiastical front by voting to
abolish episcopacy – a signal capitulation to the Puritan
left wing. On the 19th, Charles published a manifesto in
which he told his supporters, 'You shall meet with no
enemies but traitors, most of them Brownists, Anabaptists
and Atheists; such who desire to destroy both Church and
State, and who have already condemned you to ruin for
being loyal to us.' By this time he was marching down
through Staffordshire, and Essex had taken up his command of the parliamentary army near Northampton.

# VI

# THE CIVIL WARS AND
# INTERREGNUM, 1642–60

The Civil Wars were a unique occurrence in modern British history, and the events of these campaigns have been recounted again and again without adding significantly to our knowledge. Modern research, focusing on social, administrative and governmental problems, is still patchy in its results.

First, it is clear that this was no bitter ideological struggle – despite the novel theories put about by both sides and the fury generated in London in 1641 and 1642. We must always keep in mind the fact that fully half the upper classes, including half the Long Parliament itself, took no part in the wars at all. Many families were divided, with members on both sides; and though this caused initial bitterness, in the end it encouraged moderation. Without Parliament's aggressive intransigence in the autumn of 1642, the King would have been hard put to it to raise an army in the beginning, and though, as the wars developed, the magic of his presence and the authority of his office gathered men to him, support often collapsed in his wake. This was particularly noticeable in the Midlands. His only other significant outposts were in Devon and Cornwall, under Sir Ralph Hopton, and in Yorkshire and Northumberland, overrun by the private army raised by the Earl (now Marquess) of Newcastle. But both sides were hampered by the provincialism of their followers, and their unwillingness to serve outside their own region; a tendency evident even in the redoubtable Eastern Association, formed by Parliament out of the East Anglian counties, plus Essex, Cambridge and Hertford. (In any case, the basic purpose of such county associations was defensive.) Parliament's avowed aim was to reach a settlement with the King, and an active Peace Party emerged in Lords and Commons almost as soon as the war started, retaining its influence at least down to the winter of 1644–5.

Parliament's possession of London was an obvious advantage; certainly it gave Lord Essex the military initiative and internal lines of communication, if he could use them. But the City was a fickle and unruly jade, difficult to control and expensive to feed; the mobs which had yelled for Strafford's head and the Queen's impeachment were soon out in the streets again demanding peace and cheap bread. In the field of finance and organization Parliament had a clear superiority, thanks to Pym's new assessment of 1642; and the county committees for the assessment soon developed into a regular provincial government; additional duties were allocated to them by ordinance, others they assumed themselves. In 1643 Pym also imposed an excise on tobacco, beer, wine and cider, soon to be extended to other popular commodities – another long-lasting innovation, and one rejected by the parliaments of 1610 and 1628. The royalists had to find money in a much more sketchy and *ad hoc* manner, by voluntary contributions, involuntary fines and downright looting. Even in this sphere Parliament was much more efficient, as it showed by the Sequestration Ordinance of 1643, which placed the estates of known royalists under the control of local commissioners and diverted their rents to the rebel government.

Parliament also controlled the navy, but this was more

ornamental than useful; apart from the evacuation of Essex's cavalry from Cornwall in 1644, no attempt was made to move men by sea. Perhaps the planners were chastened by Buckingham's experience. Command of the sea would have been crucial if Charles had been able to call on help from abroad, but Spain, France and Holland were still engrossed in the Thirty Years War, and no country was willing to assist a monarch who was known to be seeking help anywhere and everywhere and who might at any moment make a firm alliance with one's enemy. Moreover, in the context of recent European history, the petty skirmishes in England seemed unimportant and unlikely to reach any dangerous conclusion. Charles struggled on alone; his family links with the House of Orange and the House of Bourbon, and his pre-war entente with Spain, availed him nothing.

With the advantage of hindsight, it is clear that Charles's failure to win an immediate victory and reoccupy London was ultimately decisive. At Edgehill in October 1642 the royalists showed an overwhelming superiority in cavalry, led by the King's Palatine nephew, Prince Rupert, but the overall direction of the army was weak; a marginal victory was not consolidated in the field, nor followed up. When Charles advanced on London in November he was halted by the City trained-bands at Turnham Green. Instead of crossing the river and executing a flanking movement into Kent, where he would have found plenty of support, he retreated tamely to his new headquarters at Oxford.

However, he was competing in the field, which no one would have predicted six months before, and he was more than holding his own. Already there was deep dissatisfaction in London with the tactics of the Lord General, Essex. Moreover, the King's participation remained essential to any peace settlement, and agitation for peace was growing; in May 1643 a royalist plot was discovered involving several sitting members of both Houses. This is reflected in the 'Propositions of Oxford', submitted to Charles in February 1643; they marked a significant retreat from the 'Nineteen Propositions', though the demand for the abolition of episcopy and the exclusion from pardon of some of his principal followers rendered them unacceptable.

In the campaigning season that followed, the royalists again took the initiative. In a series of victories culminating in the battle of Roundway Down in July, Sir Ralph Hopton consolidated his grip on Devon, Cornwall and Somerset, and Rupert seized Bristol, the country's second port. In the north, Lord Newcastle defeated Sir Thomas Fairfax at Adwalton Moor in June and occupied the whole of Yorkshire, except for Hull. The King wanted to capitalize on these victories by making a three-pronged attack on London, but his strength soaked away into the ground. The western army refused to advance any further, and though Newcastle did march south into Lincolnshire he came up against strong opposition from the Army of the Eastern Association, with Oliver Cromwell its cavalry general. He had to retreat, and as a *pis aller* Charles set about the siege of Gloucester. Essex marched from London to raise the siege, and the two armies fought a bloody but indecisive battle at Newbury in September.

Both sides were now dissatisfied with their progress, and were seeking reinforcements. In September 1643 Charles ordered his lieutenant, the Marquess of Ormonde, to negotiate a year's truce with the rebel Catholic Confederacy in Ireland. All he got out of it was the repatriation of the remnants of Strafford's Irish army; in return he compromised his reputation still further by appearing to endorse the prospect of an independent Catholic Ireland. But Pym's deal with the Scots the previous month also involved a compromise with religious extremism. In return for military aid the Scots demanded the reform of the English Church on strict Presbyterian lines, a concept which had never had much support at Westminster, and now had less. On the outbreak of war church reform had been shelved; the Prayer Book was not proscribed, there had been no formal move against the Laudian clergy, and even the bishops survived, though in a state of suspended animation; Parliament had resolved to abolish them in 1642, but nothing had been done to translate this into law. Pym had to play for time. In the Solemn League and Covenant with Scotland, now to be imposed on all office-holders, Parliament agreed to reform the English Church 'according to *the word of God and* the example of the best reformed churches', but the words in italics, inserted by Pym's envoy, Sir Henry Vane, offered infinite room for manoeuvre. To interpret the word of God he summoned the Westminster Assembly of divines, which sat until 1648, but it was stiffened by a strong minority of experienced laymen, and all its decisions were subject to parliamentary approval. The event was to show that there was a great difference between approving church reform and giving it legal backing.

Pym died in December 1643, leaving the moderate or 'middle' party in Parliament leaderless. (Hampden had been killed in action the previous summer.) The initiative fell to the brilliant Sir Henry Vane, though his 'Independant' party did not command a parliamentary majority, and during 1644 he moved steadily closer to Oliver Cromwell, the rising star of the army. They shared a belief in complete religious toleration and a growing conviction that the constitutional impasse could only be bridged by extreme measures, perhaps even the deposition of King Charles. But the implementation of their programme demanded complete military victory, and it was becoming clear that this was something the conservative, upper-class parliamentary generals did not want. Essex himself, the Earl of Manchester, Cromwell's own commander in the Eastern Association, and even Sir William Waller, whose initial victories in the south had given him the nickname 'William the Conqueror', hoped for a negotiated settlement on a basis of mutual exhaustion.

However, the campaign of 1644 opened with a bang. The Scots crossed the border, Fairfax erupted from Hull, and the Marquess of Newcastle was squeezed. Lord Manchester led the Army of the Eastern Association into Yorkshire to join Fairfax in the siege of York while Rupert marched north to the rescue, and the five armies, three parliamentarian and two royalist, met at Marston Moor, near York, on 2 July. For the first time Parliament's cavalry, led by Cromwell and the Scots David Leslie, mastered Rupert's horse, but the victory was not followed up. To Cromwell's disgust Manchester took his army back into East Anglia, while in the south the King virtually destroyed Waller's army at Alresford and Cropredy Bridge. Essex advanced into Cornwall, was trapped at Lostwithiel, and had to evacuate his horse by sea, leaving the infantry to surrender. Even then, by October Essex and Waller had reorganized their forces, and joined Manchester in an attempt to stop the King raising the siege of Donnington Castle. But despite Parliament's overwhelming superiority in numbers, the second battle of Newbury was indecisive, and in a famous confrontation after the battle Cromwell accused Manchester of pulling his punches because he did not want to defeat the King conclusively. Manchester did not deny it.

Returning to Westminster for the winter, Cromwell, with the support of the Independants, demanded a clean sweep of the military high command and the establishment of a national army subject to direct central control. He got his way. The Self-Denying Ordinance forced all members of both Houses to resign their commands, and a 'New Model' Army was formed under Sir Thomas Fairfax, its pay guaranteed by a new assessment. Cromwell was reappointed general of horse and second-in-command. The peace proposals submitted to Charles at Uxbridge marked a return to the 'unconditional surrender' terms of 1642, with the additional requirement that he implement the Solemn League and Covenant.

Charles refused, but with the new campaigning season the New Model Army at once seized the initiative and held it. It destroyed the King's main army at Naseby in June 1645, and his Western Army at Langport in July. Rupert surrendered Bristol, and after a quarrel with the King went abroad. In the spring of 1646 it proved impossible to raise a new royalist army of any significant size; the King surrendered to the Scots army in May, and the following month Oxford capitulated.

The first Civil War had been a traumatic experience, of course, but its impact is still very difficult to assess. The principal armies were small and their casualties in proportion, and atrocities were rare enough to attract a great deal of adverse comment. But in every area, even those apparently outside the war zone, there were continual skirmishes and scuffles, often the result of local feuds, and the emergence in 1645 of the Clubmen, associations of peasants grimly determined to keep both armies off their land, suggests a fair degree of agricultural disruption. Internal trade and distribution were also affected. On the other hand, Parliament's high taxation was successfully levied up to the end of the war, which suggests that agricultural produce continued to be sold and rents continued to be paid; and the administration of justice, by local magistrates and judges of assize, held up remarkably well – and continued to do so up to 1660.

But in any evenly matched civil war the victor is likely to be as unpopular as the vanquished, and from 1642 to 1645 the Long Parliament's unpopularity increased in proportion to its power. The mandate on which it had been elected in 1640 had long ago expired, and it was reduced to about 150 Members of Parliament and 25 peers. The 'recruiter' elections ordered in August 1645 brought in 244 new members over the next eighteen months, but only increased the average attendance at divisions from 105 to 155; in any case, these elections were of doubtful legality. In 1646, the Lords slumped to between twelve and eighteen. In most areas the arbitrary rule of the county committees was deeply resented, and had exacerbated existing differences among the local gentry. Taxation was at an unprecedentedly high level, and was punitively enforced, yet Parliament persistently refused to publish its accounts. The excise was bitterly unpopular, and it affected most of the population; and the financial sacrifice was the more resented because of Parliament's palpable lack of war aims, apart from the defeat of the King.

The war aim which had the strongest appeal to the public was religion, and here Parliament's record was particularly deplorable. The Westminster Assembly had speedily drawn up a new Directory of Worship, promulgated by ordinance in 1645, but Parliament proposed no alternative form of church government; it did not even enforce the Directory. The bishops still remained, powerless as they were, nor was the Book of Common Prayer proscribed, though the statutes enforcing its use had been suspended. Meanwhile zealots in the Commons had pushed through a sabbatarian ordinance so rigid that even travel was forbidden on a Sunday, and in 1644 another ordinance forbad the celebration of Christmas – measures not likely to commend them to the uncommitted majority. In fact, after Pym's death the difficulty of dealing with their sectarian and congregationalist allies forced the parliamentary leaders back on a strict Presbyterian solution in alliance with the Scots, thus the Propositions of Uxbridge, in 1644–5. In 1645, Parliament itself took the first steps in the same direction. Laud was tried for treason, found guilty and executed. Lay preaching was forbidden, and in August an ordinance was passed for the erection of Presbyterian church government, but without any coercive clauses to give it teeth. Both measures were fiercely opposed by the Independants.

The precise distinction between Presbyterians and Independants at this stage is so subtle that it has exercised the talents of some of our leading professional historians over a number of years to little avail. It ought to be easy to distinguish between advocates of a strict Presbyterian form of church government, and those who believed in congregationalism, the *independence* of each individual congregation without reference to any superior authority under God. True enough, but these terms also implied a political orientation, and many used or accepted them without much regard to their religious meaning. In political terms, a 'Presbyterian' believed in the absolute necessity of a negotiated compromise with the King, and the reimposition of tight ecclesiastical discipline (but they found Anglican discipline satisfactory enough in 1660). An 'Independant' took a much harder line: the coercion of the King and perhaps even his deposition, the reduction of monarchical authority and the introduction of complete religious toleration, though many Independants accepted the need for some centralized ecclesiastical organization. Fearing chaos in religion and government, a majority in Parliament fell back on Presbyterianism, which at least had the advantage of being amenable to lay control. It was a policy which enjoyed little popular support, but the King was still the key to the situation, and the fact that he was in the hands of the Scots, who were heavily committed to Presbyterianism, was a factor which could not be ignored. Thus the Propositions put to him at Newcastle in June 1646 reiterated the demand made at Uxbridge in 1644-5 that he surrender much of his executive power and sign the Solemn League and Covenant. Its urgent need of money also obliged Parliament to add to the list of prominent royalists whose estates were to be confiscated; it hesitated to impose further taxation, which in the circumstances might well be refused and would certainly be bitterly unpopular. (It was the King's good luck that in defeat he could postpone the settlement of his debts to another day.) Similarly, the belated decision to abolish episcopacy by ordinance in October 1646 was dictated as much as anything by the need to lay hands on the income from the bishops' lands.

While Charles temporized – there was little else he could do – Parliament scraped together the money to pay off the Scots Army in February 1647 and received the King in return. Once he was safely established at Holdenby House, Northants, a settlement was in sight, and in view of Charles's mounting popularity with the public at large, his public attitude of studied moderation, and Parliament's obvious weakness, it seemed likely to be a compromise settlement acceptable to both parties. With the Scots gone, the highly expensive army could now be reduced, and with it most of Parliament's problems; plans were put in hand to demobilize many units and ship others to Ireland, which was still in revolt. Their pay was in arrears, but this was so usual in the seventeenth century that it did not seem a serious obstacle. Indeed, the remaining regiments formed before 1645, outside the New Model, were demobilized without fuss.

But the reaction of the New Model Army was immediate and remarkable. Each regiment chose its own 'agitators', who demanded full arrears of pay and a watertight indemnity for their conduct during the late war. Receiving no satisfactory response, they then called a general meeting at Newmarket, where an Army Council was set up, consisting of the generals plus two officers and two men from each regiment. This Council ordered the King to be brought over from Holdenby, and on 14 June 1647 it issued a Declaration of the Army, the first of many.

Their aims and motives are still a matter for debate. Until quite recently it was accepted orthodoxy that the rank and file were sectarian zealots, 'Saints in Arms', with a mission to reform both Church and State on egalitarian lines. This is scarcely surprising, because it was a view industriously put about at the time by the army's friends as well as its enemies, and enshrined in many of its public appeals, beginning with this Declaration of 14 June, which made the celebrated assertion: 'We were not a mere mercenary army, hired to serve any arbitrary power of a state, but called forth and conjured by the several Declarations of Parliament to the defence of our own and the people's just rights and liberties.' It went on to demand direct political concessions; it called upon Parliament to remove those of its members hostile to the army, to curb the authority of county committees, to pay off all arrears and publish detailed accounts, to pass a comprehensive

Act of Oblivion, and then dissolve itself and hold new elections.

However, it is doubtful if this represented the views of a majority of the troops. Whatever the Army Council now said, the New Model *was* a mercenary army, recruited in the war-weary winter of 1644–5 by the inducement of better and more assured pay or by forced impressment, and it had always been subject to a much stricter discipline than the other Civil War armies. True, some of its chaplains were vocal and publicity minded sectarian zealots, but many more, perhaps a majority, were orthodox, conservative congregationalists, even Presbyterians. As for their 'agitators', the name is synonymous with 'agents'; they were, in fact, shop stewards. Like most shop stewards they were politically to the left of the men who chose them, but their prime concern in the summer of 1647 was with such bread-and-butter matters as pay, arrears and indemnity. The Declaration only touched on such matters as the scope of the King's future authority in very general terms, and its most radical demand was that the term of future parliaments be limited.

The most that can be said of this army is that it did have a sense of accomplishment, arising from total victory in battle; it was very conscious of being an élite corps. Its collective self-confidence was enhanced by the bastard Calvinistic belief that success was a sign of God's favour, and by a passionate desire that its past sacrifices should not be thrown away. It also had an awareness of the apposition between military and civilian society which was something new in England.

In a comparatively short time many of the agitators became deeply infected by Leveller ideas, but the Levellers originated outside the army; they were an urban, indeed a metropolitan party, drawing their strength from the support of the London unemployed, and their ideas principally from John Lilburne. Lilburne in turn drew much of his inspiration from Sir Edward Coke's *Second Institutes*, published in 1642. Coke lent his enormous authority to what was later to be regarded as the Whig view of English history: that absolute kingship was a Norman device unconstitutionally imposed on the free and equal society of Anglo-Saxon England; but the principles of that society had been reaffirmed in Magna Carta, had never been lost sight of, and were now under the guardianship of Parliament. From this Lilburne further concluded that all Englishmen were born equal, and had equal political rights, and though it is still a matter for debate whether he envisaged the introduction of adult manhood suffrage, he certainly called for the enfranchisement of all freeholders, which would have produced a massive increase in the electorate. At the same time he called for the abolition of the monarchy and the House of Lords, the wholesale revision and codification of the Common Law, and the enforcement of religious toleration. Not surprisingly, he spent most of 1647 in gaol, and his campaign for working-class support in London was disrupted. To him and his followers the mutinous army offered a new and secure base for their operations. Subsequent infiltration was rapid, and *The Case of the Army Truly Stated*, issued on 15 October 1647 by the Army Council, was a considerable advance, in radical terms, on the Declaration of 14 June from Newmarket.

The reaction of the generals was mixed, and particularly Cromwell's. Though he was a passionate believer in toleration, and at Westminster was accounted an advanced radical, he shared all the prejudices of the conservative small-gentry class from which he sprang. He was much more likely to be guided by his religious than his political beliefs. His religious position has always defied precise analysis, but in a general sense there is no doubt that his military victories had gone to his head, and now and later he was quite capable, at least at intervals, of visualizing himself as a kind of Davidic hero, sent by God to rescue the English nation. What is sinister is Cromwell's isolation. Apart from his commander-in-chief, the aloof, self-effacing Sir Thomas Fairfax, his sole confidant was his friend and son-in-law Henry Ireton. But he left Ireton in Ireland in 1650, and he died there in 1651. After that he talked a little to the lawyer Bulstrode Whitelocke, but only as one on whom he could try out the occasional idea.

To Cromwell, the New Model Army was an instrument which up to 1647 had done great things for God, and might yet do more. So he proceeded cautiously, lest the instrument break in his hands. At one time he would treat the troops like wayward and indulged children unwilling to recognize their father's authority; at another time like malign spirits who threatened to sabotage the great mission to which they were all committed. His first reaction, in May 1647, was to disown the 'agitators' in the interests of military discipline, but once it was clear that they could not be detached from the army as a whole, and when Parliament proscribed them and ordered the army to disperse, he was left with little choice. It was now up to him and Ireton to reach a new agreement with the King which would short-circuit both Parliament and the Army Council. A crisis in London also cleared the air. Terrorized by mob violence, the Speaker and a group of Independant members fled to St Albans in August and requested the army to restore order. The army advanced on London, and in the modern idiom 'liberated' it – by purging the Lords, Commons and City government. Parliament's legal authority was already dubious, now its political authority was tottering.

Meanwhile, after discussion with Charles, Ireton and the Council of Officers had produced a constitutional scheme much more advanced than the Uxbridge or Newcastle Propositions (to which Parliament was still committed), but at the same time more moderate. The 'Heads of the Proposals' obliged the King to meet Parliament at least once every two years, but Parliament also had to face a new election every two years, making it more accountable to the people. The more notorious pocket boroughs were to be suppressed, and the counties were to be represented in proportion to their tax commitment. Control of the armed forces was to be vested in a council of state, but only for ten years. An elaborate scheme of 'composition' was designed to bring the royalists back into political society by stages, and the bishops were to be retained, though without coercive powers – naturally, since there was to be complete religious toleration. Finally, as a concession to the Levellers, it was proposed to implement at least part of their social programme, notably the reform of the common law and the abolition of the excise and tithes.

Charles toyed with this scheme for some weeks, but he was also in touch with Parliament and with the Scots. Early in November he fled to Carisbrooke Castle on the Isle of Wight, where he enjoyed a measure of independence, even if he could not escape altogether to the Continent. On 26 December he finally signed an 'Engagement' with the Scots: in return for their assistance in subduing England, he agreed to give Presbyterian church government a three-year trial. The Scots invasion in the early summer of 1648 coincided with royalist risings in Essex, Kent and South Wales.

.     .     .     .     .

The King was, and still is, accused of deviousness, hypocrisy and treachery in concluding this agreement with the Scots, but such terms are inapplicable to a monarch negotiating with men in open rebellion. Nor had the leaders of the Long Parliament scorned to invoke the aid of the Scots when it had suited them. As for the army, its position was almost deliriously unconstitutional. When Charles asked Henry Ireton whether the Long Parliament would accept the 'Heads of the Proposals', he replied that they 'would purge, and purge and purge, and never leave purging the Houses, till they had made them of such a temper as to do his Majesty's business'. But it was doubtful if he could do any such thing. Though the Presbyterian leaders had been expelled, Parliament still obstinately clung to the Newcastle Proposals, which it reaffirmed in the Four Bills of December 1647. The army had no legal standing, Parliament was thoroughly discredited and the economy seemed on the point of collapse. Poor harvests in 1647 and 1648 pushed up food prices, and this was blamed on the excise; a trade recession, combined with army demobilization, pushed up the number of unemployed. Highway robbery and begging became serious social problems. The inflation which had been a feature of the economy since beyond the memory of any man now living was about to come to an end, but the tapering off of prices created as many problems as it solved. In these circumstances opinion must swing back towards monarchy, if only because the King's present helplessness absolved him from present blame.

Moreover, with the army divided as it was, there seemed no reason why the Scots should not do the King's business. His flight to Carisbrooke was greeted by the troops as a betrayal, and it remained doubtful how far they would obey their generals. In November, Cromwell and

Ireton were forced to summon a meeting of the Council of the Army at Putney Church to discuss the new constitution put forward by the Levellers: the Agreement of the People, which posited a republic with a unicameral legislature elected by universal manhood suffrage, or something very much like it. The celebrated Putney Debates developed into a backs-to-the-wall defence conducted with obstinacy and skill by Cromwell and Ireton, but their authority was seriously challenged, and all winter the Council of Officers and the Council of the Army struggled to produce a version of the Agreement of the People acceptable to both sides. At Corkbush Field, Cromwell himself laid about the troops with his sword, and one of the 'agitators' was tried, sentenced and shot on that place. Would the regiments follow their leaders into battle?

However, at the renewed threat of civil war, the scattered components came back together with a series of resounding thuds. In January 1648 news of the 'Engagement' with the Scots forced Parliament to pass the Vote of No Addresses, breaking off all negotiations with the King, while the New Model Army returned to its duty and obedience. As an act of faith they evacuated London and assembled at Windsor for a vast prayer meeting, which turned into an orgy of self-recrimination, the one unifying factor their disgust with the King. In the words of one participant:

Presently we were led and helped to a clear agreement amongst ourselves, not any dissenting: That it was the duty of our day, with the forces we had, to go out and fight against those potent enemies which that year in all places appeared against us, with an humble confidence in the name of the Lord only, that we should destroy them . . . [and moreover,] that it was our duty, if ever the Lord brought us back again in peace, to call Charles Stuart, that man of blood, to an account for the blood that he had shed, and mischief he had done to his utmost, against the Lord's cause and people in these poor nations.

Nor did the Lord hide His countenance from His People. Cromwell smashed the Scots army at Preston in August 1648 and a spontaneous *coup d'état* in Edinburgh brought back an anti-royalist régime. The risings in England and Wales were speedily suppressed.

The first Civil War had petered out in a mood of exhaustion and mutual reconciliation; there was some talk of 'war crimes' trials, but the 'criminals' were abroad, and there was no attempt to apportion 'war guilt'. The end of the second Civil War was very different. After the siege of Colchester the royalist commanders were court-martialled and shot, and the leaders of the Scots invasion were reserved for a more formal trial on capital charges. In these circumstances, and even without the army's resolution at Windsor in April, it was unlikely that the principal war criminal would escape. Cromwell was absent in Scotland, Fairfax was as unobtrusive as ever, and Ireton was left to take the lead. Incensed by the news that Parliament was incorrigibly negotiating with Charles at Newport, Isle of Wight, notwithstanding the Vote of No Addresses, Ireton issued a 'Remonstrance of the Army' to Parliament calling for the King's trial (20 November). Receiving no reply, on 1 December he ordered the army to reoccupy London, and five days later Colonel Thomas Pride was ordered to purge the Commons of dissidents, reducing it to a 'Rump' of about 150 Members (increasing to about 200 the following year as some of those who had prudently stayed away came back). The Lords, now reduced by desertion to about a dozen, refused to pass the ordinance setting up a High Court of Justice to try the King, and the Rump, drawing freely on Leveller ideas, therefore declared:

> That the people are, under God, the original of all just power; that the Commons of England in Parliament assembled, being chosen by and representing the people, have the supreme power in this nation; [and] that whatsoever is enacted and declared for law by the Commons in Parliament assembled hath the force of law, and all the people of this nation are included thereby, although the consent and concurrence of the King and House of Lords be not had thereto.

Thus the army, itself an unconstitutional body, was now shackled to the remnants of a discredited Parliament, many of whose members had been elected nine years before, in a different era.

As for the King's trial, it was an extraordinary gamble. If he had pleaded 'not guilty' and prepared his defence the whole episode could have been prolonged for weeks and months, giving time for reaction to mount up, inside as well as outside England. For the crowned heads of Europe, however indifferent they had shown themselves to Charles's previous troubles, could not be expected to countenance his trial and execution. But the regicides were lucky; Charles refused to plead, which meant that he could also be denied the chance to speak; his trial opened on 20 January 1649, it was over on the 27th and he was executed on the 30th. But on the scaffold itself he had the chance to make a memorable statement, driving home the points made in 1642 in his 'Answer to the Nineteen Propositions'. He pledged himself to 'the freedom and liberty of the people of England', but he defined this in terms which could not but appeal to a nation weary of war and argument and apprehensive of lower-class radicalism in politics and religion. Of the people he said: 'Their liberty and freedom consists in having government, those laws by which their lives and their goods may be most their own. It is not their having a share in the government, that is nothing appertaining to them. A subject and a sovereign are clean different things.'

The dignity and pathos of his death enhanced his general popularity, which had been growing since 1646 in inverse proportion to his power and authority, and had even survived the publication of his secret correspondence, captured at Naseby. The *Eikon Basiliké*, 'The Portraiture of his sacred Majesty in his Solitude and Sufferings', was published immediately after his death and became an immediate best-seller, despite the government's frenzied attempts to suppress it and counteract it. A mixture of pietistic moralizing and shrewd historical revisionism, it portrayed Charles not only as a martyr for the Church of England but as a moderate, peace-loving, generous ruler who had been betrayed by the excesses of some of his followers and overwhelmed by the intransigence of his opponents. It was, apart from the Bible and perhaps Foxe's *Acts and Monuments*, the most influential book of the century, and it is still seriously undervalued. It confirmed that his trial was a serious error, if not a grievous sin, and induced in the nation a decided swing back to constitutional royalism and a modified Anglicanism. It was only military power that delayed the consummation of this reaction for as long as eleven years.

The new regime was consciously conservative from the beginning, a trend confirmed by the return of several

Members of Parliament who had absented themselves during the King's trial. Indeed, Charles's execution must be seen as an act of revenge, or an admission of total failure to reach agreement with him, rather than an attempt at constitutional reform. No replacements were available; Charles II, acknowledged by the royalists, was abroad, and so were his brothers, James and Henry. The monarchy and the House of Lords were only abolished after some hesitation, and then because it would have been pointless to do otherwise. And though the army and Parliament had both been free with their appeals to 'the people' and 'the people's rights', the new republic, or 'Commonwealth', was not instituted out of deference to the Levellers; it expressed the classical republicanism of men like Sir Henry Vane; blatantly oligarchical, on the Venetian model, it was the product of the study, not the field. Executive power was vested in a Council of State numbering forty, thirty-one of whom were to be Members of Parliament, and the remainder army officers. As for the increased representation of the people, franchise reform and new elections were postponed to another day.

This is not surprising, because the new Commonwealth was at once thrown on to the defensive, at home and abroad. France, Spain and Holland were equally horrified at Charles's death, and only their exhaustion after the Thirty Years War, and the continuing struggle between France and Spain, deterred them from direct intervention; as it was, they launched an all-out privateering campaign against English shipping. The Scots government, too, refused to accept the abolition of monarchy, and made warlike noises; Ireland was still substantially in the grip of the Catholic Confederacy; at home the ejected Presbyterians were preparing to make common cause with Charles

II, and the Levellers, furious at the turn of events, began a serious attempt to take over the army. Other groups, even more radical, were also coming to the front. The emergence of the Ranters, the Shakers, the Anabaptists, the Quakers and the Familists worried even the most devoted advocates of religious toleration, and the Fifth Monarchists' belief in the imminent return of Christ to reign on earth for a thousand years with his saints had obvious and profoundly disturbing political implications. Economic depression and continued unemployment enhanced the general working-class unrest, and it was no coincidence that in April 1649, with food prices still rising, Gerrard Winstanley and his Diggers made their famous occupation of common land on St George's Hill, Surrey, denouncing property as 'a Norman invention'.

So, 1649 was a year of repression. Cromwell and Fairfax forced a confrontation with the Levellers; two regiments mutinied, but the ringleaders were shot and their leading supporters cashiered. Lilburne was imprisoned, and though his trial for high treason in October ended in his triumphant acquittal, this only led to the revival of the High Court of Justice to hear cases involving state security. Lilburne spent much of the 1650s in prison, in the Scillies and Jersey, and the Levellers were broken as a serious political force, though their assassination plots against Cromwell were a continuing nuisance, and in the abortive rising of 1655 many of them joined the royalists. Meanwhile the government passed a Press Licensing Act in September 1649 which was the first attempt at a general censorship since 1640, and called forth a famous protest from John Milton, in *Areopagitica*. In October it imposed the 'Engagement', a new oath of loyalty to the republic, on all office-holders, clergy and officers of the armed forces, and in January 1650 it was made applicable to the whole adult male population at will. (Fairfax retired rather than take it, making way for Cromwell as Lord General.)

But in the military sphere the republican government was triumphantly successful. In July 1649 Cromwell at last sailed for Ireland at the head of a powerful army which carried all before it; the atrocities at Drogheda and Wexford (much criticized since) broke Irish morale, and though the fighting did not end until 1652, latterly it was very much a mopping-up operation. Then began the great resettlement of demobilized English troops on the confiscated lands of Catholic rebels, which changed the face of Ireland and created lasting bitterness: the last stage in a piecemeal process of colonization and exploitation which had begun in Elizabeth's reign.

Meanwhile, against all advice, the young Charles II went to Scotland, took the Solemn League and Covenant and was crowned king. Cromwell decided to take the war to the enemy; he invaded Scotland and routed the Scots at Dunbar in September 1650. As a result the Presbyterian ascendancy at Edinburgh collapsed, Charles II threw off the patronage of the Kirk, assembled a new, more broadly based army, and invaded England, where he was joined by many royalists in what seemed likely to become a third Civil War. However, he was comprehensively defeated by Cromwell at Worcester on 3 September 1651, exactly a year after Dunbar, and after six weeks on the run in England he escaped to the Continent for good. Royalism was destroyed as an overt political force, and Scotland was forcibly united with England – an ironic realization of James I's great dream.

At sea it was the same story. Revitalized by new commanders transferred from land duties, like Robert Blake, John Lawson, George Monck and William Penn the Elder, the Navy swept the Channel of Dutch and

French privateers, and in 1650 extended English maritime authority into the western Mediterranean. So strong was the republic that in October 1651 it passed the first of the Navigation Acts, designed to break the hold of the Dutch on the carrying trade between Europe and America and within Europe, and it embarked on the resultant war in 1652 with the utmost self-confidence.

However, the triumphant republic, having for the first time realized England's full military potential, fell away. The price of glory was high. The assessment was re-introduced, the excise was stepped up, the estates of leading royalists were thrown on to the market and so were the bishops' lands (forgotten was the idea that these should support a learned ministry), and Charles I's great art collection was auctioned off in 1651, a transaction still regretted by many art historians. The republic had no appeal to the upper classes: it was ruinously expensive, and it had no leaders apart from Cromwell, who was not himself a republican.

The tension between Parliament and the army which had led to Charles I's death continued. Cromwell made it his job to remove the mutinous elements from the army, but the radicals persisted – some of them, like the Fifth Monarchist Thomas Harrison, on Cromwell's own general staff. Moreover, the Rump seemed unable to satisfy even the army's most obvious and material demands; after all these years, arrears of pay had not been brought up to date, nor had a full Indemnity Act been passed. But the Council of the Army had by no means lost its taste for politics, and its demands now centred on reform of the common law and the regularization of religion within a framework of general toleration. In neither sphere was much advance made up to 1652. The Church Question was still fluid, as it had been since 1640. Parliament had finally imposed a

Presbyterian form of church government too late, in 1648; it had been swept away in the ruin of the political Presbyterians on the King's death. There was now no recommended form of prayer or worship, no means of ordaining or appointing parish clergy, no means of ejecting the incompetent or the heretical. Adjacently, there was a furious dispute as to whether the clergy should continue to be supported by tithes, or by voluntary contributions. Anglicans were still worshipping in the old way, clandestinely, and it is reasonable to suppose, though difficult to demonstrate, that large numbers of people were staying away from church altogether. In February 1652, after much prodding from John Owen, the Puritan Vice-Chancellor of Oxford University and Cromwell's chief adviser in spirituals, the Rump finally appointed a high-powered Committee for the Propagation of the Gospel. Unfortunately it came down in favour of tithes, and its report was shelved.

But the Rump's most glaring offence was its failure to redeem the promise, made in the Act abolishing the Kingship in 1649, that it would authorize new elections as soon as possible (under the Act of 1641 only Parliament could do so). War in Ireland and Scotland gave it a plausible excuse for postponing action, but even after Worcester all it would do was to promise a dissolution not later than 3 November 1654. A menacing petition from the army in August 1652 accelerated this process, and a Bill of election was about to be passed when Cromwell came down to Westminster on 20 April 1653 and forcibly dissolved them.

Cromwell's character remains very much an enigma, but it is clear that much of the praise lavished on him then and since is misplaced. In the early 1650s he alone stood between the English people and a peaceful and permanent settlement; without his leadership and his military genius, the republic would have foundered in its first two years; single-handed he postponed the inevitable restoration of the monarchy for another ten. Moreover, his increasing authoritarianism and his unbalanced violence so weakened the cause for which he struggled that after his death his bewildered and demoralized successors had to recall Charles II on his own terms, without imposing on him conditions which would have made the introduction of authoritarian government impossible and the Revolution of 1688 unnecessary.

To the end he maintained his dignity, his sense of fairness, and above all his sense of humour; nevertheless, continued military victory, culminating in the 'crowning mercy' of Worcester, gave him an undue confidence in the possession of God's peculiar grace – the antinomian pitfall which awaited all Puritans. In 1652 his mind was moving along strange paths – thus his famous remark to Bulstrode Whitelocke, 'What if a man should take it upon himself to be king?' Yet it is evident that, throughout 1652 and into 1653, Cromwell alone stood between Parliament and the overwhelming pressure of a victorious army, a pressure exercised equally by left-wing cranks like the Fifth Monarchist Thomas Harrison and right-wing politiques like John Lambert, after Cromwell and Monk easily the most able of the New Model generals. According to his own explanation and that of his aides, Cromwell lost patience with the Rump because it was trying to perpetuate its own existence, and planned merely to fill up the House by fresh 'recruiter' elections. But it has now been demonstrated that the Bill of Elections in 1653 (never seen from that day to this) in fact provided for a normal general election, excluding only proven royalists. In other words,

Cromwell refused to face the electorate without some decisive reform of the representative system. It was an act of high and doubtful presumption.

Indeed, Cromwell now abandoned the electoral representative system altogether. The separatist Puritan congregations in the provinces were requested to send up lists of 'persons fearing God, and of approved fidelity and honesty', and from these the Lord General and his Council of Officers chose 140 delegates, who were invited to assemble at Westminster on 4 July. The use of the term 'parliament' was carefully avoided, but the new assembly at once assumed this title, and adjourned to St Stephen's Chapel.

The 'Barebones Parliament', as it came to be known (or the 'Little', or 'Nominated' Parliament), was Cromwell's unique personal contribution to the solution of current constitutional problems; just as his artless offer of a union of England and Holland was his solution to the problem of foreign relations. Like most seventeenth-century experiments, the Barebones Parliament has a real and a legendary aspect. In legend it was a babel of God-besotted fanatics, but in reality, and despite the eccentric way in which it had been chosen, it contained a majority (perhaps 90 out of 140) of normal or 'usual' parliamentary gentry. It brought upon itself its own destruction by a wholesale assault on the most powerful vested interests in the land; it proposed to abolish tithes, the Court of Chancery, the universities and even the public ministry; its institution for the first time of civil marriage was an important but unpopular landmark. Its real failure was that it never even addressed itself to the task of framing a new constitution. The conservative majority rallied, came down to Westminster early in the morning on 12 December 1653, and dissolved themselves, handing back their powers to the

Lord General forthwith. A substitute was immediately to hand; four days later Cromwell went down to the Court of Chancery and took the oath as Lord Protector under the 'Instrument of Government'.

The 'Instrument', drafted by John Lambert and the Council of Officers, was a reworking of Ireton's 'Heads of the Proposals' of 1647. The government was vested in a Protector and Parliament, with a built-in provision for a permanent army establishment of 10,000 horse and 20,000 foot, plus the sum of £200,000 a year for the civil government; all this was beyond Parliament's power to alter. Parliament was reduced from 513 to 400 members, including representatives from Scotland and Ireland, and to achieve this the English boroughs were reduced to one member each, part of the surplus being allocated to the counties in proportion to their tax commitment, and the rest simply suppressed. Obviously the aim was merely to broaden and deepen the middle-class electorate, and this was confirmed by the provision that voters and candidates alike were to have at least £200 in real or personal property. Royalist delinquents were forbidden to vote for the first parliament or sit in the first four. This parliament was to meet at least once every three years and sit for five months, though in between sessions the Protector could issue ordinances which had the force of law until they were rejected by the next parliament.

Perhaps unwisely, Cromwell postponed the first meeting of Parliament until September 1654 while he ruled by ordinance; in particular, a new treason ordinance and several taxation ordinances. He made peace with Holland and also promulgated his own religious settlement by putting into effect the recommendations of the Committee for the Propagation of the Gospel, instituting a central committee of 'Triers' to vet aspirant clergymen, and a roving committee of 'Ejectors' to remove the incompetent or eccentric.

As soon as he faced Parliament, however, the basic constitutional dilemma was exposed. Cromwell himself had put his finger on the problem in March 1653, when his officers were pressing him to disperse the Rump. 'If they destroyed that Parliament,' he said, 'what should they call themselves; a state they could not be?' They answered that they would call a new parliament. 'Then,' said Cromwell, 'Parliament is not the supreme power, but that is the supreme power that calls it.' The problem, in fact, was how to erect a new constitution in which those who were to operate the constitution were divorced from those who had made it. The Americans, in 1787, the French, in 1792, found the solution by calling a constituent convention, which reproduced artificially the genesis of the constitution by the consent of society, telescoping into a few months a process believed to have taken millennia. The constitution made and ratified, those who had framed it were disqualified from operating it. But if one element in the constitution – in the case of the 'Instrument' the chief executive – had framed the constitution, then any other element, in this case the legislature, could claim to amend it. This is precisely what happened. A minority of republican members, allowed to flourish by Cromwell's disastrously inept parliamentary management, rejected the whole idea of single-person government, be he king or protector, and declined to ratify any of Cromwell's ordinances.

He peremptorily dissolved them as soon as their time was up, but the patent illegality of the government, even by his own loose standards, now brought on a revolt of the lawyers. (Six high court judges had already resigned rather than serve the republic in 1649.) Juries refused to convict offenders against the treason ordinance, and two high court judges were dismissed for querying its validity. The Chief Justice himself, Henry Rolle, resigned because he doubted the legality of the customs ordinance. There were embarrassing appeals against the assessment. The situation was saved by Cromwell's decision to declare war on Spain and the discovery of a widespread royalist-leveller conspiracy, which petered out in Penruddock's Rising in Wiltshire. Even then, Cromwell had to transport many of the rebels to the West Indies without trial, because it was doubtful if he could find juries to convict them; in the interests of internal security he consented to the imposition on the normal local government system of ten of his major-generals with wide powers of surveillance and superintendence.

Paradoxically, the universal unpopularity of the major-generals redounded in Cromwell's favour. His control over the army was now stronger than ever. The more dangerous incendiaries in the high command, like Harrison and Edmund Ludlow, had resigned in protest at the establishment of the Protectorate. Selective demobilization in 1654 was accelerated in 1655, and the assessment was halved; most of the remaining troops were scattered in garrisons throughout the British Isles, or fighting in Flanders and the West Indies. The Protector himself had now abandoned military uniform, had taken up residence at Whitehall, and had assumed many of the external trappings of royalty; his supporters were known, apparently without irony, as 'the Court party'. The war against Spain was popular and superficially successful; Jamaica was seized in 1655 and in the same year Blake destroyed the fleet of the Dey of Tunis; Mazarin was making overtures which resulted in the Anglo-French treaty of 1657 and the seizure of Dunkirk in 1658. A nation starved of victories since 1588 gloried in England's commanding position in Europe, within the British Isles and on the high seas. Moreover, trade was booming again, harvests were flourishing and prices had finally levelled off.

For the moment, at least, nothing was to be expected from the exiled Charles II, who was now allied to Spain, the national enemy. This left the conservative middle and upper classes a choice between Cromwell as a civilian dictator and the continued rule of the generals. The result was inevitable, and in the second Protectorate parliament, which met in September 1656, a strong group of royalists (or, more accurately, 'monarchists') took control, aided by the Council of State's clumsy decision to exclude the known republican members. Cromwell publicly disowned the council's action, though he took no steps to rectify it, and he ostentatiously threw over the major-generals. The result was the 'Humble Petition and Advice', which invited him to assume the hereditary kingship, with a substantially increased income, and nominate an upper house of Parliament.

Cromwell's reasons for refusing the kingship have been exhaustively canvassed, without much result. He kept his own counsel, then and later. Counter-pressure from the army was undoubtedly a factor (politically weak as the army now was, he dare not court its outright hostility); his own personal scruples were another. He knew that neither of his sons, Richard or Henry, was competent to succeed him, he was also aware that the restoration of the legitimate monarchy was inevitable in the long run, and he must look to the safety of his family (as it was, his widow and his surviving children were not seriously molested by Charles II's government, which would not have been the case had he founded a rival dynasty). In the end, the Commons were persuaded to drop their demand that he declare himself king; instead he was granted the right to name his successor, which at once provoked the resignation of John Lambert, and the right to nominate to 'The Other House', as the new second chamber was rather lamely called. Unfortunately, these nominations weakened the loyalists in the Commons, and when the republicans were readmitted for the second session in January 1658, they at once assumed the ascendancy. Parliament had to be dissolved in confusion after sixteen days, with nothing done. In the meanwhile, despite the new taxation granted as part of the 'Humble Petition', the government was running a deficit of half a million pounds a year, with a debt of one and a half million, most of it represented by arrears of pay: the army, £537,474, the navy over £300,000, the militia, over £100,000.

These arrears conditioned the attitude of the armed forces after Cromwell's death on 3 September 1658, the anniversary of Dunbar and Worcester. Such was the force of his personality that the machine continued running for six months as if he had never died. The royalists were prostrate, the European powers assumed that this formidable military dictatorship would continue, though perhaps reverting to republican institutions. Cromwell had failed to nominate a successor after all, but the Council of State put up his ineffectual elder son, Richard. Richard called a parliament, which the Council decided was to be elected on the old franchise in the old way, jettisoning the new-fangled redistribution of seats attempted in the 'Instrument'. But all this was irrelevant. Richard was the tool of the army chiefs, Charles Fleetwood and John Disbrowe, but their plans were frustrated by a bloodless revolt of the

army, led by the garrison colonels, who proved unexpectedly radical. The new parliament was dissolved, Richard
was deposed (though so shadowy was his power that the
fact of his deposition went unrecorded), and the Rump of
1653 was recalled. Unfortunately, the Rump, though
radical enough, proved alarmingly anti-military; it at once
initiated a purge of the officer class, and cut the pay of the
remainder. At this stage the balance was tipped by the
Presbyterians; their rising under Sir George Booth in
Cheshire brought the formidable John Lambert out of
retirement, and it was he who provoked a confrontation
which led directly to the second forcible dissolution of the
Rump in October 1659. But news that George Monck,
Commander-in-Chief of the Army of Occupation in
Scotland, was mobilizing his forces, brought about a
sudden *volte face*, and in December the Rump was back at
Westminster.

Cromwell's failure to make any proper disposition for
his successor practically ensured the restoration of the
monarchy on minimum terms. The appalling political
chaos, and the economic slump, were all the harder to take
because of the superficial stability of the preceding years;
they produced a violent reaction which had been latent in
the public consciousness since 1649, if not before. The
ineffectuality and irresponsibility of the restored Rump
confirmed this reaction, and the inability of the rival
generals, Fleetwood, Lambert and Monck, to work together
left the army divided and impotent. It was inevitable that,
sooner or later, one of the generals would swim with the
current. (It was the same with the navy; the death of
Robert Blake in 1657 left the navy uneasily divided
between the putative royalists, headed by Edward
Montagu, and the 'Commonwealthsmen', headed by
John Lawson. Montagu opened a tentative correspondence

with the King even before Monck, but Lawson came in early enough to escape the fate of Lambert and Fleetwood.)

George Monck was a professional soldier and a former royalist; he had a stricter control over his men than any other commander apart from Cromwell. The Army of Scotland had been isolated from the recent contestations south of the border, and Monck took care to keep it so. It was he who peremptorily ordered the restoration of the Rump in December, and in return received a commission from the Rump's Council of State naming him commander-in-chief of the armed forces in the three kingdoms. Raising another foot regiment as he came, named after the border town of Coldstream, he invaded England on 1 January 1660 and marched steadily south. Facing him were armies much superior in numbers, but the troops had no confidence in their officers, nor the officers in their generals, nor the generals in themselves. Meeting with no resistance, he occupied London on 3 February, divided up the English army and dispersed it to remote garrisons and, after lengthy consultations and negotiations, removed the guards which had surrounded St Stephen's Chapel since December 1648. The members excluded by Pride returned, and voted for the election of a new parliament; thus the Long Parliament at last dissolved itself, nearly twenty years after its election. The new Parliament assembled on 25 April 1660, with the significant addition of the House of Lords, and was presented with a letter from Charles II and a conciliatory Declaration, issued at Breda on Monck's prompting. Charles offered four basic concessions: a free and generous pardon, arrears of pay for the armed forces, confirmation of titles to land, and a limited freedom of conscience. Even then, all these concessions were, very properly, made subject to parliamentary approval. It was

179

received with rapture. After the minimum debate Charles was proclaimed king, and urgently summoned to return to his sorrowing and repentant people. He landed at Dover on 26 May and entered London on the 29th, his thirtieth birthday.

# VII

# THE RESTORATION, 1660

Obviously the Restoration of 1660 restored something, but it is not clear what. By simply overriding any Act or ordinance which had not received the royal assent, the Convention Parliament of 1660 turned back the clock to the summer of 1641. This left the Act of 1642 excluding the bishops from the House of Lords, which was repealed by the Cavalier Parliament in 1661. It was thus a decisively negative settlement, and the only important positive enactment, the Militia Act of 1661, which placed the command of the armed forces unambiguously in the King, only confirmed the general desire to return to the *status quo ante bellum.*

There had been a shift in the balance of power, but no one would acknowledge it. The only advance in the power of Parliament – as distinct from restrictions imposed on the King – was the Triennial Act of 1641, which on the dissolution of the Long Parliament at last took effect. This was a muddled measure – it was never clear whether it was intended to secure regular general elections or regular sessions of Parliament – but in any case it was decisively amended in 1664 so as to make it permissive, not mandatory. The fact that, since 1642, Parliament had defeated the King's father twice, executed him, abolished the upper house, conquered Ireland and Scotland and lorded it over Western Europe, was simply ignored. True, these stirring events had much less effect on the composition or attitude of Parliament than might have been expected, but surely they could not be ignored altogether?

But the failure of Parliament to assert itself in 1660 was just one aspect of a general trend which still defies analysis – the collapse of Puritanism. This vital intellectual and spiritual force, credited with the downfall of the monarchy (and not only by nineteenth- and twentieth-century historians but also by acute contemporaries like Thomas Hobbes), abruptly faded away in 1660, and with it the 'Good Old Cause', and all those other dreams of a restricted monarchy, general toleration, a New Deal and a New Age. The Convention Parliament of 1660 was thought to have a majority of 'Presbyterians', but in the end they could not even secure that modest 'liberty for tender consciences' promised by Charles II at Breda. In fact, the Presbyterians were as averse as the Anglicans to extending toleration to the working classes, and the other Nonconformist sects were regarded, with some superficial plausibility, as political incendiaries, responsible for the worst excesses of the Great Rebellion. This hypothesis was confirmed by a singularly ill-timed Fifth Monarchy revolt in London in January 1661. Venner's Rising, with its slogan of 'King Jesus, and their heads upon the gates!', at once sabotaged the prospects of the Savoy Conference, called by the King to find a basis of accommodation between Presbyterians and Anglicans; but it was also undermined by the intransigence of the Puritan divines, who did not realize that their lay support was melting away. George Monck himself, now Duke of Albemarle, was typical of those who realized that conformist Anglicanism was the religion of the successful; another was Anthony Ashley Cooper, raised to the peerage as Lord Ashley in 1661.

The wraith of Puritanism continued to fade in the face

of persecution. The Corporation Act of 1661 was a straight-forward security measure, obliging all local government officers, elected or appointed, to take the oaths of allegiance and supremacy, the notorious 'non-resistance oath' (to the effect that 'it is not lawful upon any pretence whatsoever to take arms against the king'), and an oath abjuring the Solemn League and Covenant of 1643 – and lest this provision be thought redundant, it is worth noting that a resolution to burn the Covenant only passed the Cavalier Parliament by 228 votes to 103. By adding the require-ment that all such officers take the Anglican communion, the leaders of the restored Church unhesitatingly placed the holiest of Christian sacraments at the disposal of mammon.

The Uniformity Act of May 1662 imposed all these oaths on the clergy, plus the obligation to accept the Book of Common Prayer and the Thirty-Nine Articles in their entirety, plus ordination by a bishop. It was not expected that more than a proportion of clergymen would comply, perhaps not even a majority, but Parliament approached its distasteful task with utter ruthlessness; the church settlement had been delayed since 1640, and could hang fire no longer. In the event, nearly 2,000 clergy (out of approximately 9,000) gave up their livings, and the great purge which had been impending ever since the Reforma-tion now took place. Yet it is a serious misnomer to represent the Settlement of 1662 as a triumph for the Laudians, or even for the Church. Laud's view of liturgy and ceremonial was substantially accepted, and during the reign of Charles II the Church swung decisively away from Calvinism towards some modified form of Arminian-ism – though it is significant of a changed climate of opinion that this last was scarcely noticed outside the universities – but the new constitutional position of the

Church accorded more with the ideas of Pym than Laud. The Uniformity Act itself acknowledged a right in Parliament, resisted by every monarch since 1559, to define the parameters of the national faith, and regulate the order of service. Parliament even secured the right, rejected by James I, to veto canons drawn up by Convocation. Parliament's refusal to revive the Court of High Commission removed a key weapon of royal superintendence and control over the clergy, and the wholesale ejection of ministers in 1662 and their replacement by men nominated mainly by lay patrons inaugurated the famous eighteenth-century alliance between squire and parson, with the latter still in a decidedly inferior social position.

Moreover, in 1661 and 1662 the Church at last surrendered its claims to a monopoly of Protestantism. The Uniformity Act imposed the usual fines for non-attendance at Church, but not until 1664, in the first Conventicles Act, were legal measures taken to suppress dissenting congregations, and another year went by before the Five Mile Act was passed to restrict the activities of dissenting ministers – and then largely because of their much-publicized services in London during the Great Plague. Technically these statutes were intended to eliminate religious dissent, but both of them contained a measure of toleration disguised in negative form; the Conventicles Act exempted worship within the family or the household, whatever the numbers involved, and the Five Mile Act did not touch ministers who kept away from the towns or from their previous parishes. The Conventicles Act lapsed altogether in 1668, and it was renewed in 1670 with a drastically reduced scale of punishments (though these now embraced ministers as well as their congregations), and with other clauses, threatening to punish magistrates and constables failing to enforce it, which tell their own story.

Nevertheless, the idea of a radical Nonconformist plot to overwhelm the establishment continued to be a factor in politics at least up to 1688. It was fuelled by Venner's Rising in 1661, and by the Derwentdale Plot in 1663 (a matter taken much more seriously by contemporaries than by subsequent historians). There was then a lull; but the Rye House Plot of 1683 and Monmouth's Rebellion in 1685 confirmed the establishment in their worst fears. It is easy to slight Judge Jeffreys, but in 1685 he was expressing the prejudice of all his generation when he said, 'Good God! That we should live in such an age, when men call God to assist them and protect them in rebellion!' In contradistinction, the fact is that all the Nonconformist sects after 1660 were imbued by a profound political quietism; to the extent that when they were offered freedom of worship by successive kings, in 1672 and 1687, there was a very serious debate whether to accept it or not. The Dissenters soon slumped to a very low proportion of the population – though exactly what proportion we cannot discover – and from then on recruitment was slight. By the 1680s it was becoming increasingly difficult to replace the original ministers ejected in 1662, who were now dying off.

As Puritanism fell, so the Church of England rose, but it only rose towards an Indian summer. In common with all other hierarchical churches, including the Roman Catholic, its power over men's minds was being eroded. The scientific spirit and the rationalist approach were the dragon's teeth of Puritanism. The nature and extent of Puritanism's contribution to the new natural science is still fiercely debated. No question but that the Puritan pursuit of natural learning was inchoate, over-confident and intellectually disorderly; but the savants who flourished in the general breakdown of educational and intellectual supervision in the 1640s and 1650s came to realize that there was now a natural science, quite distinct from religion. Taking their inspiration from Bacon's *Novum Organum* (1620), a book whose posthumous influence was incalculable, they proposed the thorough reform of education and the law and the wholesale encouragement of technology and invention by the State, in the confident expectation that through what Bacon called 'The Great Instauration' perfectibility was attainable now, in a world in which intelligence was set free from the trammels of the imagination. This may seem a strange doctrine for the Puritans to embrace, but stranger things arose in the ferment of the Interregnum: divorce was seriously discussed, and strongly advocated by Milton, who had an unhappy marriage behind him; the institution of civil marriage was also canvassed, and even introduced by the Little Parliament of 1653; and there were even moves to ameliorate the inferior social position of women.

Unfortunately, all such schemes were woefully unsuccessful. Plans for a new technology never left the drawing board, the campaign for a new system of education foundered on the indifference of government – for the Interregnum governments proved no more liberal than their predecessors. Cromwell bowed to public pressure for law reform, but even he was defeated by the inertia of the legal profession, and the example set by his Chancery ordinance of 1654 was ignored in 1660. (Legal reform had to wait until the 1870s.)

But it was not all in vain; the spirit of rational inquiry could not easily be exorcized. The Puritan emphasis on the confrontation between the individual and God was soon deflected towards a preoccupation with the individual alone, and in this they, or their successors, were fortified by Descartes, to whom the universe was an objective, uncar-

186

ing machine. The Royal Society 'for improving natural knowledge' came under the patronage of Charles II, that great improviser, in 1662, but it had grown out of the meetings of various groups of savants in London and Oxford in the previous decade. In fact, William Harvey, whose discovery of the circulation of the blood (in *De Motu Cordis et Sanguinis*, 1628) and the fundamentals of reproduction (in *De Generatione Animalium*, 1653), flourished originally under Charles I, and Robert Boyle, the father both of physics and chemistry, began his life's work in the 1650s (his most famous work, *The Sceptical Chemist*, appeared in 1661). But the tide rolled on, and Newton's epoch-making work on optics, physics and astronomy (the *Principia Mathematica*, 1686) was published in the reign of James II, not usually regarded as the most enlightened of rulers, and under the auspices, as President of the Royal Society, of Samuel Pepys. John Locke, in *An Essay Concerning Human Understanding* (1690), completed the ruin of previous philosophical and moral systems by rejecting totally the theory of innate ideas and arguing instead that human personality owed everything to upbringing and education. None of these men – all of them devout Christians – willed the end, but they used the means by which reason supplanted faith, and before their attack organized, hierarchical religion continued to crumble all over Europe, not least in England, where the confidence of Anglican churchmen was further undermined by their failure to eliminate Dissent and their failure to accommodate to the vagaries of political obligation.

For among the most famous children of the new scientific age was Thomas Hobbes, who reacted to the Great Rebellion by propounding a theory of political obligation based on the unchanging laws of geometry and the constitution of the human body. The result, in *Leviathan* (1651), was a theory of life and politics which was based entirely on fear, not love, force, not persuasion, which had no place in it for man's higher nature, and reduced religion to a matter of superstition. Moreover, it posited a theory of absolute despotism which drove the theory of the Divine Right of Kings to its utmost logical conclusion and beyond. It would have been better if Hobbes's critics could have ignored him, as they ignored the agrarian republican theories of James Harrington (*Oceana*, 1656), another spawn of the Interregnum. But it was a tribute to Hobbes that his enemies could never leave off publicizing and propagating his views by opposing them; and though he did not find in Charles II the platonic philosopher-king who would put his theories into practice, the bases of political obligation were never the same again after *Leviathan*.

The economic parameters of society were changing, too. The landed classes as a whole had stood up remarkably well to the penal fines and high taxation imposed on them by the Interregnum governments. Few royalists had to sell their lands to pay fines, and those whose estates were confiscated received them back after the Restoration; the immediate social effects of the Interregnum were surprisingly muted. But a dragging burden of debt lasting over generations, the return of high taxation, especially after the Revolution of 1688, and a sharp fall in agricultural prices at the end of the century forced many small landed families 'out of business', a concealed, long-term effect of the Civil Wars. The larger the estate the more economical it was to manage, the easier it was to pay non-graduated taxation, and the easier it was to find the capital for agricultural improvement; manuring, marling, draining, planting root crops to feed winter cattle and improving the breed of stock. The preservation of such estates from the depredations of improvident heirs or the temptation to sell was also facilitated during Charles II's reign by the introduction of a new system of entail known as the 'strict settlement'.

It is much too early to talk of a 'decline of the gentry' in the late seventeenth century, or a 'rise of the nobility', but it is noticeable that from the 1670s through to Anne's death the parliamentary history of England is punctuated by disputes between the two Houses of a kind which had not arisen before 1640, and on the crucial constitutional questions of the period – the Exclusion Bill of 1680, James II's use of dispensations in 1685, the Partition Treaties in 1701, *Ashby* v. *White* in 1704 – the Lords' intervention was decisive. By the reign of William III the interference of the Lords was continually resented and feared by the Commons. Throughout the century there was a belief in aristocratic leadership, but when it was forthcoming it was found to be oppressive. Increasingly, Parliament was managed, or intended to be managed, from the upper house by newly ennobled careerists: Clarendon, Arlington, Shaftesbury, Danby, Rochester, Nottingham, Somers, Halifax (both of them), Godolphin, Marlborough, Oxford, Bolingbroke. With only one exception, these men were raised to the peerage, from comparatively modest beginnings, by the monarch they served; they were ministerial peers. Nottingham was the only one who inherited his peerage, and his father, the first of the line, was a career lawyer. (Bolingbroke and Charles Montague, Lord Halifax, were of ancient lineage, but they were born into penniless cadet branches of their families, and had to make their own way in the world.)

The rise of a wealthy career aristocracy was just one symptom of England's increasing prosperity. The slumps and depressions which had been a feature of the first half of the century recurred in the second half, but their effect was muted; for instance, England withstood the disastrous harvests of 1697–8 with ease, while financing a major war on an unprecedented scale; earlier she withstood the enormous dislocation of the Great Plague of 1665 and the Great Fire of 1666 in successive years (again during a major war) with much greater ease than she thought she had.

Bumps were ironed out. World inflation levelled off as mysteriously as it had arisen; economic theorists lost their obsession with the trade balance and bullion reserves. The Navigation Act of 1651 was re-enacted in 1660 in a more realistic and at the same time a more rigorous form. Together with the Staple Act of 1663, it required that goods be imported to England either in English ships or ships of the country of origin, and closed off the colonial trade to foreign shipping altogether. The American and West Indian colonies rapidly emerged as the staple suppliers of tobacco, raw cotton, rice and sugar to Europe, and it was all transhipped through England. In the reverse direction, foreigners trading with the colonies had to ship their goods through England, adding to their costs and putting them at a disadvantage with English manufacturers. It was a closed system, rigidly enforced. The growing of English tobacco was suppressed by statute, so was the export of Irish cattle; Scotland was excluded altogether, and put on a level with France or Denmark.

It was a policy designed to supplant the Dutch, and at the same time emulate them. Initially its weakness lay in a sheer lack of merchant ships and seamen, but this was made good with remarkable rapidity. Rising population provided a surplus of men to man the ships; the navy, by now a major industry, was in the forefront of technological advance. The effect was cumulative: naval wars were consciously undertaken to secure more trade, more trade led to more wars, naval architects fashioned bigger and better ships, naval press-gangs sucked in more and more men, who in peace-time constituted a reserve of trained mariners. The three Dutch wars of this period (1652-4, 1665-7, 1672-4) were inconclusive, unheroic and politically unsuccessful, but they were a slow, mangling, chewing process which inflicted wounds on the Dutch which could never be healed; a struggle the Dutch could not win, the English could not lose. Already it was coming to be understood that the real focus of the war was not on the battle fleets, slow and virtually unsinkable, noisily banging away at each other for hours and even days without result, but on the vulnerable merchant convoys on which the Dutch depended not only for their wealth but their very being.

With their tiny population (of about two million) and their inability to feed even that number from their own resources, the position of the Dutch had always been unreal, and dependent on their neighbours' inactivity or lack of enterprise. They successfully defended their monopoly of the spice trade, but just at the time when, because of the new practice of wintering cattle, the demand for spices to disguise the taste and smell of 'high' meat slackened. They lost Brazil to the Portuguese in the 1640s, they lost New York to the English in the 1660s, and with it their foothold in North America. It is symptomatic that competition for the lucrative Newfoundland cod fishery was now between the English and the French, not the English and the Dutch. Cromwell's initiative in clearing the western Mediterranean in the 1650s gave the Levant Company an all-important hold on the luxury trade with the Middle East and Central Asia; again, in the 1660s and 1670s England's rivals in the Mediterranean were the French, not the Dutch. The American colonies, or 'plantations', hitherto little regarded, now began to pay a dividend. Virginia, the Carolinas and Jamaica (captured for Cromwell in 1655) steadily increased their export of tobacco, rice and sugar to Europe (via England, of course), and New York opened the way up the Hudson river valley to the lucrative fur-trapping areas of the midwest. Only the Puritan colonies of New England served no obvious economic purpose, and they caused constant trouble and irritation to the government at home. It was not forgotten that such incendiaries as the young Henry Vane and Hugh Peters had returned in 1640 from New England, nor that it sheltered three of Charles I's murderers. After a long legal battle the Massachusetts charter was confiscated in 1684, and James II united Massachusetts, Connecticut, Rhode Island, Vermont, Maine and New Hampshire in one Dominion of New England under Sir Edmund Andros, an experiment which did not survive the Revolution of 1688. Meanwhile the East India Company, disdaining the spice trade it had lost, found a major outlet in the export to Europe of cheap Indian cotton goods, a traffic so lucrative that in 1698 it was supporting two companies, with a combined capital of £3·9 million. (They were reunited in 1708.) So important was this trade that the company was allowed to flout mercantilist theory; lacking suitable exports to exchange for Indian cloth, it bridged the gap by buying it with silver. (In fact, the 'loss' of bullion was made up by England's invisible exports, in banking and insurance services and maritime transport.)

The wars of attrition seriously wounded the Dutch, but it was the close Anglo-Dutch alliance of the years 1689–1713 which administered the kiss of death. However, succeeding to Holland's inheritance, England found herself under the same pressure. Under Louis XIV and

Colbert, France emerged as a major mercantile and colonial competitor, in the Channel, the Mediterranean, Canada and later India. While she fought Holland in two wars under Charles II, England tried to erect a closed-tariff system against France, seeking the extra taxation she needed to fight the Dutch by swingeing duties on French imports, particularly of wines and spirits. The more her wealth depended on her shipping, the more vulnerable she was in war, and after 1689 she had to suffer from the French what she herself had inflicted on the Dutch; the loss of the Smyrna convoy in 1693 was a crippling blow, and by 1704 her merchant shipping losses were so extensive that her ability to continue the War of the Spanish Succession was in some doubt. Nevertheless, the trend was always onwards and upwards, and the ability of the English to finance nearly twenty years of almost continuous warfare on a world scale (1688–97, 1702–13) mystified even themselves. The great victories of Marlborough provided the one quality previously lacking, an ability to compete on land in the major European theatres of war, and confirmed England's rise to 'great power' status.

Charles II seemed the very man to take advantage of the prevailing trends – for there was no reason why the monarchy should stand in opposition to the general national development. He was thirty when he came back to England, mature and wise, with an abundance of political experience behind him. He was shrewd and accommodating, and much more resilient politically than any other member of his family; he had learned to ride humiliation and survive with his identity intact, and, when he wanted to be, he was a master of political timing. Lord Halifax said of him, 'As a sword is sooner broken upon a feather bed than upon a table, so his pliantness broke the power of a present mischief much better than a more immediate resistance.' A child of the new age, a friend of Hobbes, a patron of science and technology, witty and convivial, he appealed at once to a new generation of courtiers alienated from the 'puritanism' of their fathers (whether it was spelled with a small 'p' or a large). To them his cynicism, his sexual athleticism, his worldly wisdom were more attractive than otherwise, and to them he offered leadership, or at least 'spokesmanship'.

At the same time he was not at odds with the older generation. He had a personal appeal for men like Clarendon, the veteran Earl of Southampton and the Duke of Ormonde, which offset their disapproval of much that he did and said. Whatever his character, he was also a symbol of national unity after the disorder and social instability of the previous twenty years. The Church, shorn of much of its power and prestige, was for that very reason more dependent on the monarchy than ever and willing to exalt its moral authority. The new cult of monarchy found expression in the near-deification of Charles I. In the new order of service for 30 January, reserved by Parliament as a day of fasting, repentance and self-abasement in perpetuity, the late king appeared as a saint-like figure of overpowering sweetness, moderation and humility, tormented and destroyed by cruel and bloody men. Masochistic preachers did not hesitate to draw the obvious comparison between him and the Saviour of the World, a comparison the more apt in that Charles I was now held to have offered himself as a sacrifice to expiate the sins of his people. The anniversary of Charles II's return, 29 May, was also celebrated with ecstatic pomp. Then, and on 30 January, and on any and every occasion, the pulpits of the Anglican Church rang with exhortations to perfect obedience.

Nor were such exhortations entirely necessary. Charles

II had been recalled with the general approval of the great majority of the nation, and the enthusiastic support of many. He had no visible enemies, nor serious critics. The new government he formed under Edward Hyde, Earl of Clarendon, embraced all significant political interests and groupings, ex-parliamentarian as well as royalist. The Act of Oblivion, passed by the Convention in 1660 with strong royal support, was a constructive and statesmanlike attempt to wipe out the animosities, enmities and prejudices of the previous twenty years, and to a great extent it succeeded. The Cavalier Parliament of 1661 contained a substantial minority prepared to oppose the government on key measures, but this was in no way a permanent, 'formed' Opposition, and it was not sponsored or led by any major political figure – not until 1668, when Sir William Coventry resigned from the government and moved to the back benches. The Stuart monarchy had been given a completely new start, and there seemed no reason why it should not move with the tide of general European development, which was now firmly in favour of royal autocracy and against the direct participation of elected assemblies in government, a process evident not only in France and Spain but in most of the German states.

Experience of the Interregnum had thoroughly discredited republicanism, and deterred the restored régime from making any adjustment to an out-of-date electoral and representative system. In an era of expanding trade, the House of Commons remained essentially a body of landowners, and many of them small landowners at that. The extended rule of the Long Parliament, with its oppressive taxation, its by-passing of legal procedures, its support of an ill-disciplined and radical army, produced an inevitable disillusionment with representative institutions. Up to 1640 Parliament was expected to solve everything; in

1660 it could solve nothing, only return tamely to 1641. Moreover, the Militia Act gave Charles II the undisputed control of the army, and unlike his father he at last had an army to control: only two regiments, but they were crack regiments, Monck's Coldstream Guards and Lord Oxford's regiment of horse, 'The Blues'. There were other regiments at Dunkirk initially, and in Portugal and Tangier, an English Catholic regiment in the French army, as well as substantial mini-armies in Scotland and Ireland under the King's direct command. True, the events of the Interregnum had strengthened the existing prejudice against a 'standing' army, but the army existed, and its use could be justified and condoned by the latent menace of 'Puritan', 'Leveller' or 'Oliverian' conspiracies, or the need to fortify the nation against external aggression from Holland or France, which was how the rulers of many German states justified their swollen military budgets in the second half of the seventeenth century. Tough, resilient, interested in trade, technology and manufactures, it was easy to see Charles declining into old age as a Hobbesian philosopher-king, with an efficient council, a watchful army and a compliant and infrequently summoned Parliament. His chief minister, Clarendon, dreamed similar dreams (though without the Hobbesian element).

As it was, in the first few vital years of the Restoration, Charles squandered all his chances. He was not a lazy man, but he lacked concentration, his interests were too diversified, and he did not apply himself to the business of governing. He had a knack of managing men which his father conspicuously lacked, but he relied too much on it. By leaving much of the responsibility to Clarendon, he ignored his father's last advice, which was to beware of putting too much trust in a single minister; then he under-

mined Clarendon's authority by permitting the 'young
bloods' at Court (Bennett, Clifford, Buckingham, Ashley) to oppose him publicly. When Clarendon went hard
on the rocks in 1667 it was too late for Charles to jump
clear. But whenever he had a chief minister (Danby in the
1670s, Rochester in the 1680s) he could not resist tampering with his power in this way; otherwise he favoured
loose ministerial coalitions like the Cabal, whose jarring
internal disputes he viewed with complacency, though they
weakened his own authority and made continuity of
policy impossible.

He was glad of any opportunity to enhance the power
of the monarchy, but unlike his brother James he gave no
continuous thought to it. In any case, though he was a
supremely able tactician he was a poor strategist, and it is
to be doubted if he had a long-term policy at any stage.
He announced in 1660 that he did not intend to go on his
travels again; this was understandable in the beginning,
but throughout his reign the concept of survival too much
dominated his thinking. In addition, he had the usual
Stuart failings: he did not understand finance, and when
he chose good finance ministers it was by accident, or as
a by-product of other intrigues. His over-spending on the
Court and on his own pleasures was perhaps not so spectacular as James I's, but it was just as heavy, and it kept
him poor even when his income was rising, as it was for
the second half of his reign. He was a very bad public
speaker, and just as incompetent at dealing with Parliament as his father and grandfather, though the fact is disguised by his agility in avoiding direct confrontation and
his willingness to compromise when hard pressed. All in
all, it is not so surprising that the affairs of the monarchy
should remain at a standstill during his reign: what *is*
surprising is that they should have gone backwards.

# VIII

# CHARLES II, 1661–85

As usual, the main problem facing the new government in 1661 was financial. Accepting, roughly, the principle their grandfathers had rejected in 1610, Parliament voted the Crown the not ungenerous sum of £1,200,000 a year for its normal peacetime expenditure, mainly from customs and excise duties; though it is a mystery to this day how this figure was arrived at. Unfortunately, the tax yield fell short of the estimate by about £300,000 a year. Parliament was well-meaning, it experimented with various short-term direct taxes, but it could never bridge the gap; in 1660 and 1661 the taxpayer had already dipped deep into his pocket to pay off the Cromwellian army and navy, and this was not the time to approach him again. The proceeds (£400,000) from the sale of Dunkirk to France in 1662, and the dowry brought by the Portuguese princess, Catherine of Braganza, when she married Charles the same year, brought the crown's average annual income for the years 1661–5 slightly above Parliament's estimate, but the King, in process of consolidating his regime, could not afford not to be generous to his followers, and though Parliament had accepted responsibility for his and his father's just debts, it did nothing about them, then or later. There was a strong suspicion that the Treasury was less than competently managed by the veteran loyalist, the 4th Earl of Southampton.

In fact, Charles's ministers soon separated out into two

groups: the veterans, who accepted public responsibility without always having private control, and younger men, like Lord Ashley (Chancellor of Exchequer), Sir Henry Bennet (Secretary of State), Sir William Coventry (Secretary to the Admiralty), and Sir Thomas Clifford (Comptroller of the Household), who had the King's ear but disowned responsibility. To these last must be added George Villiers, 2nd Duke of Buckingham (Master of the Horse), who seemed to have inherited from his father the evil role of favourite. The King himself seemed to take little interest in government, and what little interest he took was not sustained. His reckless pursuit of pleasure, his flouting of conventional morals, deepened the disillusionment which was probably inevitable after the heady excitement of the Restoration. To a generation raised on Cromwell's oaken austerity, his conduct was particularly deplorable, as we can see from Pepys's comments. (In his diary Pepys, quite rightly, applied higher standards to public figures than he was willing to apply to himself.)

It was fortunate for Charles that Clarendon drew much of the resulting unpopularity on himself. It is typical that the legislation against Dissenters should be labelled 'The Clarendon Code', though Clarendon himself was not the driving force behind it. Public opinion was ambivalent. It feared Puritanism as a national movement, but it sympathized with the travails of respected local pastors; it accepted the bishops as necessary props to a shaky social order, but it had no affection for them and considerable distrust. Anticlericalism remained the predominant English attitude towards religion.

Clarendon attracted further disfavour by the marriage in 1661 between his daughter Anne and the King's younger brother, James, Duke of York. Clarendon set his face against it, but this was not a fact which could be decently publicized. James was now heir presumptive, and he was already unpopular with the public, though it is not clear why. (The existence of a married, adult prince of the blood royal, unknown for nearly two hundred years, was another drain on the government's finances.) Abroad neither King nor ministers had any clear policy. In exile, Charles had been the ally of Spain, but she was clearly prostrate now after forty years of war ending with the Peace of the Pyrenees in 1659. In view of the Navigation Acts an alliance with the Dutch was improbable, especially since the Dutch Republic, under pressure from Cromwell in 1654, had passed the Perpetual Edict barring Charles's young nephew the Prince of Orange from executive power. Should England, then, resort to Cromwell's ally, France? While they dithered, a new alliance between France and the Netherlands was signed in 1662, leaving England without an ally at all, and the golden bait of the King's hand was thrown away on lowly Portugal. In the circumstances, the decision to sell Dunkirk back to France, though economically defensible, was bitterly unpopular. (This is one of the few instances in which ill-formed popular clamour was justified. The demilitarization of Dunkirk featured largely in the Peace of Utrecht, and it was still causing trouble to the English government in the 1730s.)

Public clamour, encouraged by the trading interests, also led to the Second Dutch War (1665–7) – that, and a restless instinct for aggression, inherited from Cromwell in the 1650s. True, the Dutch were England's principal trading competitors, but the experience of the First Dutch War (1652–4) strongly suggested that the way to defeat them was not in battle. (The fact that none of these Dutch Wars lasted more than two years is in itself suggestive.) The Navigation Act, strengthened and reimposed in 1660, could be left to do its work. It is remarkable that Charles and James not only succumbed to this jingoistic clamour but positively welcomed it. They hoped to recoup the fortunes of their family through war, though their father's experience strongly suggested the futility of such a course.

In fact the war was a disaster for the Crown. The peace terms granted by the exhausted Dutch at Breda in 1667 were in fact quite handsome; notably, they confirmed England's possession of New York, captured in 1665. Dutch convoy losses were spectacular. But a series of bloody and expensive fleet actions produced no tangible result, a fact it was easy to blame on the royal admirals, James and Rupert; and the Plague and the Fire had a disastrous effect on public morale. The epidemic of bubonic plague in the summer of 1665 was the worst this century; it killed about 70,000 Londoners and paralysed the port for six months. The Great Fire of September 1666 was probably less damaging, but it was more spectacular, and it left its mark on the City for at least another twenty years, something we tend to forget. (Wren's new St Paul's Cathedral was not opened until 1697, and was not declared finished until 1711.) Early in 1667 Charles decided to cut his losses and withdraw from the war, but in June, with the peace negotiations under way, a Dutch raiding force attacked Sheerness, broke the boom across the Medway, sank three first-rates at their moorings and towed two others back to Holland, one of them being the flagship, *Royal Charles*.

Clarendon was promptly dismissed, but this was not enough to appease the public, enraged as they were at the mismanagement of the naval war, in such sharp contrast to the achievements of Cromwell's admirals, nor to allay the suspicion that some of the large sums voted for the war had been embezzled. This last was almost certainly untrue; the government was incompetent rather than dishonest; but an independent commission of inquiry appointed by Charles under strong parliamentary pressure failed to deliver a conclusive verdict, and the accusation was left hanging. This was unfortunately typical. Clarendon's impeachment, which would almost certainly have failed, was side-stepped; he was sent into exile instead. Similarly, a lengthy inquiry into the navy, extending into 1668, cast considerable doubts on James's capacity as Lord High Admiral, and on that of other members of the Navy Board, but only Commissioner Pett, from Chatham, was sacrificed.

As a result, the slump in the prestige and popularity of the Crown persisted. A regular opposition was forming in the Commons, soon to be known as the 'Country Party', and in 1668 it acquired a leader in the able and highly respected Sir William Coventry, former Secretary to the Navy. As befitted a Country Party, they were convinced of the existence of widespread corruption in high places, and they were deeply suspicious of the King's foreign policy, whomever he chose to ally with. Most damaging of all, they were beginning to suspect his loyalty to Protestantism.

Despite his punctilious attendance at Anglican church services, there were many who believed that Charles had been converted to Rome during his exile. We now know that he was not finally received into the Catholic Church until he was on his deathbed, but it is probably fair to regard him as a 'church papist'; in other words, like many of his Catholic subjects, he conformed on Sundays but his beliefs did not lie that way. As early as 1662 the favour he showed to Catholic courtiers, and his reluctance to enforce the penal laws, roused suspicion (he had, in fact, been holding secret pourparlers with Catholic spokesmen for a modified toleration). An explanatory proclamation on the matter had not helped, nor had his attempt in 1663 to secure parliamentary sanction for his right to dispense individuals from the provisions of the penal laws. Moreover, after some brief initial enthusiasm his marriage to a Catholic princess was as unpopular as his father's had been, especially when by 1667 it was realized that Catherine of Braganza was sterile. Clarendon was even accused of deliberately choosing a sterile queen so that his son-in-law should succeed to the throne. Even at this early stage, and before James's conversion, this prospect was viewed with alarm, and when Lord Roos secured a divorce in the House of Lords in 1670, the King's ministers took an unwonted interest in the proceedings.

These ministers organized the government with great efficiency, and they were assisted by the fact that Clarendon's fall had been preceded by the death of Lord Treasurer Southampton. Sir Thomas Clifford and Lord Ashley took over the Treasury, and with the assistance of one of the greatest of Treasury secretaries, Sir George Downing, overhauled the King's finances. The yield of the customs and excise was increased, and arrangements were made to pay debts in strict rotation – payment 'in course' – thus enhancing the government's credit; the exchequer certificates now issued as a record of debt circulated as an embryo paper currency. Foreign policy was directed by Henry Bennet, Earl of Arlington, with some intermittent assistance from the maverick Duke of Buckingham, who had inherited his father's charm and brilliance but not even his modest abilities. Unfortunately, he had been raised with Charles as a boy and was still one of his closest friends. The roster was completed by John Maitland Earl (later Duke) of Lauderdale, the High Commissioner for Scotland. Like his successor in the next reign,

John Drummond, Earl of Melfort, Lauderdale had considerable influence on English affairs, though it is now difficult to assess with accuracy. Perhaps his greatest contribution, which lies outside our scope, was his success in imposing autocratic royal government on Scotland; apart from a minor rising in 1679, Scotland was to cause little concern to the English government until after the Revolution.

But the ministers were not popular. The very fact that the initials of their names could be juggled into the opprobrious term 'C–a–b–a–l' is significant; they were regarded as a secretive and rather unsavoury junta. Disunited amongst themselves, they found it impossible to present a united front, and therefore to offer national leadership independently of the King. In contrast to Clarendon, and later Danby, their religious views were motley and decidedly unorthodox: Ashley and Lauderdale were some kind of Presbyterians; Buckingham was a freethinker; and Clifford and Arlington were strongly inclined towards Catholicism. As a group they presented an appearance of sophistication and expertise, but their shallowness and instability were easily detected.

Meanwhile, in the aftermath of the Second Dutch War, problems of foreign policy arose which were not to be settled in this reign. Rivalry with the Dutch was still predominant in the public mind, but at the same time the increasing power of France under Louis XIV was giving cause for concern; ideally Parliament would have opted for no binding foreign alliances at all, but in the circumstances this was unrealistic. In 1668 Arlington and Sir William Temple, the English ambassador at The Hague, executed a remarkable diplomatic *coup*. In 1667 Louis XIV had taken advantage of the distractions caused by the Anglo–Dutch war to claim part of the Spanish Netherlands (roughly modern Belgium) on behalf of his wife, and occupy it; now a hastily formed alliance between England, Holland and Sweden gave him pause, and eventually brought him to arbitration.

The Triple Alliance could have formed the basis of a new anti-French coalition of the kind which eventually emerged in the 1680s (without England). In 1677 and 1678, 'the Triple League' was even held up by the government's critics in Parliament as the ideal example of a forceful Protestant foreign policy. Unfortunately, ten years earlier they were still too suspicious of Charles, and not yet ready for an alliance with the hated Dutch. Disillusioned by the Triple Alliance's lukewarm reception in Parliament, Charles drifted with public opinion towards a third war with Holland, but this time in alliance with France, the boom nation in Europe. The result was the notorious Treaty of Dover, signed in May 1670.

This treaty has always been regarded as Charles II's bane. But it was a realistic and perfectly workable agreement for the dismemberment of the United Provinces, by now equally odious to both nations, and it was to England's natural advantage rather than France's. England was to take most of the coastal strip, France the south-east provinces, and the remainder was to constitute a new hereditary principality for Charles's nephew William of Orange, still barred by the Perpetual Edict from holding executive office in the Republic. Though the French were to do the bulk of the land fighting, while England merely blanked off the Dutch navy, Charles was to receive three million livres a year for the duration. Charles also inserted a secret clause undertaking to declare himself a Catholic at the appropriate time, and for this Louis agreed to provide another two million, plus the promise of military support if necessary.

This *catholicité* clause was Charles's own idea, and Louis XIV was distinctly lukewarm, fearing that it would impede the war effort. His motives remain a mystery. Some have seen it as part of a broader plan at this time for a royalist–Catholic *coup*: in 1669 and 1670 Clifford was regaining control of Parliament, though not always by the most scrupulous means; Scotland and Ireland, with their armies, were being brought under closer control from London – there was even talk of an Anglo-Scottish Union; and in 1670 Charles and James had long interviews with the Internuncio from Brussels, who was on a secret mission to England. But the Crown was still weak, its financial credit was still frail, and public opinion was decidedly wary of Rome; a skilled tactician like Charles must have known that this was not practical politics. The straightforward personal explanation is the best: that Charles was indulging his favourite sister, Henriette-Anne, Duchess of Orleans, who had been raised a Catholic in France and acted as a plenipotentiary in the negotiations. Certainly his interest in this aspect of the treaty rapidly waned after her premature death in June 1670. On the other hand, he may have been motivated by envy of his brother, who was secretly converted to Rome in 1668; if James could indulge his religious feelings in defiance of the political consequences, why not he? He was furious with James, ordered that his daughters, Mary and Anne, be brought up strict Anglicans, and forbad him ever to announce his conversion or admit it.

In the end, the time was never appropriate for Charles's conversion, but in the treaty as published the extra two million was added to the existing subsidy, so Louis XIV could regard himself as outmanoeuvred. But Charles had given Louis a potent blackmail weapon for the future; also the others in the secret, James, Clifford and Arlington. On the eve of the war, in March 1672, Charles issued a Declaration of Indulgence suspending the penal laws against Protestants and Catholics alike, ostensibly as a bid for national unity, but almost certainly under pressure. At the same time he tried to strengthen the ministry by making Clifford Lord Treasurer, with a peerage, and Ashley Lord Chancellor, with the title of Earl of Shaftesbury.

Initially the war was popular enough, and its motivation was obvious; it opened in advance of the declaration of war with an attack on the Dutch Smyrna convoy. Shaftesbury, heartened at the prospect of toleration for Dissenters, was still firmly behind it in February 1673, when he made his celebrated 'Delenda est Karthago' speech to the House of Lords. Popery was hated as much as ever, and the rise of French power was alarming; but the Dutch were still the national enemy, and relations between the two countries remained tense right down to 1714. France, on the other hand, was still in a sense England's traditional ally, favoured by Charles I and Cromwell alike.

But it was a gamble, and the more so because of Charles's financial improvidence. He could only find funds for the war by diverting the income of the Exchequer from the repayment of previous debts, and this 'Stop of the Exchequer' ruined the government's credit at the outset. The main sufferers were the goldsmith bankers; Danby later agreed to pay interest on their debts, but their case for capital repayment was finally rejected by Lord Chancellor Somers in 1697. This would not have mattered at all if it had been followed by resounding military success, but it was not. James fought an indecisive fleet action at Sole Bay, and his heavy losses were blamed on the failure of the allied French squadron to engage. On land the

207

picture was worse. The invading French carried all before them, but they were soon halted by William of Orange, who was elected stadholder and commander-in-chief after a popular uprising which overthrew the republican government; he ordered the dykes to be cut, flooding the lowlands. The *blitzkrieg* planned by Charles and Louis, with the United Provinces occupied by the autumn, and a peace signed by Christmas, went badly wrong. Charles was faced by the prospect of a lengthy war, with the added embarrassment of waging it against his own nephew.

English public opinion, inflamed by vigorous Dutch propaganda, swung behind the young stadholder, pictured as the heroic swordbearer of Protestantism against the hydra of Rome. The war, and the Declaration of Indulgence, were now seen as part of an international Catholic conspiracy, and this was near enough the truth to be dangerous. Charles put off the next meeting of Parliament as long as he could, until February 1673, but when it met Peter du Moulin's celebrated pamphlet, *England's Appeal from the Private Cabal at Whitehall to the Grand Council of the English Nation*, was in circulation and avidly read. The Commons held up supply for the war while they protested against the Declaration of Indulgence; when the Lords abandoned him on 1 March Charles gave way. A week later he finally cancelled the Declaration. He got his supply, but at the prorogation on 29 March he also had to accept the Test Act, which imposed on all office-holders not only the existing oaths but a declaration denying the transubstantiation of the elements in the mass; they also had to furnish a certificate showing that they had recently taken Anglican communion. The requirement that this be registered in a court of law in public session made evasion impossible.

The Test Act confirmed the public's worst fear, for that

summer not only Lord Clifford but the Duke of York resigned their offices rather than comply. A query still hung over the King himself, who was the only office-holder not covered by the test. The campaigning season again brought no result, just another two costly and inde-cisive fleet actions, and in August Spain and the Empire entered the war on the side of Holland, extending its probable duration almost indefinitely. Still worse, in the autumn news leaked out that James, whose first wife had died in 1671, was on the point of marrying Mary of Modena, a bigoted young Italian Catholic whose family were traditionally clients of France.

In a short parliamentary session in October, Shaftes-bury joined the furious opposition to the Modenese marriage, and was dismissed. By January 1674 the rout was complete, with Arlington and Buckingham, sum-moned before parliamentary committees of inquiry, des-perately accusing each other of responsibility for the events of the previous two years. At the risk of alienating Louis XIV, Charles had little choice but to pull out of the war, and he took the unusual step of communicating the terms of the Treaty of Westminster (February 1674) to Parliament beforehand. The rest of the Cabal resigned or were dismissed, with the exception of Lauderdale, leaving the initiative to Sir Thomas Osborne (later Earl of Danby), who had succeeded Clifford as Lord Treasurer the previous year.

In terms of parliamentary politics and diplomacy, the period from 1674 to 1678 is one of the most complex in English history, and certain guiding factors must be kept firmly in mind.

First, Charles was faced by an utterly recalcitrant parliament, now thirteen years old, and the ominous thing was not so much the attitude of the Commons as that of the

Lords, where a formidable aristocratic clique, led by Shaftesbury, a disillusioned Buckingham and the young George Savile, Viscount Halifax, campaigned vigorously for a dissolution, which must result in a resounding defeat for the government. The Country Party in the Commons, while receptive to leadership from above, found it difficult to mobilize the rest of the House behind a policy which must result in a good proportion of them losing their seats – a hazard the Lords did not face, of course. Thus a lot of opposition campaigns in the Commons were mere shadow-boxing. For instance, it was Shaftesbury, Wharton, Salisbury and Buckingham who protested in February 1677 that after a prorogation of more than a year Parliament was automatically dissolved, and went to the Tower for their pains. The Commons resolved that the prorogation was unconstitutional but the continuation of Parliament was not.

In the meanwhile Danby dug himself in. He rectified government finance by nursing the Customs and Excise, and a steady increase in English overseas trade resulted in a corresponding stabilization of crown revenue, at around the one and a half million pound mark. Up to 1678, England also enjoyed the advantages of peace while her two principal trade rivals, France and Holland, were at war. To undo the harm done by the Cabal, Danby fostered the image of a Protestant monarchy; he tried to step up the persecution of Roman Catholics, he rigorously enforced the Test Act, and in 1675 he even tried to introduce a supplementary test, forswearing any attempt to alter the government in Church or State. This failed, but he showed his resilience by beating off an attempt to impeach him, he overhauled government management in the Commons, and was not above resorting to some judicious bribery. The continuance of his government was a triumph of improvisation, his brinkmanship was alarming, his 'Church-and-King party' was largely a sham, but his was essentially a long-term programme, designed to come to fruition in 1684 and 1685. At the moment he was 'locked onto' Parliament, unable any more than Queen Elizabeth's ministers to contemplate government without it; but the long prorogation of 1675–7 was a straw in the wind, and the revised Triennial Act of 1664 gave the King plenty of room for manoeuvre.

Unfortunately, while the war in Europe continued, England must at least seem to have a foreign policy, and this meant continual resort to Parliament. Both sides were now bluffing. Charles wanted to get back into the war, if only to get his feet under the conference table at the end of it, but he did not want to fight France and he did not want to put himself in the hands of Parliament again as he had in 1674. Similarly, Parliament bayed for him to re-enter the war on the side of the Dutch, but they were markedly unwilling to entrust him with a large army for that end; so, for every step they took forward they took two back, and a hundred years later Whig historians were stupefied to find that some of the most Protestant and patriotic of the opposition leaders had been secretly in league with the French ambassador. As for Danby, he wanted a resplendently Protestant foreign policy without paying anything for it, and this he triumphantly achieved by the marriage in October 1677 of William III to James's elder daughter Mary, the ultimate heir to the throne (James's second wife being childless). At the same time Danby was quite willing to pander to Charles's desire to keep on good terms with Louis XIV; thus the secret treaty of February 1676, by which he promised not to re-enter the war on the side of Holland.

However, by the winter of 1677–8 the war was clearly

drawing to a close, and the peace terms were being thrashed out at Nijmegen. Charles hastily signed a treaty with the Dutch, and with grudging support from Parliament shipped a force of 12,000 men to Flanders in May 1678. But this was too transparent; rather than admit him to the conference table, the French and the Dutch hurriedly wound up their negotiations, leaving him stranded, so much so that in June 1678 Parliament gladly voted the money to disband and pay off the army. Unfortunately, Charles used the money to keep up the army another few months in a last desperate attempt to influence the peace terms – in vain.

So the Peace of Nijmegen proved as deep a humiliation to Charles as the Treaty of Westminster in 1674. His general credibility was nil, he had succeeded in alienating both France and Holland, and when Parliament met in October he had to explain as best he could why he still had an army afoot and what he had done with the money voted for its disbandment. This is why he and Danby were unable to withstand the shock of the Popish Plot, which burst upon them in August and September. Titus Oates's tale of a Catholic conspiracy to assassinate the King was quite incredible and inconsistent within itself, as was the supporting testimony of other witnesses, even more disreputable, who jumped on the bandwagon. But the government was undermined by two pieces of extraordinary ill-luck: the mysterious murder of a noted London magistrate, Sir Edmund Berry Godfrey, which was at once attributed to the Catholics, and the discovery of distinctly treasonable material in the papers of Edward Coleman, a former Secretary to the Duke of York and a notorious Court Catholic.

The depth and extent of the subsequent furore are still extremely difficult to assess. Coleman was tried, sentenced and executed, but not before he had irredeemably compromised the duke. He was followed to the scaffold by a number of Jesuits, in 1679; but the Jesuits, hated and distrusted by most English Catholics as much as by the Protestants, were fair game. The campaign against the secular priests was much less vigorous, as it was against the Catholic gentry and aristocracy, and seems to have been confined to areas in which there was a larger-than-average Catholic population; London, the Marches and Wales, Lancashire and Yorkshire. Much of the excitement was dying down by the end of 1678, and though Parliament lashed itself to a perfect state of fury about the whole thing, and the opposition fished industriously in these troubled waters, only one anti-Catholic measure reached the statute book: the second Test Act of November 1678, excluding Catholics from Parliament and the Court; and even then, amazingly enough, James's supporters were strong enough to have him exempted. What wrecked the government's precarious balance was the discovery in December of Danby's secret negotiations with Louis XIV, which led to his immediate impeachment, of course, and a hasty prorogation. Charles made an informal agreement with the opposition to save Danby in return for a dissolution, and a new parliament met in March 1679, the first for eighteen years.

Charles's skill in handling the subsequent 'Exclusion Crisis' has been much exaggerated. When it became obvious that the elections had completely destroyed the former Court party and returned a House of Commons potentially as dangerous as that of 1640, he lost his nerve. His decision to send James abroad could only lead men to suppose that James was indefensible, and his solemn oath before the Privy Council that he had never been married to the mother of his eldest son, James Scott, Duke of

Monmouth, at present Captain-General, lent undue weight to that young man's pretensions. (Because of Charles's indulgent affection for him he was a useful political tool, but no one of any weight regarded him as a serious candidate for the throne. The Whig leaders did not run him as such until late 1680 or early 1681, and then only in frank acknowledgement of his illegitimacy.) Next, Charles was slow to recognize that the opposition leaders could not or would not honour their undertaking to save Danby, and it was five weeks into a stormy session before he was safely in the Tower, where he stayed five years. With no substitute for Danby available, Charles then had to take the leaders of opposition, including Shaftesbury, Halifax, the Earl of Essex and William Lord Russell into a re-formed and slenderized Privy Council of thirty, from which all the old courtiers were excluded. He then proposed statutory limitations on the powers of his successor, which produced the inevitable riposte in a Bill simply to exclude James from the succession altogether, which passed the Commons on 21 May. The minority of 128 against the Bill, in a House of 335, showed the mobilization of opinion against it, and it would certainly never have passed the Lords; but Charles ducked the confrontation for which James, from exile, was calling, and prorogued Parliament on 27 May. Even more disastrously, he then dissolved Parliament in July and summoned another for October, obviously hoping that the election results of February had been a vote against Danby, not the Crown. He was wrong; the elections produced much the same House of Commons, now resentful at being put to the expense of defending their seats.

A lucky illness felled Charles at the end of August, and brought James back. With the King apparently dying and

Monmouth still Captain-General, garlanded with the cheap laurels won that summer in the suppression of the Covenanters' Rebellion in Scotland, the situation was menacing. James demanded a confrontation and got it; and up to a point it was successful. Parliament was prorogued to December, then in November it was announced that unless there was some significant change in Europe it would not meet for another year. Shaftesbury was dismissed the council, and the fact that most of his associates hung on until January 1680 was, in the circumstances, an admission of weakness. Halifax, refreshed by an earldom, stayed on. Monmouth was dismissed the Captain-Generalship and sent into exile; when he at once returned he was comprehensively disgraced. James retired briefly to Scotland, but returned in February 1680. There followed an extraordinary lull; Shaftesbury organized a nation-wide campaign of petitions, calling upon the King to meet Parliament, but the number of counter-petitions 'abhorring' the practice confirmed the strength of conservative opinion. 'Petitioners' and 'Abhorrers' settled out that winter into 'Whigs' and 'Tories'. Meanwhile James's brother-in-law, Lawrence Hyde, was straightening out the royal finances, disordered by the political crisis and a trade recession in 1679. Two more of James's associates, the young Earl of Sunderland and Sidney Godolphin, were labouring to build up an anti-French coalition in Europe, consisting of England, Holland, the Empire, Spain, Brandenburg and some of the lesser German Protestant States. (Charles remained convinced, as before, that the solution to his problems lay abroad.)

The bubble burst in June 1680, when a group of Whig lords headed by Shaftesbury suddenly presented James before the Middlesex grand jury as a popish recusant, and the Duchess of Portsmouth, Charles's principal mistress, as a common prostitute. This blow to the King's prestige in a most sensitive area, followed by a Court defeat in the City of London elections, effectively torpedoed his new anti-French foreign policy; all that was left was a treaty with Spain, now the weakest of the 'major' powers, signed that month; the other putative allies drew back, fearing that England was lapsing once more into chaos. Charles could only go on. There was no precedent for dissolving a parliament without meeting it, so he ordered a session for 21 October. He sent James back to Scotland, but after some hesitation he rejected the advice of Sunderland and Godolphin that he sacrifice the duke and concentrate on safeguarding the Princess Mary's rights as next heir.

In the second Exclusion Parliament Charles had his back to the wall, but the Whigs were now outmanoeuvred. A second Exclusion Bill passed the Commons, but it was rejected by sixty to thirty votes in the Lords, the King making his wishes unequivocally clear beforehand. Charles then put forward, through Lord Halifax, an even more specific scheme of statutory limitations on the future James II. Vague Whig threats of revolt in London came to nothing, nor dare they impeach James, which was the next obvious step. James's adamantine obstinacy meant that if he were impeached, or excluded by statute, he would fight, and in Scotland he had an effective power base, with some prospect of French aid and a considerable prospect of support in England – much more than his father could muster in 1642. After the events of mid century this generation would not trifle with civil war, and even by appearing to bring the nation near it the Whigs were fatally compromising their standing. The parliamentary campaign petered out in attacks on the King's advisers and the judges, and the session ended in January 1681 with four rather infantile and desperate Commons' resolutions, one of them calling for the reinstatement of Monmouth. Charles dismissed all his ministers who had voted for exclusion, dissolved Parliament, and summoned another to Oxford in March.

The elections again returned a majority in favour of exclusion, but in ultra-Tory Oxford they were disorientated and deprived of popular support. They were now driven to the last desperate step of openly espousing Monmouth's candidature; indeed, Shaftesbury made a spectacular personal plea on the steps of Christ Church Hall that Charles legitimize his son. Charles's answer was to put forward once more his scheme of limitations, this time with William and Mary as Protectors of the kingdom. On the face of it, it was an offer no reasonable set of men could refuse, and when the Commons riposted with yet another Exclusion Bill Charles felt strong enough to dissolve them after a session of only one week.

This was the key moment. Many members of both houses had come to Oxford with armed retainers (indeed, some of them were charged with treason as a result), and some were in favour of continuing the session in defiance of the King. But constitutional conventions were too strong, and the King had taken the precaution of bringing a regiment of cavalry with him. They eventually dispersed, in confident expectation of another parliament that autumn, a parliament which never came.

A few days before he dissolved the Oxford Parliament, Charles concluded an informal verbal agreement with Louis XIV. In return for a subsidy of two million livres for 1681–2, and one million in each of the succeeding years, Charles agreed not to summon a new parliament nor to implement the Anglo-Spanish Treaty of 1680. Ever since 1678 Louis had been deaf to periodic appeals for help like this, sometimes from Charles, more often from the Duchess of Portsmouth. But he was now mildly alarmed at the prospect of Monmouth's accession as the spokesman of an anti-French Whig oligarchy; he may have visualized James as a king who would face so much opposition at home that he would inevitably be a client of France abroad; and, feeble as it was, the Anglo-Spanish Treaty of June 1680 gave him cause for concern.

It used to be argued that it was this secret agreement which nerved Charles to make a stand against the Whigs, and indeed made it financially possible. This last is patently untrue; thanks partly to Lawrence Hyde, who has been under-estimated as a finance minister, Charles's finances were now in a better shape than at any previous stage, and the French subsidy of £175,000 for 1681-2 contrasts with a Crown income from other sources of nearly £1,300,000. The decision to abandon Tangier in 1684, sometimes held up as evidence of financial stringency, was inevitable on military and logistic grounds. On the other hand, in the last years of his reign Charles completed an expensive remodelling and beautifying of Windsor Castle, whose present form owes much to him, and embarked on the planning of another great palace at Winchester.

Nevertheless, Charles was always psychologically dependent on his magnificent cousin, and the restoration of Louis XIV's friendship probably nerved him to a confrontation. If so, he paid a high price. For the next four years foreign affairs were the weakest element in Charles's policy, and reduced England to a humiliating position in Europe. He had to stand aside while Louis XIV consolidated his grip on the Rhine frontier, securing Strasbourg in 1681 and Luxembourg in 1684; and in 1683-4, when war broke out between France and Spain, and Charles was called upon to honour the treaty of 1680, he could only offer his mediation, which was humiliatingly refused. This policy, or non-policy, also drove a wedge between Charles and William of Orange, who strained his own political influence in an attempt to bring the Dutch Republic to war with France in 1684, and blamed the King for his defeat. Prince William's increasing disposition to meddle in English politics in 1680 and 1681 had angered Charles, but in view of the continued failure of the Duchess of York to bear a son he remained the ultimate heir presumptive (for at no time was it supposed that Mary would reign alone), and James himself realized that this dynastic split was weakening and potentially dangerous.

Otherwise the power of the monarchy revived with remarkable speed. At first the measures taken by the government were tentative and probably defensive in character, but it soon became apparent that the violent Whig assault mounted in the exclusion crisis had been succeeded by a Tory reaction just as violent and even stronger. By taking the nation to the brink of another civil war, the Whigs had given the upper classes a profound shock, and the Church's unhesitating support for James from the beginning set up a strong undertow. The pamphlet debate on the right of parliament to alter the succession ultimately strengthened the doctrine of divine right and passive obedience, adding to them a third tenet, that of 'hereditary succession', which decreed that the Crown must pass in the direct hereditary line come what may. Conservative ideology was also reinforced by the belated publication in 1680 of Sir Robert Filmer's *Patriarcha*, written in the 1640s. Filmer's theory that the absolute authority of kings was based, with overwhelming divine sanction, on the natural authority of fathers over children, chimed in with the social assumptions of the age, and was generally and enthusiastically accepted. Though it was despised and derided by subsequent generations, it is noteworthy that John Locke felt impelled to compose an answer to it at once (published in 1689 as the celebrated *Two Treatises of Civil Government*), and so did Algernon Sidney. Dryden's *Absalom and Achitophel* (1681) was an elegant, if rather smug, commentary on the whole matter.

Moreover, the very success of the Whigs in the elections of 1679–81 told against them, especially since it was accompanied by increasing mob participation, and by published proposals to reform the electoral system and broaden the franchise in the corporations. Worse still, the lower-class Dissenters were blamed – probably quite wrongly – for the undermining of vested political interests in so many localities. A substantial majority of Members of Parliament who had been panicked by the Popish Plot into supporting Exclusion now took stock, and decided that the evils to be expected from a Catholic ruler were far outweighed by the evils attendant on any alternative proposals. This was symbolized by the return to Court of prominent exclusionists such as Lord Townshend and William Lord Cavendish, heir to the earldom of Devonshire.

The Tory reaction got under way with the trial and execution of two comparatively minor tools of the Whig opposition, Edmund Fitzharris and Stephen College, in the spring of 1681. Shaftesbury was then charged with treason, for conspiring to levy war against the King at Oxford, and was fortunate to be released by a Whig grand jury in London. This provoked the government to an all-out effort to secure a Tory Lord Mayor in 1682, and with him Tory sheriffs and Tory juries, and Shaftesbury fled to Holland, where he died in January 1683. Meanwhile, the government issued a writ of *quo warranto* against the City's charter in 1682, and after a long struggle in the courts it was confiscated in 1683, and replaced by another which gave the Crown absolute political control. Similar proceedings were initiated against other parliamentary boroughs renowned as strongholds of Whiggism or Dissent or both, and most of them surrendered without a struggle. By the end of the reign, fifty-one new charters had been issued, and another forty-seven were in the pipeline. Another twenty-one in the first eighteen months of James II's reign brought the total up to 119, which meant that the Crown could now influence to some degree the election of 238 members, not counting those who already stood for the Cinque Ports, naval towns like Chatham, or boroughs controlled by the Duchy of Lancaster.

Equally important, as early as December 1681 the Privy Council ordered local magistrates to enforce the Corporation Act of 1661, and empowered the county authorities to act in case of neglect. At the same time the personnel of county government, the Lord Lieutenants, deputy lieutenants and justices of the peace, was comprehensively purged. With the vigorous support of the bishops, these new Tory spokesmen now attempted, arguably for the first time, the full enforcement of the Clarendon Code. Over the period 1682-6 the persecution of Dissenters was at its height, the Quakers suffering particularly. Finally, in the summer of 1683, the Rye House Plot delivered the remaining Whig leaders into the government's hands. A conspiracy by a few radical ex-Cromwellians to assassinate Charles and James, once discovered, was easily blended by the government with a much less substantial plot for an aristocratic *coup d'état* which had never got beyond the stage of talk. Monmouth, Essex, Lord Russell and Algernon Sidney were rounded up; Essex committed suicide in the Tower, Russell and Sidney were found guilty of high treason and executed; several lesser Whigs fled to Holland, followed by Monmouth, whose royal blood saved him from something worse than exile.

It is strange that we do not know who originated and conducted this skilful campaign against the Whigs. Not Charles himself, who had by now lapsed into petulant and indifferent senility, and was up to his old game of playing his ministers off one against the other. Nor does it fit the character of Lawrence Hyde (created Earl of Rochester 1682), who was his chief minister in so far as he had one. Suspicion points to Edward Seymour, who held no ministerial post but was high in favour from 1680 to 1682, to Sir Leoline Jenkins, a career diplomat and Secretary of State 1680–84, and to the Duke of Ormonde, who was certainly recalled from his duties as Lord-Lieutenant in Ireland to mastermind the campaign against London in 1682–3. The judges were naturally credited with a prominent role, particularly George Jeffreys, appointed Chief Justice of King's Bench in 1683. And there is no doubt that James, Duke of York, himself assumed the role of chief minister of the Crown, and even director of policy, as soon as he returned from Scotland in May 1682.

There is little doubt that James would have remained at Edinburgh indefinitely if Charles had had his way, except in the unlikely event of his returning to Anglicanism – a step which Charles constantly urged on him. Charles spoke of him with bitterness, and blamed him personally for the events of the past three years; he regarded him as a prime political liability even now, and doubted his capacity to rule. But James returned through the machinations of the Duchess of Portsmouth, backed up by Sunderland and Godolphin, both dismissed for supporting exclusion in 1680. They feared a complete Tory–Anglican domination of the government, and also wanted to ingratiate themselves with the next monarch. It is a sign of Charles's essential weakness that he allowed himself to be outwitted in these manoeuvres.

James demonstrated his ascendancy in a series of new ministerial appointments. Sunderland was received into favour and reappointed Secretary of State in 1683; Godol-. phin was appointed to the Treasury Board and in 1684 to a Secretaryship of State. James resumed control of the navy early in 1684 without official standing, and it is apparent that he was now a member of all policy-making bodies. Later that year he effected a remarkable *coup* by securing the appointment of a Scotsman, Charles, Earl of Middleton, to an English Secretaryship of State. There was always a counterpoise; Charles saw to that by holding onto Halifax, James's most detested critic, who was given a marquessate and appointed Lord Privy Seal in 1682. There was also an ambiguous incident in the summer of 1684 when Rochester, James's brother-in-law and close friend, was 'kicked upstairs' from the Treasury to the Lord-Lieutenancy of Ireland. But there is no doubt that James was now in effective control, and was initiating new policies, particularly in Scotland and Ireland, which smoothly developed into his own reign. Ormonde was re-called from Dublin in the autumn of 1684, the Irish army was detached from the Lord-Lieutenant's control, and a campaign began to break the military power of the Anglo-Irish Ascendancy. In Scotland the Earl of Middleton and James's tool John Drummond of Lundin (later Earl of Melfort) were preparing the ground for a meeting of the Edinburgh Estates in 1685, to be presided over by James himself, which would finally consolidate the Crown's authority there. In England he was actively preparing to implement a scheme, in his brother's name, for the *de facto* toleration of the Roman Catholic aristocracy and gentry. But at this stage, on *g* February 1685, Charles

223

was stricken by a coronary thrombosis, and died two days later, having been received into the Catholic Church. The ports were closed, the Lord Lieutenants alerted, but James II was proclaimed king amid moderate public enthusiasm and with no signs of overt opposition.

Nor is this surprising. In character and temper James was an Anglican Tory of the old school, a bent confirmed by his marriage to Clarendon's daughter and his close friendship with Clarendon's son Lawrence Hyde; not to mention men of similar disposition like George Legge, Lord Dartmouth, or Richard Graham, Viscount Preston. He was much more affected than Charles II by their father's death, and often spoke of it; he was deeply impressed by the Church of England's undeviating support for Charles I, and for himself during the exclusion crisis. To him it was the bedrock of the social order. His conversion came comparatively late in life, and there seemed much truth in his insistence that it was a personal decision. His Italian wife, twenty-eight years his junior, had no important influence on him until 1687 at the earliest, and he had significantly few Catholic friends or associates, apart from Scotsmen and Irishmen (and his partiality for them predated his conversion). Moreover, he had very little contact with the native English Catholics, and he was never the head of any 'Catholic interest', whatever his enemies said. His Catholicism was of the Court, and ultramontane; his favoured spiritual advisers were drawn from the Society of Jesus. Everyone would have been happier had he been Protestant, of course, but his refusal to conceal his religion was a point strongly in his favour, and contrasted with his brother's duplicity; for no one had much doubt that Charles II had been a Catholic, and James himself offered support for this view by publishing two of his brother's private meditations on the matter after his death. These contrasting traits had a wider application. James was known as a straightforward man, an implacable enemy and an unshakeable friend; this was a relief after the tortuous duplicity of Charles II, and was much nearer the hearts of the kind of men who could offer him important support. He was a man who made himself readily understood.

His unyielding conservatism, and his sympathy with the Church of England, were reaffirmed in a speech to the Privy Council the day of his accession; he published it, and repeated it in his speech from the throne at the opening of Parliament in May. He had had plenty of time to compose this document while his brother lay dying, and there is no doubt that it expressed his considered sentiments; his policy revolved round an alliance between Crown and Church. If confirmation were needed, it could be found in the appointment of Rochester as Lord Treasurer, and the retention of Halifax, who was nothing if not hostile to Rome, as Lord President. He and Rochester told the French ambassador that naturally he wished to alleviate the lot of the English Catholics, but this must be a slow, inch-by-inch process, undertaken in the closest cooperation with the Church of England. He said, with typical bluntness, 'I have been reported to be a man for arbitrary power, but that is not the only story has been made of me, and I shall make it my endeavour to preserve this government both in Church and State as it is now by law established.' His decision on the very first Sunday of his reign to attend mass publicly in the Queen's chapel caused a slight *frisson*, but no more; again, it was a sign of his robust manliness, compared with his brother's rather feminine duplicity. This was to be a new era of firm leadership and open government, and one of his first steps was to eject from Whitehall his brother's unsavoury troupe of mistresses, comedians, panders and yesmen, and issue new regulations for the more austere governance of the Court.

His success was confirmed by the composition of the new House of Commons summoned in May, which was overwhelmingly royalist in sentiment. When every allowance is made for the recent pressure on the boroughs, it was a vote of confidence in James and in all he represented. He is often accused of handling this parliament incompetently, but in fact his brusque, no-nonsense approach was much more in keeping with contemporary expectations of kingship, and again, it contrasted well with his brother's evasions and empty suavities.

Nor were more practical aspects neglected. By 1685, Charles II's annual income had risen to £1,370,000; James's first parliament cheerfully confirmed this, and added supplementary short-term grants, to 1688, for the refitting of the navy and the suppression of Monmouth's Rebellion, which brought the total to nearly £2 million. James was the first monarch since Henry VIII to have no financial worries. He had at his disposal an army of nearly 10,000 men, recently strengthened by the withdrawal of two crack regiments from Tangier, and over and above this small but useful forces in Scotland and Ireland. The English army was increased to about 17,000 men to deal with Monmouth. In 1685 James also inaugurated a planned three-year programme for the refitting of the navy. This was small beer compared with the forces at Louis XIV's disposal, but it was quite adequate to overawe any opposition in the three kingdoms. And as at home, so abroad. James's overtures to Louis XIV in the first five months of the reign, which met with a crabbed refusal, have been much publicized by Whig historians; not so well publicized are his conscientious efforts to find a *modus vivendi* with his difficult Dutch son-in-law, which culminated in William's dispatch of troops to assist in the suppression of Monmouth's rebellion in July, and the formal renewal of existing treaties between England and the Netherlands in August. With our foreknowledge of the Revolution, only three years away, we tend to ignore the fact that in 1685 the monarchy was at the very zenith of its power, and well up with current trends in Europe, which were towards centralized and militarized royal power, with elected assemblies playing at best a formal role. Nor is it likely, when we consider William III's career in Holland, that he would have reversed this trend had he succeeded his uncle in the normal course of events; rather he would have encouraged it.

# IX

# THE REVOLUTION, 1685–8

The Revolution of 1688 is almost unique among modern revolutions or uprisings in that it had no obvious social or economic motivation. It came suddenly and unexpectedly upon a nation which was enjoying unprecedented prosperity and social tranquillity. Even if it is considered as a religious phenomenon, it did not represent a division in the majority Church, as in 1642, but a general reaction against a minority sect; indeed, 1688 did much to bridge the gap between the Anglicans and the Protestant Nonconformists, which had been opened in 1642 and held open in 1662. The Revolution hinged almost entirely on the relationship of the King with the upper classes, in Church and State.

The turning-point in James's reign came early, with the landing of the Duke of Monmouth in Dorset in June 1685, at first demanding a parliamentary inquiry into his father's death, then making an outright bid for the throne. He had strong radical and republican support, and the rebellion should be seen not as an attempted dynastic *coup* but as the last stand of the 'Good Old Cause'. His tatterdemalion army was routed at Sedgemoor, he was captured and executed, and his supporters in the West Country were brutally decimated by Jeffreys in the famous Bloody Assizes that autumn, for which he was made Lord Chancellor. But the issue had been more evenly balanced than appeared; James had had to borrow two English regiments from the Dutch army before he dare release his own regiments guarding London. The episode intensified his existing sense of insecurity.

Moreover, though the parliament of 1685 was overwhelmingly loyalist, it was also militantly Anglican. Despite strong rumours beforehand, James did not propose any statutory amendment to the penal laws against Catholics; in fact the Commons gave grave offence by demanding that they be enforced. In the first week of his reign, in pursuance of a policy decided upon by his brother, James issued confidential orders for persecution of Catholics to cease, but his legal authority for so doing was slender. As it was, the question of the penal laws was not raised again until 1687; instead, James turned to the Test Act. In the autumn, during the parliamentary recess, James let it be known that he intended to retain the additional regiments recruited that summer, bringing his army up to about 20,000 men, and when Parliament met in November he told them, for their information, that he intended to keep nearly ninety Catholic officers whom he had commissioned, and whom he had dispensed from the provisions of the Test Act. (He did not demand the repeal of the Act, though he is supposed to have lobbied for this beforehand; it is not even clear that he was asking for permission to use his power of dispensation; all he was seeking, it seems, is a confrontation.) This brought him into direct conflict with the nobility. The Commons were bullied into quiescence, but so vocal were the Lords that he had to prorogue Parliament after only ten days. One of his sharpest critics, Henry Compton, bishop of London, was dismissed the Privy Council and his post as Clerk to the Closet. Halifax had already been dismissed in October, a sign of James's hardening attitude.

This attitude was dictated by a growing sense of

isolation, of defensiveness, and was intensified by a mounting religious mania, which provoked comment even from Catholic observers in London in the spring of 1687. This was associated, perhaps, with his first known quarrel with the Queen; with the backing of the priests at Court, she now secured the ejection of his mistress, Catherine Sedley, a Protestant. (All his life James, who was a lusty and amorous man, found sex a problem; in old age he believed that his deposition in 1689 was a punishment for his adultery.) From the autumn of 1685 he spared neither money nor effort to propagate the Roman faith. Priests and monks were encouraged to return from abroad, small religious houses were re-established in London, together with a first-class Jesuit school which attracted Protestant pupils in considerable numbers. A Catholic press was set up to flood the market with cheap works of devotion and proselytization. A formal diplomatic correspondence was resumed with the Holy See, for the first time since 1558, and envoys were exchanged, though the Pope would not designate his a nuncio until 1687. However, he did appoint a Vicar Apostolic for the English Catholic Church, John Leyburn, and James was soon requesting the appointment of bishops.

All this seems very superficial to us. James's relations with Innocent XI were in fact poor, and no amount of bishops seemed likely to improve the conversion rate, which was low, and continued so throughout the reign. He was far from enjoying the support of the English Catholics themselves, who were anxious to preserve a working relationship with the Protestant majority and secure a long-term agreement with William and Mary. His sole positive achievement in 1686 was to secure a verdict from the high-court judges in the collusive action *Godden* v. *Hales* which confirmed his right to dispense with the provisions of the Test Act. This was only used to bring a few Catholic peers on to the Privy Council as figureheads, and confirmed what he had announced the previous November. However, if his activities were superficial, that only made them the more noticeable, and there were several riots and rabbling of priests in London, Bristol and Gloucester, which should have served as a warning. The external patade of Catholicism was alarming, especially when it was combined with an apparent campaign against the established Church.

By the summer of 1686 James's honeymoon with the Church of England was over, and with it his gradualist approach to religious toleration. But it is difficult to say what replaced it. His establishment of a Commission for Ecclesiastical Causes in July was regarded with deep foreboding. The new court bore a distinct resemblance to the notorious High Commission, suppressed by a statute of 1641 confirmed in 1661; but no statute could prevent the King delegating any of his powers to commissioners, as he did for the navy, and in the case of a Catholic king who was head of a Protestant Church it was only proper that he should. The commission was entirely staffed by Protestant bishops, law officers and cabinet ministers, and it had no power over laymen. True, it had obviously been formed to deal with the bishop of London, who had refused to silence the anti-Catholic sermons of John Sharp, vicar of St Martin-in-the-Fields; but, whatever the merits of the case, James was not the first masterful monarch to pursue a squabble with an individual cleric to inordinate lengths without endangering the Church as a whole. Nevertheless, when William Sancroft, Archbishop of Canterbury, was barred from the Privy Council for declining to join the commission, and the commission then suspended Compton, the Church was deprived of important leadership at a

critical juncture, especially since James kept the archbishopric of York vacant from April 1686 to November
1688. When it became known that James was seeking the
appointment of Catholic bishops, and a cardinalate for his
Jesuit favourite, Edward Petre, contemporaries drew the
obvious conclusion. They may have been wrong. The
Pope refused to promote Petre, and when four Catholic
bishops were appointed in January 1688, it was to new
districts independent of the Anglican hierarchy; and apart
from one isolated case (that of Edward Sclater, always
cited) there is no evidence of James's trying to intrude
Catholics into Anglican livings or benefices. All the same,
the suspicion is understandable.

It is natural that James's disillusionment with the
Church should bring in its train the fall of his brothers-in-
law, Lord Treasurer Rochester and the 2nd Earl of
Clarendon, Lord Privy Seal and Lord Lieutenant in
Ireland, in January 1687. The fact that the process was so
long-drawn-out testifies to James's instinctive loyalty to
relatives and lifelong friends. The turning-point came in
November 1686 when James put Rochester to the ultimate
test by demanding that he turn Roman Catholic. There is
some rather fragile evidence to suggest that he tried this
tactic on other ministers, but it was soon abandoned.

The fall of the brothers Hyde was also associated with a
New Deal for Ireland. James's policy in Dublin, like most
of his policies, was contradictory. In 1685 he had appointed
his friend Richard Talbot, Earl of Tyrconnell, Lieutenant-
General of the Irish army, on the understanding that he
would purge the officer class of the Anglo-Irish Protestants. But James himself was a child of his age, race and
class, deeply committed to the maintenance of the
Ascendancy; he appointed Clarendon Lord-Lieutenant
and repeatedly affirmed his support for the hated Act of

Settlement of 1662 which had perpetuated minority rule in Ireland. Under growing pressure to alleviate the lot of his Irish co-religionists, he at length agreed to the unprecedented appointment of a Catholic and a native Irishman, Tyrconnell; but only as Lord Deputy, with the constant threat of having a new Lord Lieutenant appointed over him. (One never was; on the other hand, the Act of Settlement was never repealed, only by the Jacobite 'Patriot Parliament', which met at Dublin in 1689.)

Similar vacillation was evident in England. Having dismissed the Hydes, the chief sponsors of an Anglican policy, in the first three months of 1687 James proceeded to bring pressure on the members of his predominantly Anglican parliament to support the repeal of the Penal Laws and Test Act, in the process known as 'closetting'. The results were ambiguous, but a corresponding inquisition in the Court and in the army and navy produced a large number of dismissals, notably that of Admiral Arthur Herbert, second-in-command of the Fleet and at the same time Master of the Robes. The King's policy on religion was still surprisingly opaque; the persecution of Dissenters was slackening noticeably, a trend which had begun back in the spring of 1686 with the Quakers, who had a powerful friend at Court in William Penn. But no official announcement was made at this stage. In December 1686 he also began what his suspicious Protestant subjects saw as an attack on the universities, with the appointment of the Catholic John Massey as Dean of Christ Church, Oxford. (Obadiah Walker, the incumbent Master of University College, had already turned Catholic.) In January 1687 he forced a Catholic Master on Sidney Sussex College, Cambridge, and he tried to repeat this at Magdalen College, Oxford, in April. The resistance of the Fellows was unexpectedly fierce, and it took a visitation from the Ecclesiastical Commission in October to bring them to heel. Then the college was comprehensively romanized, and received a Catholic president in Buonaventura Gifford, one of the new English Catholic bishops, in March 1688. Almost certainly James's aim was simply to secure the entry to the universities of candidates for the Roman priesthood on the same terms as Protestants, but it is not surprising that his aims were exaggerated by his opponents. Also his violent and arbitrary removal of men from posts like masterships of colleges, which were regarded as a species of freehold, made nonsense of his repeated assurances that he had no designs on his subjects' property.

However, long before this his conduct had attracted unfavourable attention abroad. Louis XIV was alarmed at the increase in the English army, and James's naval rebuilding programme; the emergence of an independent England would disturb the delicate balance imposed by the Truce of Ratisbon in 1684 between France, Spain and the Empire. Throughout 1686 there were sporadic quarrels between the two kings; James's attempts to prevent the absorption into the French state of William III's family principality of Orange, and his efforts on behalf of English Protestants stranded in France after the Revocation of the Edict of Nantes, caused Louis disproportionate irritation. On the other hand, the Revocation (by the Edict of Fontainebleau, 1685), and the ruthless persecution of the French Protestants which followed, reflected on James as a fellow Catholic monarch. In 1687 James made matters worse by trying to intervene in Louis's long-standing quarrel with Pope Innocent XI; as a new convert, with very little experience of Continental Catholicism, James was horrified by Louis's violence towards the head of their Church. Though many of his subjects suspected the existence of a secret Anglo-French alliance, and some even assumed it, relations between the two countries were in fact edgy for most of James's reign.

As for William III, the *détente* between him and his father-in-law in 1685 was short-lived. There followed a succession of petty disputes – over the chaplains appointed from England for the Princess Mary, over the English envoys at The Hague, over the activities of exiled English Whigs in the Netherlands, over the command of the Anglo-Scots brigade in the Dutch army, over the principality of Orange – which had a cumulative effect, especially since an exchange of special missions in 1685 had failed to solve the outstanding maritime and colonial disputes between the two powers. In the autumn of 1686, William was also alarmed at James's active naval and military preparations, which seemed to portend a fourth Dutch war, and by persistent rumours throughout Europe that he intended to divert the succession to Anne or even to his illegitimate son by Arabella Churchill, James FitzJames, later Duke of Berwick. The appointment of Tyrconnell was interpreted as a prelude to the detachment of Ireland from England, and therefore another threat to Princess Mary's inheritance. In February 1687 William's confidential emissary Dykveldt arrived in London for secret talks with James, on these and other matters. Dykveldt also had talks with a number of noblemen who were deeply critical of James's policy; with the Earls of Nottingham and Shrewsbury, with Halifax, Bishop Compton and some of the dissident Catholic peers. He took back with him letters from them to William, and thereafter William maintained a regular though infrequent correspondence with Halifax and Nottingham, and they had further discussions with another of the Prince's envoys, Zuylestein, when he came over on a formal mission in August. In the same month, Shrewsbury, who had been disgraced for his refusal to comply with James's policy, went over to The Hague. But it is unwise to deduce from this that any 'conspiracy' existed, and certainly not in the spring of 1687, when it seemed equally likely that William and James would reach an accommodation.

In fact, Dykveldt was confronted soon after he arrived with a direct request that the Prince and Princess endorse James's proposals for a general religious toleration, which were now far advanced, though not publicly announced. This was a master-stroke. Though the reaction of Members of Parliament individually 'closetted' was unpromising, the compliance of the heir to the throne with the King's policy would cut the ground from under their feet, and enable him to summon Parliament, which still stood prorogued. On 4 April James felt confident enough to issue his Declaration of Indulgence, akin to his brother's in 1672, suspending the Test Acts and all the penal laws against Protestant Dissenters as well as Catholics. On the face of it, he had no reason to expect a refusal from William. In the Dutch Republic most religious minorities, including Catholics and Jews, had long enjoyed *de facto* toleration, and William and Dykveldt were Calvinists in belief, congregationalists in religious observance – the English Dissenters were in a very real sense their co-religionists. A state-imposed toleration extending through the next reign could not easily have been reversed and in the circumstances William's refusal was not only unexpected but unenlightened. Undoubtedly he was influenced by the advice of James's opponents in England, by the King's campaign against Magdalen, Oxford, and by his monumental tactlessness in staging a public entry for the newly designated papal nuncio, Ferdinand d'Adda, archbishop of Amasia *in partibus infidelium,* which provoked a confrontation in April between him and the loyalist Duke of Somerset. All the same, the final decision was postponed until Dykveldt's return to Holland in June; William then wrote to James saying that he and Mary heartily endorsed the suspension of all persecution for religion, but they must insist on the retention of the Test Act and the privileged position of the established Church. Even then, it is important that their attitude was not made public until December.

William's refusal made Parliament redundant, and James dissolved it in July 1687, but no alternative policy presented itself. It must be supposed that the numerous Protestants still enjoying favour and high office, like Godolphin, Ormonde, Middleton, Churchill and Dartmouth, had endorsed the King's policy of toleration, but otherwise he was not even sure of the united support of the Catholics, and the greater part of the Anglican Church, at all levels, was alienated from him. The London pulpits rang with exhortations to stand fast against the persecution soon to come. As for the Dissenters, the King's attitude to them, and they to him, was mixed. James still found it difficult not to regard them as infidels and republicans. On their side, they were naturally suspicious of overtures from a Catholic monarch who had so spectacularly quarrelled with the Anglicans, his cossetted favourites only two years before. In any case, the Dissenters had dwindled in numbers since 1660, and they had turned their backs on the political activism of their Puritan fathers and grandfathers. The new Edict of Toleration received its warmest welcome from working-class sects like the Baptists, who were politically weak and regarded with general aversion. The middle-class Dissenters, who did enjoy political influence and considerable wealth, tended to hold aloof. Moreover, the Anglicans at once realized the necessity of making a counter-bid, which they did in a barrage of pamphlets, of which Halifax's *Letter to a Dissenter* is only the most notable. The upshot was that the least the Dissenters could now expect from the Church was freedom of worship, and there was a chance of 'comprehension' – a relaxation of forms which would permit the reabsorption of the right-wing, upper-class Presbyterians. Many lay Dissenters and former Whigs joined James in the winter of 1687–8, particularly as election agents, but most of them were political adventurers, and even if they could secure a majority in the next parliament, and this was a big 'if', they were likely to drive as hard a bargain as their Angli- can predecessors.

Notwithstanding all this, in October 1687 James launched an unprecedentedly thorough campaign for elections which were at first announced for January 1688, then postponed into the spring. Lord Lieutenants were required to put their deputy lieutenants, the county justices and other prominent gentry to an inquisition as to their voting intentions, and those whose answers were deemed unsatisfactory were dismissed, as were several Lord Lieutenants. Every effort was made to recruit Catholics and suitable Dissenters as magistrates and sheriffs. In November, a Committee of Regulation in London began revising the membership of parliamentary corporations in the same way, using powers conferred on the King by the new charters issued since 1681 (see p. 221 above: a further twenty-one *quo warranto* actions had gone through in 1686). This process was accelerated, perhaps even initiated, by the unexpected news that the Queen was pregnant, publicly announced in December, known at Court in November, and perhaps known to James even earlier.

From the first the news was greeted with some scepticism; after all, Mary Beatrice had not conceived since 1681, and by 1687 even devoted Catholic royalists like Tyrconnell had given up hopes in that direction. The intemperate optimism of the Court Catholics, and their immediate assumption that the child would be a prince, did not help. Conversely, the Protestants ought to have been thrown into a state of despair, but there is no sign of this. In fact, Mary Beatrice's record in childbirth was abysmal, a fact widely attributed to venereal disease contracted by James in the late 1660s; there was a fifty-fifty chance that the child would be a girl, who would rank in the succession after Mary and Anne; and even if it were a boy James was now an old man by seventeenth-century standards; in the winter of 1687-8 he lapsed into a petulant and aggressive senility. He was unlikely to survive long, and unless the Catholics could extend their power base his widow would soon lose control of her son's upbringing. The conversion rate to Catholicism was still slow, and so continued; up to the end James was reliant on Protestants like Jeffreys, Godolphin and Middleton to run the government and even to man embassies in Catholic countries abroad.

Indeed, news of Mary Beatrice's condition had a more immediate impact on William. His first act, in December, was to send back to England his close confidant Henry Sidney, to contact the dissident nobility and watch over his interests. This was the tentative beginning of the 'conspiracy' beloved of Tory historians. At the same time he sent the Scotsman James Johnstone to organize routine 'intelligence' and arrange with the famous publisher Jacob Tonson the dissemination of anti-government propaganda. The first and most important result was the publication in December or early January of the officially inspired *Reflections on Monsr Fagel's Letter* which for the first time made public the Prince and Princess's stand on the Test Act.

This infuriated James at a time when Anglo-Dutch relations were in any case fast deteriorating. In the spring and summer of 1687 several prominent English officers, cashiered for their refusal to support his policy, took service in the famous Anglo-Dutch Brigade, formed in 1678 as part of the Dutch army, and consisting of six seasoned regiments, three Scots, two English, one Irish. Home recruitment to the regiments was now forbidden, and in October 1687 James secured Louis XIV's grudging and hesitant agreement to pay and maintain them if they were recalled. Opposition at Court delayed this decision until January 1688, when the States General's unlooked-for refusal, backed up by William, brought the two countries to the brink of war. Nor did the episode improve relations with France. Louis had bargained on weakening the Dutch army by pulling out the Anglo-Dutch Brigade; in fact, though James managed to recall many of the officers, who held his commission, the troops stayed. He now proposed to form new regiments in England under these officers, and others recalled from the Imperial service. Louis only agreed with the greatest reluctance, and the final stages of the negotiations were disfigured by petty disputes over details – whether the troops be paid from 1 April or 1 May; even whether the date should be New Style, as in France, or Old Style, which was ten days behind. (Why this should be so it is difficult to say; there is no evidence that James was particularly short of money. It may be part of the general deterioration in his character noticeable at this time; but he had always been a man keen on money; before his accession he had always cultivated his considerable investments in overseas trading companies, and his post-office monopoly, most assiduously.) Louis's cup was filled to overflowing when he now requested James's token support in a naval demonstration to arrest an impending brushfire war between Sweden and Denmark, and James refused.

By now it was clear that the Truce of Ratisbon could not hold up another year, or even six months. Any assessment of the English Revolution must take account of the fact that a major war was expected to break out in Europe in 1688. Louis XIV's ambitions on Germany now focused on the Archbishopric of Cologne, and this in turn impinged on his quarrel with the Pope. The Archbishop-Elector was dying, and Louis exerted all his influence to replace him by his obedient agent in the Rhineland, Cardinal William von Furstemberg; at the same time he intended to prosecute his tenuous claim, in abeyance since 1684, to the Palatinate. Time was of the essence, for the Emperor Leopold I was now winding up his long war against the Turk; Budapest fell in 1686, Belgrade in 1688; any year now the Emperor would turn back towards the West with a seasoned army, and secure in the support of (non-French) Catholic Christendom. At the same time war was clearly imminent between England and Holland, though no one could make out whether James intended another commercial and maritime war, or whether William meditated a sudden attack on England to force his uncle to change his policy – though not, it must be stressed, to depose him. But whatever the truth, England was very much a side-show. James would be a reluctant ally of France in the coming war, and it was unlikely now that he could mobilize the country behind him; better that he should fight his own war with William III, and thus neutralize one of Louis's most dangerous enemies. As for Louis, after his experiences in 1672 and 1673 he had no intention of becoming embroiled in another land campaign against the Dutch. All these factors contributed to England's increasing isolation, of which James was only intermittently aware. He still subscribed to the sadly out-of-date idea that the Protestant powers, led by his nephew, were organizing a war of religion against him.

Meanwhile at home, James's electoral campaign was proceeding with frenetic vigour. Contemporaries found it difficult to assess its potential success, and so have historians; unfortunately it was a campaign which never came to fruition. Macaulay dismissed it as a 'complete and hopeless failure', but modern historians are not so sure; J. R. Jones, for instance, sees the effort involved as 'impressive and exceptional', which it certainly was. It was the first attempt to bring the English electoral system under centralized control, and as such it set an example which was ignored until the nineteenth century. It was this more than any threat to religion which united the nobility and gentry against James. Unfortunately, time was denied him. The elections had to be postponed into the spring of 1688, and in March Lord Sunderland, backed by the professional civil servants actually operating the campaign, persuaded him that they must be postponed again. James felt that his honour was involved, and he re-issued the Declaration of Indulgence in April with a new codicil committing himself to meet Parliament in November at the latest – thus binding his ministers' hands as well as his own. In April, professional agents were dispatched from London to secure detailed information on the constituencies: the nature of the franchise, the size of the electorate, the local interests involved – another lead which was not taken up; even great 'electoral' ministers of the next century like Walpole, Pelham, Newcastle and John Robinson relied on information gleaned *ad hoc* from provincial correspondents, and the first comprehensive survey of the boroughs was undertaken privately by Thomas Oldfield as late as 1792.

Some experienced observers, well represented by Halifax and Nottingham in their letters to William, believed that James was doomed to failure. Halifax summed it up in a famous passage: 'To men at a distance the engine seemeth to move fast, but by looking nearer one may see that it doth not stir upon the whole matter, so that there is a rapid motion without advancing a step, which is the only miracle that church hath yet shown us.' To others, however, it seemed that James could secure a parliament which would increase his income, and if he were once willing to purge the army thoroughly (which he had not yet done), success would tip the balance of the see-saw, and many men who were now uncommitted or even mildly hostile would slide down to his end. This was the message conveyed by Edward Russell, when he went secretly to see William in May on behalf of a number of opposition notables. William replied that if he were to come over with an army he must receive a written invitation from a quorum of leading men, and even then he must await the death of the Great Elector, which would take Brandenburg out of the French camp – a timely reminder that the English Revolution hinged on continental diplomacy. (The Elector duly died early in June.)

The Invitation requested by William was dispatched on 30 June, signed by Russell himself, the Earls of Danby, Devonshire and Shrewsbury, Viscount Lumley, Henry Compton and Henry Sidney. With the possible exception of Danby, none of these were men of pre-eminent political importance, and Halifax and Nottingham, who were, refused to sign. But the birth of a Prince of Wales, James Francis Edward, on 10 June left William with little choice but to move now or relinquish his interest in England.

The gloomy prophecies of the Invitation – that, left alone, James would have consolidated his régime to such an extent that by the spring of 1689 he would be immovable – were confirmed by William's own intelligence agents in England. The one ray of hope was that Mary Beatrice's confinement had been as mysterious as her whole pregnancy; it was a month earlier than forecast, with the Princess Anne out of London and no other trustworthy or unbiased witnesses present. Before the end of the month rumours were spreading that it was all a fraud; that the Queen had never been pregnant, or that she had miscarried of a dead child, and the new prince was a by-blow smuggled into the palace somehow (the famous warming-pan came later). The authors of the Invitation took all this perfectly seriously, and so, after some hesitation, did William; indeed, this was now his only real excuse for intervening. The Revolution was to hinge on this unfortunate ambiguity, which no one today takes seriously at all.

By this time James's position had deteriorated. In May he had ordered the Anglican clergy to read his reissued Declaration of Indulgence from the pulpit, a procedure for which there was some precedent in 1629 and 1681, when the clergy had read out long statements published by Charles I and Charles II explaining their sudden dissolutions of Parliament. But the Archbishop of Canterbury and six of his bishops now drew up a petition protesting against the order on the grounds that the suspension of legislation by the Crown had been declared unconstitutional by Parliament, in 1673, and partly, no doubt, as a result the greater part of the clergy refused to comply. Understandably infuriated, James then had the 'Seven Bishops' arraigned on a charge of seditious libel. The issue was not in doubt, though the King's more responsible advisers tried to restrain him from a confrontation which could bring him no advantage whatever the result. After lengthy delays, which allowed public opinion to rally markedly in the bishops' favour, they came before King's Bench on 29 June. But Lord Chief Justice Wright handled the case flabbily, allowing the defence to turn it into a debate on the legality of the suspending power, and two of the puisne judges, Holloway and Powell, summed up against the King. Next day the jury returned a verdict of not guilty.

In retrospect, it is clear that this began the slide which ended in James's deposition. The legality of his main policy, to which he was committed, had been challenged and found wanting. He had obviously lost control of the high court, if he had ever secured it. For though much is made of James's frequent purges of the high court bench, these continued because the purges were never fully effective. For instance, Sir Edward Herbert, who had stage-managed the case of *Godden* v. *Hales* in 1686, had to be demoted to common pleas in 1687, and Wright, Holloway and Powell had been appointed by James in place of less amenable men. Even Lord Chancellor Jeffreys was far from impeccable; James had been seeking a replacement for him for two years. Meanwhile the clergy had also defied the King to his face, and seemed likely to get away with it, for though James's first thought was to invoke the Commission for Ecclesiastical Causes, even he thought better of it. Finally, the trial marked an important stage in the emergence of a new *détente* between the Church and Dissent. In their petition, itself drawn up in consultation with Dissenting spokesmen, the bishops had pledged themselves to toleration, and soon after his acquittal Sancroft set up a joint committee to frame specific proposals for the next parliament; in other words, the Church was now running openly against the Crown in the toleration stakes. James continued with his plans for Parliament, and the writs were issued early in September, but he was now forced to make an important concession, to request the repeal of the Penal Laws, leaving the Test on one side and thus bringing himself into line with William. Unfortunately the Test operated against Dissenters as well as Catholics, and in any case he delayed an announcement on the matter until after the news of William's coming had broken, so that together with all his other concessions at that time it was dismissed as patently insincere.

Rumours of William's intentions were circulating as early as June (in fact, before he had made up his mind), but James should not be criticized too harshly for disbelieving them. All Europe was now mobilizing for war, England and Holland included, and the specialized transport ships which would have given the game away were kept dispersed until the last moment. Quite reasonably, James did not believe that either the Princess Mary or William's Catholic allies would permit an invasion for dynastic or religious reasons; nor did he believe that the Dutch would allow the Stadholder to commit part of their army to England at a time when a general European war was imminent. In fact, William's political ascendancy in the Netherlands was now almost complete, and for England he had recruited a new mercenary army, chiefly from Denmark and Germany, with the Anglo-Dutch Brigade, of course; he had also borrowed from Brandenburg a highly experienced mercenary general, the Duke of Schomberg. The fleet was to be commanded by Arthur Herbert, dismissed by James in 1687.

But Herbert's appointment, superseding the Dutchman Evertsen at the head of what was essentially a Dutch fleet, emphasized the danger of a clash between the navies of two powers habituated to antagonism and with many old scores to settle. This apart, there was the sheer hazard of transporting an army of 12,000 men, with transport and equipment, across the Channel in the teeth of the autumn gales; it called for a fleet of 225 transports, escorted by 50 warships (much larger than the Armada of 1588), which was in fact dispersed by a gale on its first emergence in late October. William is rarely given credit for the brilliant logistical organization of the first successful invasion of England since 1066.

Louis XIV, having better sources of information, was convinced of William's intentions in the first week of September, James about a fortnight later (18 September seems to have marked the turning-point). But the armed forces had been on a war footing since June, all leave had been cancelled in August, and there seemed little else James could do. Louis XIV's decision not to interfere is crucial in retrospect, but at the time it was perfectly justifiable, and James seemed to expect no more. In July Louis had lost the second round of a desperate struggle to seat Furstemberg as Archbishop-Elector of Cologne, and unless he made a military intervention in west Germany, his whole diplomatic position there was in danger of collapse. The imminence of war with Spain, and his continuing quarrel with Innocent XI, had caused him to transfer most of the French Atlantic fleet to the Mediterranean; he could only launch an overland attack on the Netherlands, which was not in itself attractive and would involve surrendering his claims in Germany. It did not seem that James's position was so dangerous as to warrant such a sacrifice – if, indeed, it was dangerous at all. James expressed himself entirely satisfied with his army and navy, which were certainly large enough to deal with William; he had declined offers of French naval assistance in June and again in August, and had publicly rejected Louis's attempts to bring diplomatic pressure to bear on the Dutch government early in September, making it clear that he had no wish to appear as an ally of France. And even if he could not throw William back into the sea, he could surely hold him, and civil war in England, plus a war between England and Holland, could only redound to Louis's advantage. On 14 September he committed his armies to an all-out attack across the Rhine, aimed at the Palatinate.

James's reaction suggests that his confidence in his armed forces was not all that great. Certainly there were rumours of disaffection in the army as well as the navy, and, in any case, James now betrayed a marked deterioration in character, which intensified as the crisis mounted. Beginning on 21 September, he embarked on a policy of concession which was so precipitate as to be wholly implausible. He announced that elections to Parliament were to be free of government interference, and that his proposals for toleration were limited to the repeal of the penal laws; county officials and magistrates dismissed over the past two years were reinstated by a stroke of the pen; the Lord Lieutenants were ordered to restore the corporations to their former state; Magdalen College was turned over to its (Anglican) Visitor, and it was announced that the City of London charter would be restored as soon as possible. A new Anglican ministry began to take shape round Dartmouth and Middleton, and James sent for Rochester to head it; he lifted Bishop Compton's suspension, dissolved the Commission for Ecclesiastical Causes, and opened discussions with Sancroft and some of the bishops on further concessions.

Unfortunately, on 25 September, he also withdrew the writs for Parliament, and the proclamation of the 28th announcing the impending invasion made his motives embarrassingly clear. The bishops rejected his overtures, and so did Rochester – the bishops even refused to issue a statement deploring William's conduct – with the result that James now swung the other way. He gave private assurances to the Roman Catholics, the policy of concession was halted, though not reversed, and he refused to withdraw his Declaration of Indulgence or reissue the writs for Parliament. Sunderland, dismissed on 27 October, was made a convenient scapegoat for the events of the past month, and much else.

William finally sailed on 30 October, with the assistance of a 'Protestant wind', blowing due west. There is some evidence that he originally intended to sail up the east coast and land in Yorkshire, where Danby was preparing to raise the county while Lord Devonshire took care of the Midlands. But instead William took advantage of the prevailing wind to pass the Straits of Dover on 1 November, leaving the English fleet stranded in the Thames mouth. He landed at Torbay in Devon on 5 November (an auspicious anniversary), quickly disembarked his army, and took Exeter. There he remained for a fortnight, consolidating his base and circulating copies of his official declaration, dated 1 October, calling simply for the election of a free parliament and a public inquiry into the birth of the Prince of Wales.

Whether by accident or design, the Prince's landing-place was well chosen. He could ignore for the moment the efforts of powerful noblemen like Danby and Devonshire, who might have been in a position to bring pressure to bear on him. In fact, their risings in the North and Midlands were entirely successful, but he took no notice at all until the Princess Anne, an important dynastic pawn, took refuge with Devonshire at Nottingham on 26 November;

he then peremptorily ordered her to join him at Oxford on his march east. Meanwhile he left James two alternatives, neither of them attractive: he could advance into the west, leaving London unguarded in his rear, or he could dig in round London, surrendering the initiative to William and condemning his army to a period of waiting calculated to sap their morale. He compromised by ordering the army to rendezvous at Salisbury, roughly halfway. Lord Cornbury, son of the Earl of Clarendon, at once defected to William with his regiment.

Cornbury's defection naturally unsettled James. He could trust no one. He reached Salisbury on 19 November, and stayed till the 25th. On the news that William had left Exeter on the 21st on his long march east he convened a council of war, and he accepted the advice of Feversham, the army commander, for a policy of inaction while he returned to London and tried to rally political support. But that night Lord Churchill, another personal friend and protégé, fled west to William, with the colonels of the Tangier regiments, Kirke and Trelawney, and the Duke of Grafton, a guards colonel and an illegitimate son of Charles II. On his way back to London he was deserted by his son-in-law George of Denmark, by the young Duke of Ormonde, spokesman for the Anglo-Irish nobility, and by Lord Drumlanrig, son of the greatest lord in Scotland, the Duke of Queensberry. When he reached London he found that his daughter the Princess Anne had also fled.

His military situation was now desperate. The rank-and-file of the army stood firm, and would probably still have fought with brute courage and blind obedience, given leadership; but only the Catholic officers could now be relied on, and they, contrary to popular belief, only constituted about 10 per cent of the officer corps, and they were scattered through the regiments. The Duke of Beaufort and the Earls of Bath and Bristol, regarded as firm loyalists, had virtually surrendered the West of England, and news was coming in that Danby and Lumley had secured the North-East of England from Hull to Newcastle, while the Earl of Derby was in control of Lancashire. The Earl of Devonshire and Lord Delamere between them had secured Derbyshire, Cheshire and Nottinghamshire. James even considered joining Danby, and there was some plausibility in the idea; in London he was now thrown back on the advice of Halifax, his most persistent critic among the English grandees. It was on Halifax's advice that he now decided to negotiate, and Halifax led the royal commissioners who met the Prince at Hungerford on 8 December.

James's position was still strong, probably stronger now that the idea of a military campaign had virtually been abandoned. William was in the position of aggressor, and James was free to renounce any settlement at a later date on the grounds that it had been imposed on him by force. Some of the English exiles he had brought with him pressed William to declare himself king, but this was never practical politics; he had denied any such intention in his Declaration, which had secured him the allegiance of many moderates and conservatives. At Hungerford he proposed that the elections for Parliament should go forward, and during its sitting the two armies remain forty miles from London: if the King remained in London, the Prince would join him there, with his personal guard; if not, they should both observe the forty-mile limit. Under these conditions it is almost unthinkable that James should have been superseded; it proved difficult enough even after he had fled the country in the most inauspicious circumstances. It is equally unthinkable that Parliament would have declared his son spurious; it shrank from this even in 1702. Statutory limitations could have been put on his authority, but only William and his army could have enforced them, and they could not remain in England indefinitely.

But the very strength of his position unmanned James, for his death was the obvious solution. More than once during these last weeks he reminded the French ambassador and the papal nuncio of the fate of Edward II, Henry VI and Richard II, who had been murdered by close relatives. Nor was this the product of a disordered mind. William had given specific assurances to his wife that her father's person should remain inviolate, but there were plenty of bravos in his entourage who would not have scrupled to anticipate what they took to be his secret wishes. There was already a similar, very well-known incident on William's record; the murder of the brothers de Witt in 1672. James also feared that his enemies would seize his son and bring him up a Protestant, a prospect arguably more alarming than his own death. He had sent the child to Portsmouth in November, and he now ordered Dartmouth to take him to France. Dartmouth's refusal intensified his fears; he brought the prince back to London, and found a playboy French nobleman, the comte de Lauzun, who was willing to escort the Queen and her son to France. They left on 10 December. He gave them a twenty-four-hour start and left in secret the following night. He burnt the writs for Parliament, ordered Feversham to abandon all resistance, and pitched the Great Seal into the river as he crossed over to Kent, bound for Sheerness and exile.

What followed was anti-climax. William began a forced march on London, which was a prey to rioting and general hysteria, while an *ad hoc* committee of peers struggled to restore order. They learned with mixed feelings that James had been seized by some fishermen at Faversham in mistake for a priest. He returned on the 16th, obviously very badly affected by his experiences in Kent, and almost certainly suffering from a nervous breakdown. William, who had reached Windsor, cancelled the Hungerford agreement and ordered James to leave London while his army restored order. When James requested permission to retire to Rochester it could only be with one purpose.

William's position was still baffling and precarious. As soon as he reached London he summoned all the available peers and bishops to the Guildhall and asked their advice on how to summon a 'free' parliament in pursuance of the undertaking in his Declaration. Significantly they hesitated, but on 23 December, with the news that James had 'escaped' the previous night and got clean away to France, he called another meeting, this time of all the surviving members of Charles II's parliaments then in London. Lords and Commons now agreed that the Prince should send out letters to the returning officers under his personal seal, for a parliament, or 'convention', to assemble on 22 January. In the meanwhile he was asked to assume responsibility for public order and the civil administration.

# X

# THE REVOLUTION SETTLEMENT,
## 1689–90

At the close of 1688 England's situation was unparalleled – at least for a nation which asserted, and continued to assert, that it was not in rebellion. It was a knotty constitutional problem, which the Convention could only solve by some notable 'double-think'.

From the beginning James's case went by default; there was no question of a contest, as it were, between him and William or Mary. It was generally agreed that the King had forfeited his right to rule, and even his most stalwart defenders, like the Earl of Clarendon, acknowledged it. After all, in December a representative cross-section of Lords and Commons, including many of James's adherents, had unanimously thanked William for his Declaration, which was as devastating a critique of James's policy as could be imagined, and requested him to summon a Convention 'for the preservation of our religion, rights, laws, liberty and property', and 'the establishment of these things upon such sure and legal foundations, that they may not be in danger of being again subverted'. There was no question of recalling James, except under the strictest supervision, and not one speaker in the Convention is on record as suggesting it.

At the other extreme there was a substantial minority in favour of outright deposition. There were plenty of precedents for this in the Middle Ages, and an obvious comparison to be made between William III and Henry of Bolingbroke. As for the Prince of Wales, now he was in France he had ceased to be a viable political entity; it would be necessary to bargain with his father and King Louis for his return, and not even the most conservative royalists were ready for this. In the end, though William's Declaration had said that a full public inquiry into the Prince of Wales's birth would be one of the main items of business in the next parliament, the child was scarcely mentioned in the Convention debates, and passed over altogether in its resolutions and declarations.

Nevertheless, though the Commons might have mustered a majority for James's deposition – the issue was never put to them squarely, so it is difficult to say – the Lords would certainly never permit it, nor would a majority of the clergy approve it. Medieval precedents were cancelled out by the one great seventeenth-century precedent, the trial and execution of King Charles I, and the Church, including its lay spokesmen, had committed themselves too deeply, in honour, conscience and general psychological make-up, to extreme concepts of Divine Right and Hereditary Succession largely framed to prevent a relapse into the anarchy of the Interregnum. Nor were fears of such a relapse entirely unreal in 1689. Even before the Convention met some were suggesting that this was no ordinary parliament, charged with making minor adjustments to the existing system, but a constituent convention, with a special mandate from the people to alter the very basis of the constitution, making it a republic if needs be. (This was even implied in John Locke's *Treatises of Government* published later that year and usually regarded as an essentially conservative, bourgeois interpretation of the Revolution.) The republicans, though small in numbers, were active and vocal, and the sudden return of Edmund Ludlow, the last surviving regicide, from exile in Switzerland caused a flutter in Parliament. A speedy settlement was obviously essential, and only a compromise settlement could be passed quickly and without divisive argument.

Finally, there was William himself, whose precise position is often misunderstood. He had behaved with the greatest circumspection and self-control, but no one but the irredeemably naïve supposed that he did not have the crown in mind. It had always been a possibility, if his venture to England succeeded at all, and from the moment James fled it was a distinct probability. He continued to represent himself as commanding a police operation initiated by the English themselves, but he had a sizeable group of committed followers, including influential peers like Shrewsbury and Devonshire, who regarded him as virtually king already, and pressed him to declare himself as such, and he had already taken certain irrevocable initiatives.

For instance, his first act on assuming control of the administration in December was to order the French ambassador to leave the country forthwith; a notable act of provocation, since the two countries were not at war, and it could only be construed either as a riposte to Louis XIV's benevolent reception of James at Versailles – which in turn assumed that James was some kind of national enemy – or simply as an attempt to force the pace. In fact, war with France was not declared until May; and if James had not meanwhile landed in Ireland in March, with slight French support, and provoked a nationalist revolt, it would have been difficult to fabricate a *casus belli*. But in January, whether there was war or not, William's services as a military commander were already indispensable. Nor was his civil administration entirely passive, he was much more than a caretaker; for instance, he had lodged the Lord Chancellor (Jeffreys) in the Tower, and he had dismissed all James's high court judges *en bloc*, replacing them by others. He did not claim to be acting on James's behalf, and lawyers acknowledged that the King's legal authority had lapsed from the moment he left the country.

This is why, when the House of Commons debated the state of the nation on 28 January, they reached a conclusion in about three hours. There is much we do not know or understand about the composition of the Convention, but it is certainly anachronistic to apply to its members at this stage the party names of Whig and Tory, which had lost their meaning with the elimination of the Exclusionist leaders between 1681 and 1685 and the fall of the Restoration monarchy in the person of James II. Certainly there was a vociferous and experienced minority of 'Old Whigs' left over from Charles II's last parliament (John Trenchard, Hugh Boscawen, Francis Winnington and a few others), whose vigour and loquacity later propelled the Convention into the strangest follies; but they lacked leaders in the Lords, where, with the exception perhaps of Delamere, the Whig peers were now firmly established and conservative. Also, the voting record clearly reveals a conservative majority in the Commons, even if it lacked speakers and spokesmen. So, although there was much airy talk of the original contract between king and people, which James had, of course, broken, thus forfeiting the crown, it led nowhere. Strangely enough, the idea of a regency met with little support either. The solution found – a bizarre pretence that, by leaving the country as he did, James had by implication abdicated – was eventually put forward by the Whig jurist Sir George Treby, and supported by others of that ilk, like John Somers and Sir John

Holt. The resultant Resolution, though it ended with a firm declaration that James had 'abdicated the government, and that the throne is thereby become vacant', left the reasons for this clouded by ambiguous syntax and open to a number of conflicting interpretations. Thus it passed unanimously.

The virtues of unanimity and obfuscation soon became apparent. The Lords met on the 29th, and first debated the establishment of a regency, on the assumption that James was as incapable of ruling as if he had been a lunatic or a child. The proposal was strongly supported, and the debate was long and bitter; and but for the absence of key figures like Archbishop Sancroft and Lord Godolphin, and an unexpected switch by Halifax (who was acting as Speaker in the absence of a Lord Chancellor) it would have been carried. As it was, it failed by two votes (51 to 49). Next day, the 30th, they took the Commons' Resolution into consideration, and after another tense debate substituted the word 'deserted' for 'abdicated', and struck out the last clause, on the grounds that to suppose that the throne could be vacant implied that the crown was elective.

There followed a considerable struggle. The Commons rejected these amendments *nem. con.*, and after a formal conference between the two Houses on 4 February, the Lords reaffirmed them. The Commons again reversed them, though this time the second amendment, on the 'vacancy', went to a vote, of 282 to 151, our first chance to assess 'party' strength. But the majority in the Lords had now fallen to single figures, and there was strong pressure behind the scenes. The Princess Mary, who by this time had arrived from Holland, at once rejected Danby's suggestion that she be made Queen regnant, with William prince consort – a notable gaffe on Danby's part. William let it be known equally firmly that he would accept nothing less than the kingship for life. There was even talk of popular demonstrations against the Lords. After an informal conference with the Commons on the 6th, the Lords gave way; their only condition was that the crown pass to William and Mary jointly, with both enjoying full regal power. On the 8th the Commons agreed; the offer was made to William and Mary on the 13th, and on the 14th they were proclaimed.

It was a compromise of which no one was particularly proud. It was an interlocking framework of ambiguities and inconsistencies. The Lords had logic on their side when they argued that abdication called for a formal act of renunciation, and they could point to the recent example of Queen Christina of Sweden in 1654; the Commons rejected the word 'deserted' because it had no legal weight, but they were to find that the legal authority of the word 'abdicated' was impossible to substantiate in this case. As for the succession, the Commons had been driven to admit, in their second conference with the Lords, that they were making the crown elective, but only for this 'turn'. In this case, the sensible thing was to make William king and Mary queen consort. Conversely, if Mary were to be queen regnant, this could only be on the hereditary principle, which then excluded William; and William's elevation prejudiced the Princess Anne's rights of succession, which Mary's elevation was supposed to strengthen. The Prince of Wales had been ignored, though the propriety of doing so was doubtful in the extreme; as Sancroft pointed out, the child had been prayed for as Prince of Wales and rightful heir to the throne by the clergy of the established Church ever since his birth. If this was wrong, then the fact should be established, if it was right, then James's 'abdication' must be broadened to embrace his son. And so on. To the left wing it seemed that Parliament had not gone far enough, to the right wing it seemed that it had gone too far, and even the middle group were far from satisfied. Halifax saw 'no great hopes of lasting peace from this settlement', and though Danby acknowledged the new king and queen, yet, he said, 'no man could affirm they were rightfully so by the constitution'.

With the crown was presented a Declaration of Rights, hastily drawn up by the Commons in the first week of February, and approved by the Lords with some amendments. It opened with a statement of the nation's 'case' against James II, went on to declare most of his actions illegal or unconstitutional, and made certain provisos for the future. Assumptions to the contrary notwithstanding, then and since, William did not accept any of this as a condition of his receiving the crown, but his speech in reply suggests that he did acknowledge it as a programme of reform, to be carried out by individual statutes. His later attitude suggests also that he expected this to be done with all convenient speed. So, after some debate, the Convention now decided to declare itself a proper and legal parliament, confer a kind of incestuous validation on all its previous actions, and extend its own existence indefinitely, ignoring the precedent of the Convention of 1660, and the example of the Scots Estates of 1689, which, after offering William and Mary the crown, with their own 'Claim of Right', dissolved themselves in May 1689. Unfortunately, apart from a few essential *ad hoc* measures, like the introduction of a new oath of allegiance, the Convention Parliament was unable to agree on any specific reform statutes, and the new king, essentially conservative and authoritarian in temper, gave them no assistance. All they proved able to do was to pass the Declaration of

Rights into law, in August 1689, as a 'Bill of Rights'; but it is doubtful if this had been their original intention, for it was a singularly defective document.

Some practical questions it did settle. Anne's succession was postponed until after the death of both William and Mary, though in view of the King's state of health, compared with his wife's, this seemed an academic matter. No provision was made for the succession after Anne, partly because of a violent squabble between the two Houses – one of many – and partly because she gave birth to a healthy son, William Duke of Gloucester, in July. All this signalled the demise of hereditary succession, and divine right was further undermined by the application of the Test Act to the monarch, who now had to make the standard declaration against Roman Catholicism, though in deference to William he was not required to furnish proof that he was a communicant Anglican. The proviso that the monarch should not marry a Catholic was a further invasion of his private life – and a considerable restriction on his diplomatic activity in eighteenth-century Europe. At the same time, a new coronation oath obliged William and his successors 'to govern the people of this kingdom according to the statutes in parliament agreed on and the laws and customs of the same', whereas his predecessors had sworn only to 'confirm to the people of England the laws and customs to them granted . . ., agreeable to the prerogative of the kings thereof, and the ancient customs of the realm'. The superiority of Parliament over the crown was later confirmed, almost unnoticed, by the Demise of the Crown Act of 1696, passed in the wake of the Assassination Plot, which decreed that Parliament should for the first time continue after the King's death, for up to six months. The Regency Act of 1706 extended this principle to privy councillors and all other officers of the crown, civil and military (except, strangely enough, the high court judges, who had to wait until 1760). Implicit here is the concept of government existing independently of the King, who is just another official, though the most important one.

As for the Bill's negative provisos, in the light of James II's experience it was unlikely, to say the least, that any future king would attempt to suspend legislation, dispense individuals in large numbers from the requirements of penal statutes, set up ecclesiastical commissions, and so on – and so it proved. The only serious issue was the army, and the requirement that a standing army should not be maintained in peacetime without consent of Parliament was reinforced by a Mutiny Act, renewable annually, which granted the King the right to try offences against military law by courts martial. The importance of this Act has been much exaggerated; it did not apply to the discipline of troops in the field, and Charles II and James II managed without it with only occasional difficulty – as did William III from 1698 to 1701, when Parliament omitted to renew the Act. On the larger issue, two decades of almost continuous war up to 1713 established a pattern which proved difficult to break, and despite occasional protests, as in 1718, eighteenth-century parliaments automatically endorsed the upkeep of a large army in peacetime. (The navy, it is worth noticing, was regarded as constitutionally inert compared with the army; as long ago as 1661 the Naval Discipline Act had granted the Lord High Admiral powers of court martial in perpetuity.)

Otherwise the Revolution Settlement is chiefly remarkable for what it did *not* settle. For instance, ever since Charles I's reign there had been intermittent pressure to restrict the King's right to summon or dismiss Parliament as he pleased. No one wanted frequent general elections, and the Triennial Act of 1641, amended in 1664, merely required the King to meet Parliament regularly – any parliament. Charles II's precipitate dissolutions in 1679 and 1681 were much more unpopular than his retention of his first parliament, which he met at fairly frequent intervals, for eighteen years. The Triennial Act was only doubtfully effective; Charles II (1681–4) and James II (1685–8) had both shown what a determined autocrat could accomplish in three years while remaining within the law; yet the Bill of Rights merely observed that parliaments 'ought to be held frequently', which might mean almost anything, and though the Convention had plans for a further Bill, nothing emerged until the next parliament, in 1692, by which time the parameters of conflict had changed.

Even stranger was the failure to deal with parliamentary elections, for James's aggressive and abrasive electioneering had done more to alienate the upper classes than anything. All the Bill of Rights did was to lay down that elections 'ought to be free' (free of government pressure, that is), without suggesting any method by which this might be accomplished. With the failure of the Corporation Bill early in 1690, William retained all the powers of interference in corporations which his predecessor had so notoriously abused, and his right to appoint and dismiss at will Lord Lieutenants, deputy lieutenants, sheriffs and magistrates. Similarly, though the Convention Parliament devoted an inordinate amount of time to an investigation of James II's alterations to the high-court bench and the pressure he had put on individual judges, they entirely neglected to make any statutory provision to prevent this for the future. William voluntarily reverted to Clarendon's practice (1660–67) of issuing patents to judges *quamdiu se bene gesserint* ('during good behaviour'), which gave them some slight technical protection against arbitrary dismissal, but he vetoed the Judges' Bill of 1692 designed to give them absolute security of tenure; Parliament had to slip this into the Act of Settlement in 1701.

The failure to curb the King's sweeping powers of appointment to office, in Church and State, in local and central government, in the judiciary and the armed forces, was decisive for the maintenance of royal power and influence down the eighteenth century. But here the architects of the Revolution Settlement were merely following the precedent set by their fathers in 1661; the Long Parliament's claim to veto or control Charles I's appointment of ministers had produced its own reaction. Similarly with elections. The illogicality of the franchise in most boroughs, the inequity of the distribution of seats as between various regions and between large towns and small, was generally recognized; this was not something that emerged with the Industrial Revolution. But the proposals of the Levellers and the experiments of Oliver Cromwell had left an indelible taint on electoral reform; it was something now associated with republicanism or lower-class radicalism. And this despite the fact that James II had left the situation more chaotic than he found it. His panic orders of October 1688 revived borough charters confiscated between 1679 and 1686 without cancelling the others, with the result that many boroughs were left with two charters and some with three, each with its claque of supporters, and each, in most cases, permitting the use of a different franchise. This exacerbated local feuds and encouraged the spread of national parties to the constituencies; it also encouraged double returns and disputed elections. Again, the Corporation Bill of 1689–90 would have rectified this situation, but it was delayed by partisan disputes at Westminster and lost with the dissolution of the Convention Parliament.

As for the Church of England, Archbishop Sancroft for the clergy and the Earl of Nottingham for the laity proposed sweeping changes. That they were not put through was not entirely Parliament's fault, for once. Freedom of worship for all Protestants was a *sine qua non* – after all, it had been guaranteed by the Seven Bishops themselves – but Nottingham's sights were set on a more constructive scheme, of comprehension. By judicious concessions on points of liturgy, doctrine and church government he hoped to bring back into the Church the more respectable, wealthy and upper-class Dissenters, mainly Presbyterian, leaving minimum toleration as a sop to the more extreme working-class Dissenters. But the plan misfired. Sancroft declined to recognize the new régime, and with him some of the more liberal bishops; at the same time Nottingham was let down by William, who alienated the Commons by suddenly proposing, apparently on his own initiative, to repeal the sacramental clause in the Test Act, which excluded Dissenters from office. Parliament rejected this with indignation, passed the Toleration Bill, but referred the Comprehension Bill to Convocation later in the year, when it was predictably talked out. So the division between Protestants created in 1662 was confirmed.

The Church was not the most pressing of William's concerns, but by the end of the year he had plenty of other reasons to be disillusioned with the Convention. For instance, it had persistently declined to bring in the comprehensive Act of Oblivion requested by William in one of his first speeches from the throne; his desire for such a measure, in imitation of the statesmanlike Act of 1660, may well have been one of his principal reasons for keeping Parliament on at all. Instead, the Commons embarked on a rancorous but unbusinesslike investigation, lasting most of the year, into the misdeeds of James II's and Charles II's ministers, preparatory to drawing up a Bill with so many listed exceptions that it must prove a source of division, not union. This was also made the excuse for a series of attacks on Halifax, now one of William's closest advisers, for his role during the Exclusion Crisis. Parliament also caused William the greatest irritation by its running criticism of the conduct of the war in Ireland, where James II had overrun most of the country and Londonderry was under close siege, despite the dispatch of a large army under Schomberg.

But Parliament's greatest sin in his eyes was its failure to settle the revenue. Here, of course, it was in a genuine dilemma. In view of all that had happened, it was unwilling to vote William a revenue for life, but how could it refuse 'Our Great Deliverer' what it had so cheerfully granted to the popish James? It pleaded the necessity for a general overhaul of the tax system (as its predecessors had done in 1625), and in the meanwhile voted him James II's revenue on a three-monthly basis (though, again, this was unpleasantly reminiscent of the Long Parliament's treatment of Charles I in 1641). As in 1660, the King was poorly served by the Treasury, which was in fact manned by a group of inexperienced and rancorous ex-Exclusionists headed by Delamere, with Godolphin doing all the hard work; but up to a point there was much to be said for a waiting game. James II's revenue was about £1,900,000 a year, but the Commons planned eventually to reduce this; also by neglecting, as they did from time to time, to renew their authorization for periods of weeks or even months they were themselves eroding the principle, reaffirmed in the Bill of Rights, that no taxes be levied without their consent. Eventually, in November 1689, they decided to continue James's revenue, and add to it £2 million a year for the conduct of the war, the latter sum being so manifestly inadequate that William would be obliged to return each year for supplementation; even then, when the Finance Bill emerged in December it, too, was limited to a year. To add insult to injury, a strong faction in the Commons then took the unprecedented step of trying to secure a separate financial provision for Anne, which led to a bitter quarrel between her and her sister.

This coincided with the fracas over the Corporation Bill, when the old Whigs, led by William Sacheverell, showed their irresponsibility by tacking on a clause excluding from local government all those associated with the surrender of previous charters. At the same time the Commons brought in a Bill of pains and penalties, to ensure the punishment of those excluded from a very grudging Act of Oblivion, and added to their sins by criticizing William's decision to go in person to Ireland, which he regarded as a considerable sacrifice on his part, deserving of thanks. He abruptly prorogued Parliament on 27 January 1690 and dissolved it on 6 February, summoning another for March.

# XI

# WAR AND POLITICS, 1690-97

Though the Revolution had been put through with such assurance and speed it left an aftermath of doubt. Contrary to all expectations, an overwhelming majority of the clergy, let alone the laity, was willing to take the oath of allegiance to William and Mary, which was carefully pruned of any mention of right or title. But the refusal of Sancroft and six of his most respected bishops created a schism which had important symbolic implications. Were these men not the keepers of the Church's true conscience? Could she as easily as all that throw off her sworn allegiance to James? William's sympathy for the Dissenters was obvious enough, and it was unfortunate that his first episcopal appointment, to Salisbury in May 1689, was the historian Gilbert Burnet, a Scot with distinct Whig leanings. (Thereafter, under the guidance of Queen Mary and the Earl of Nottingham, his patronage was more wisely and moderately administered.)

Where the clergy led the laity were sure to follow, and no Members of Parliament refused the oaths, only four peers and a handful of ministers and officials, the only ones of any significance being the Earl of Clarendon and Samuel Pepys. The Whig peers waxed neurotic at the deficiencies in William's title; in 1690 they tried without success to amend the oath of allegiance so as to describe him as 'rightful and lawful' king. Somers put through an oath of association containing these magic words in 1696, in the wake of the Assassination Plot, only to have at least twenty peers and more than a hundred members refuse it. But it is possible to exaggerate the importance of this problem, at least up to 1700. The Church's problems were *sui generis*; indeed, as the Whigs exultantly pointed out, self-inflicted; and it was probably to William's advantage that she remained divided for this decade. The 'Oaths Controversy' was very much the preoccupation of a few specialized pamphleteers on both sides. *De facto* allegiance to the ruler in power proved sufficient, especially since the King *de jure* had always been committed to a religion regarded as loathsome and dangerous, and was now a client of the national enemy. The Jacobites were never strong enough to raise a serious rebellion, less so now than in 1715, when they could call on Scottish support, and their so-called leaders – like Ailesbury, Clarendon, Preston and Middleton – were distinctly second-rate. The return of King James always hinged on powerful outside intervention, and in this respect the crisis reached a peak in 1690. William's victory at the Boyne on 31 July 1690 scotched the threat from Ireland, and sent James scuttling back to France, but the defeat of an Anglo-Dutch fleet off Beachy Head the day before left the south coast open to invasion. If the advantage was not pressed home it was probably because Louis XIV, deeply embroiled in Germany, continued to regard the war with England as a 'side-show'. The danger was not finally contained until 1692, when Russell destroyed the French Atlantic fleet off Barfleur (or La Hogue).

The crisis of 1689–90 was accentuated by William's choice of ministers. From the beginning he seemed obsessed with the fear of falling under the direction of one man, or group of men; at the same time, he felt it necessary to satisfy all parties, as Charles II had done in 1660 (though

Charles was not fighting a major war). So, Danby was refused the Treasury, which, as we have seen, went to a group of extreme Whigs, plus Godolphin, and he was fobbed off with the Lord Presidency and a marquisate (of Carmarthen). To counterbalance him, Halifax, his chief rival and personal enemy, was made Lord Privy Seal. One Secretaryship of State went to the High Church leader, the Earl of Nottingham, who had only taken the oaths at all with some qualms, and the other to the young Whig revisionist peer, Shrewsbury, who had signed the Invitation and then gone to Holland in August 1688 to join the Prince's expedition. As a result England was without unified leadership for much of 1689 and only William's automatic assumption of full responsibility for war and foreign policy disguised the fact. The excesses of the Convention Parliament were partly due to lack of control.

In 1690 the Whigs were ousted from the Treasury, which was placed under Godolphin, and Halifax and Shrewsbury resigned in mysterious huffs. This left a ministry headed by three men, Carmarthen, Nottingham and Godolphin, who at least had in common a conservative outlook. The elections of 1690 also removed some of the wilder elements in the Convention. However, the new Parliament continued to defeat the efforts of the ministers to guide or control it.

As I have suggested already (p. 56), the idea that Parliament could be 'handled' or 'managed' to a perfection of docility and obedience, provided only the right methods were used, is a historians' myth. A biddable House of Commons was a phenomenon that appeared at most once in a generation, and then under special conditions, as in 1661 or 1685. Yet the parliaments of the 1690s were peculiarly difficult, and the more so because they could not be evaded. Mainly for financial reasons, partly on grounds of constitutional propriety, Parliament henceforward met for at least five months over the winter, sometimes longer. (The economic and social stress this imposed on members is something yet to be assessed; certainly the practice of annual sessions was not something universally welcomed.) And if government organization was deficient, the members themselves were not strictly organized among themselves, either.

Though it is difficult to avoid using the terms 'Whig' and 'Tory' in the 1690s, and they were habitually employed by contemporaries, they were not expressive of any political organization, or even any accepted ideology, less so than in 1680. The aims of pre-Revolution Whiggism had been consummated in the Revolution, and it increasingly developed into an aristocratic, oligarchic movement; radical Whigs certainly existed, but they were a minority and remained so, and Whig peers like Devonshire and Shrewsbury were never anxious to be associated with them. They survived into Anne's reign as the 'Old', or 'Country' Whigs, though some of them, like Robert Harley and Jack Howe, drifted over to the Tories.

For the logic of the Revolution had made the Tories an opposition party, if they were anything: their doctrines of divine right and passive obedience were now discredited, and in any case not easily transferable to William. They were later to find a rallying-cry in defence of the Church, but the nature of the post-Revolution church was not yet apparent. In Sir Edward Seymour, the Earl of Nottingham and the Earl of Rochester, they had able spokesmen in both houses, but they were not party leaders; Rochester was compromised by his past adherence to James II, Nottingham by his present adherence to King William. Whiggism and Toryism retained some ideological weight, in that they expressed differing attitudes towards the Revolution itself; the one welcoming it as desirable and progressive, the other lamenting it as a regrettable necessity; there was thus a foundation on which contrasting parties could be built. But the terms were still for the most part pejorative; a man who cheerfully described his opponents as 'Whigs' would himself deny the appellation 'Tory', and vice versa.

In the 1690s, in fact, the Commons was much as it had been in the 1670s, with a majority of members owning a 'Country' allegiance – the term 'Country' used either in opposition to 'Court' or to 'foreigners', and in the latter case often interchangeable with 'patriot'. The Dutch took the place of the French as false and distrusted allies. It was the 'Country' tradition that all government was by nature corrupt and authoritarian, and it was the duty of Parliament to monitor its operations ceaselessly without besmirching themselves by actually partaking in it. As one member said in 1689, 'If an angel came down from heaven, and 'twas a privy councillor, I would not trust our liberties with him a moment.'

Naturally they approached the question of taxation in no very generous spirit. In 1690 they voted William the additional excise for life, but the customs for only four years, and even then they encumbered his hereditary revenue (including the standing excise on beer, cider, tea and coffee voted to the Crown in perpetuity in 1661) with a loan towards the further cost of the war, now even more unrealistically estimated at £1,200,000 a year. (In fact, a parliamentary committee appointed in 1868 worked out the cost of the war from 1688 to 1697 at £49,320,145, though so exact an estimate was beyond later-seventeenth-century accounting methods.) In 1692, however, they were obliged to reintroduce the land tax, essentially the old 'assessment' of the Interregnum, abandoned at the Restoration, though revived for Charles II's wars. This time it was to be permanent. Another device of Charles II's reign now revived was the Parliamentary Commission. for taking the Public Accounts, which scrutinized war expenditure with grudging care; in fact, the conduct of the war in general, particularly at sea, was investigated each winter with remarkable thoroughness.

Here there was plenty to criticize. In Flanders, William was consistently outmanoeuvred by Louis XIV's marshals, and when he did fight, at Steenkirk in 1692, and Landen in 1693, the result was bloody and indecisive, and the King's decision to put the British regiments under the Dutch general de Solms was bitterly unpopular. (Another Dutch general, Ginkel, took until 1692 to wind up the Irish campaign.) John Churchill, now Earl of Marlborough, was disgraced in 1692 on suspicion of pro-Jacobite intrigue and took no further part in the war, which intensified the quarrel between his patron, the Princess Anne, and the Queen. At sea, Admiral Russell's victory at Barfleur was a welcome relief, but he was accused, with some reason, of not following it up. Nottingham's insistence on directing the sea war intensified the ideological and temperamental differences between him and Russell, and brought on Russell's resignation the following winter. The loss of the wealthy Smyrna convoy in the summer of 1692 was then blamed on Nottingham's new 'Tory' admirals, Killigrew, Delaval and Shovell.

Conscious as we are of William's many weaknesses, his chronic shortage of money, the ineffectuality of his ministers, we cannot appreciate the fear he roused in his new subjects. He was a hard man and a highly successful ruler, a professional soldier strongly suspected of autocratic tendencies. In 1675 he had made a much-discussed attempt on the liberties of Guelderland – an incident still remembered in the 1690s – and since then he had bent the stubborn republicanism of the Netherlands to his will by subtler means. He was a figure of European renown and a millionaire in his own right. He now commanded military forces and supplies of money beyond the dreams of his less able Stuart predecessors and he could plead 'war emergency' for almost any action. He was surrounded by an inner junta of Dutchmen, headed by Hans Willem Bentinck, Earl of Portland, and though they held no 'cabinet' posts – even Portland, his prime favourite, was only Groom of the Stole – they enjoyed a greater degree of confidence than his English ministers and owed allegiance only to him. Nor had they any devotion to liberty; Bentinck, Keppel, Dykveldt, Ginkel, de Solms were of the proud aristocracy of Brabant, tracing their ancestry back to the old Duchy of Burgundy, and divorced entirely from the burgher republicanism of the Dutch cities.

Moreover, there was little in the Revolution Settlement to curb this new-style, militaristic monarchy; Parliament had been too busy burying the old-style, divine-right, paternalistic monarchy of the Stuarts. It was now apparent that though William had to meet Parliament every year, he was under no obligation ever to dissolve it, and with the escalation of the war on all fronts, and its growing complexity, the amount of patronage at the disposal of the government was rapidly increasing: the number of army and navy officers had trebled, government contractors were everywhere, new government commissions and committees, fiscal, administrative and military, were being set up every year, if not every month. At the head of the government stood Carmarthen, who as Danby had managed so unscrupulously the Long Parliament of Charles II, and Godolphin, who had run the Treasury for James II; equally suspect was the Treasury Secretary, Henry Guy, another survivor from the bad old days of prerogative rule. By 1693, the parliament elected in 1690 was known as 'The Officers Parliament' or 'The Pension Parliament', supposedly packed with placemen and dependants of the Crown who moved with regimented precision in response to orders from above.

This picture is almost laughably unreal. Carmarthen had lost his touch almost entirely, and he and Godolphin were usually at odds; such 'management' as went on was entirely haphazard, and placemen voted more or less as they wished. Indeed, the decision in 1692 to appoint the Earl of Rochester to the Privy Council and Sir Edward Seymour to the Treasury Commission – the principal Tory 'wreckers' in both Houses – encouraged the belief that the way to power lay through obstruction not obedience. In any case, old traditions died hard, and not until the next reign did the government dare dismiss an official for voting with the opposition unless he did it consistently. (This was the case of Admiralty Secretary George Clarke in 1705; see p. 312 below.) Nevertheless, from 1692 to 1694 a powerful campaign was mounted in both Houses to pass a Triennial Bill, making a general election mandatory every three years, and a Place Bill, barring officeholders from the Commons. The first Place Bill, in 1692, only failed in the Lords by two votes, and William had to use his veto on the second, in December 1693. He had already vetoed a Triennial Bill sponsored by Lord Shrewsbury the previous January. His use of the veto, of course, only enhanced existing fears; neither Charles II nor James had dared attempt it.

It is usual to regard this 'Country' campaign as blinkered and reactionary, if only because it would have made the development of cabinet government, as we know it, impossible. But there is nothing particularly hallowed about our modern system of government, and it has proved difficult to export, even to some of the white 'dominions'. The American Constitution is based on precisely this 'Country' principle of complete divorcement between executive and legislature, and it has proved at least an equal success. In fact, this campaign, which continued well into Anne's reign, was a constructive attempt to adapt the existing constitution to the changed conditions of the post-Revolutionary era. Now that Parliament enjoyed a much greater and more continuous share in government, it was only proper that its mandate should be renewed at regular intervals by the electorate, though three years (arbitrarily copied from the Long Parliament, who borrowed it from the Scots), was not necessarily the right interval. It could also be argued that the executive should not be able to influence members of the legislature directly, though the end result of the Place Bill would have been to strengthen the ruler at the expense of his ministers, as in America. These were not selfish, narrow or irresponsible ideas, and it is noticeable that they were shared by a majority of the Lords. In fact Shrewsbury made the passing of a Triennial Act the condition of his return to office in 1693.

What William needed was a parliamentary manager; not because he did not understand English politics – he understood as much as was necessary – but because it was apparent that the monarch could not descend into the parliamentary arena without jeopardizing his special position; moreover, William was now absent for six months of the year at the front. Carmarthen did not measure up to the job; Shrewsbury was feckless and lazy; and Nottingham, whom the King would have preferred, was hampered by his strong loyalty to Church Toryism and his ambiguous, *de facto* attitude towards the Revolution. William's eventual choice of the Earl of Sunderland seems bizarre. But Sunderland had compromised himself so badly with all parties that his dependence on the King was absolute; he could not even be given office, only a pension. Yet he was adroit, intelligent, adaptable and immensely knowledgeable.

In the summer of 1693, given his head, Sunderland began to pull the Court party together. The leading opposition spokesmen in the Lords were bought off cheaply, and Shrewsbury was persuaded to return to the Secretaryship of State by the promise of a Triennial Act, if the Place Bill was dropped. Seymour and Rochester were ousted, and Russell was brought back as First Lord of the Admiralty, which forced Nottingham to resign in November 1693. Meanwhile Sir John Somers was promoted from Attorney-General to Lord Keeper, and John Trenchard was made Secretary of State. Their associate, Charles Montague, was already a member of the Treasury Board, and he, Godolphin and Henry Guy now began to cooperate in the framing of financial legislation. Because Somers and Montague, together with Wharton, who had been Comptroller-General since 1689, and Edward Russell, were later known as the Whig Junto, it used to be thought that this was a Junto government. This is a misnomer. Somers, Montague and Russell had been taken on as ambitious career men, suitable recruits to William's new Court party, they were closely supervised by Sunderland. Godolphin and Shrewsbury were key figures in the ministry, and Carmarthen was much more than a titular head; in 1694 he was made Duke of Leeds.

The King now agreed to a simple, declaratory Triennial Act, which passed early in 1695; in return, the Commons rejected the latest Place Bill by a large majority. This brought a release of tension; so, in a curious way, did the unexpected death of Queen Mary of smallpox in December 1694. It had been supposed that her hereditary title, her great popularity and her undeviating Anglicanism were indispensable to William, but he survived without apparent difficulty. He even survived a major scandal at the end of the session (1694–5) which confirmed the 'Country' members' worst suspicions of government. The discovery that Henry Guy had accepted bribes to expedite military contracts led to his expulsion from the House and his dismissal from the Treasury; he was closely followed by the Speaker, Sir John Trevor, on a similar charge, Paul Foley, one of the chief 'Country' spokesmen, being elected in his stead. The Duke of Leeds was detected at the same time in shady dealings with the East India Company, and impeached for the third time in his varied career. The impeachment was abortive and he continued as Lord President of the Council until 1699, but he was forbidden to attend any of its meetings.

All this shook the government badly, but not the King. The recapture of Namur that summer was his first notable success in the land campaign, and he decided to capitalize on his new and unexpected popularity by holding an election that autumn, instead of waiting another year, as he could under the terms of the new Triennial Act. He even made an innovatory pre-election tour of the Midlands when he returned from the front.

The result of these elections is difficult to assess, and the two following sessions (1695–6 and 1696–7) are poorly documented. But contemporaries had as much difficulty as we in distinguishing political alignments in a period of flux and transition. Leeds's disgrace weakened the ministry, and a permanent settlement of the revenue seemed as far off as ever. In the circumstances, William was inclined to accept the Commons' proposals for a Land Bank, a very obvious 'Country' counter to the Bank of England, founded in 1694 on the initiative of Charles Montague, now Chancellor of Exchequer. But he had to move fast to suppress another proposal for a parliamentary Council of Trade. This was an echo of the privy council Committee for Trade and Plantations set up under Charles II, and looked forward to the future Board of Trade; it was meant to fill a very obvious lacuna in government at a time when England's overseas trade was expanding so fast; administration as well as politics was in a state of flux. The attitude of Sunderland towards these manoeuvres is difficult to determine, and so is Shrewsbury's.

However, in February 1696 the political climate was temporarily transformed by the discovery of a serious Jacobite plot to assassinate William. The government Whigs, led by Somers, were quick to cash in on the predictable wave of rage, apprehension and relief which swept the country; William's unique importance as war leader and guarantor of stability was underlined, a role which could not be filled by the inexperienced Anne or her ineffectual husband, George of Denmark. As we have seen, the Whigs pushed through an oath of association which many members of both Houses could not take; it was then imposed on all local magistrates, effecting a purge which resulted in a thoroughly Whig, or at least anti-Tory, bench – a situation which persisted beyond 1714, despite the intermission of avowedly Tory governments in 1702–4 and 1710–14.

William, with the support of Godolphin and perhaps of Sunderland, who had no love for the Junto Whigs, had been groping towards a patriotic 'Country' government based on the prevailing majority in the Commons, headed by Godolphin and Robert Harley, a rising young

Whig politician who accused Somers, Montague and Wharton of betraying Whig ideals. (This government did, in fact, emerge in 1700, too late.) The Assassination Plot halted these plans, and they were reversed in the summer of 1696 when the government was hit by a serious 'cash-flow' crisis. The state of the silver currency had been giving concern for years, but the decision to remint it in the middle of a major war was bold to the point of recklessness. The return of clipped and damaged coins against new ones was an expensive operation, and the immediate loss of value of the old coins and the hoarding of the new left William with no specie to pay the Flanders army, which was soon on the verge of mutiny. The Land Bank could not meet the King's needs, but the Bank of England did. It was the end of the Land Bank.

Godolphin was finally removed in the last convulsions of the Assassination Plot. In August, Sir John Fenwick, one of the plotters still in custody, made a confession accusing Godolphin, Shrewsbury and Russell of holding a secret correspondence with Saint-Germain in previous years – something almost certainly true, of the first two at least. All three were exonerated by Parliament, and in the absence of two witnesses against him Fenwick was attainted and executed, the last use of this medieval device, and one which occasioned bitter dispute in Parliament. In the meanwhile, Sunderland manoeuvred Godolphin into resigning on the false expectation that he would be immediately reinstated, but unfortunately, at the same time, Shrewsbury's health finally collapsed, and though William would not allow him to resign until 1700, from now on he only appeared in London infrequently. William seemed to accept that he was now dependent on the Junto Whigs; Montague was appointed to the vacant First Lordship of the Treasury in April 1697, Somers was promoted to the

Lord Chancellorship, and Russell was created Earl of Orford. However, the appointment of Sunderland to public office (as Lord Chamberlain), and his continuing control over patronage and appointments, was equally significant, and so was Portland's dominating share in the peace negotiations of Ryswick, which were brought to a conclusion in September 1697. In many respects, the peace treaty was more of a truce, but Louis XIV's recognition of William as King of England *par la grace de Dieu*, and Anne as his lawful successor, was a resounding concession, and achieved England's only real aim in going to war. The peace would almost certainly bring new alignments. The determination of the Spanish Succession was a problem which could not be postponed, and in view of the Emperor Leopold's intransigence, this implied a rapprochement between the Maritime Powers and France. The Junto were essentially a war ministry, and violently francophobe. Sunderland, skilled in foreign affairs and used to working with the French, would come into his own.

# XII

# PEACE AND MATERIAL PROGRESS,
## 1697–1702

The government's failure to evolve any continuous scheme of management for the post-Revolution parliaments reflected the lack of any firm or disciplined party groupings they could use. Because they had publicly thrown in their lot with the monarchy, the very success of the Junto Whigs had rebounded on them, and split their 'party', if it is appropriate to use that term at all. The Tories, on the other hand, were weakened and embittered by the King's ostracization of their leaders; at least the Whigs had some foothold in government, even if they did not want it and could not capitalize on it.

The extraordinary thing is, that as late as 1697 not even the most experienced politician could predict the behaviour of the Commons from session to session. Sunderland, Charles Montague, Harley and Sir Edward Seymour all independently came to the conclusion that the Peace of Ryswick would inaugurate a new period of tranquillity and consolidation after the bitter turmoil of the war years. But the precise opposite was the case. No sooner did they reassemble in December 1697 than the Commons launched an all-out assault on government which was sustained for four years.

The first target was the standing army, which now amounted to about 90,000 men, costing more than two and a half million pounds a year. It represented a potential threat to English liberties in the hands of a man like William and an expense the taxpaying classes were not prepared to bear in peacetime. It was argued that foreign adventuring was now at an end, and defence was the task of the militia – never mind that reform of the militia was yet another task the Convention parliament had never got round to. The demand that the army be reduced to the token establishment of 1680 (about 8,000 men) was bitterly resisted by the King, but without success; nor did the new parliament elected in the summer of 1698 bring any relief. The Junto lost further ground, and the Commons even rejected a personal plea from William that he be allowed to retain the famous Blue Guards, the Dutch regiment which had been his personal bodyguard since 1688 and had borne the brunt of the battle of the Boyne. He talked seriously of abdicating. On the other hand, in this year Parliament took an important constitutional step, and eased William's financial position, by establishing the principle of the Civil List (initially £700,000 a year) for the personal and household expenses of the Crown; the maintenance of the civil government, the armed forces and the diplomatic service must henceforth be covered by specific parliamentary grants.

The 'Country' members had a cause which was sure of public support, and even the Junto, though they compromised themselves by backing the King as far as they could, were well aware that Portland's embassy of reconciliation to Versailles, followed by the Partition Treaty of 1698, gave an assurance of future peace, which could well make them redundant. It was now agreed between Louis XIV and William that, when the childless Charles II of Spain died, the bulk of his inheritance, including Spain itself and the Indies, should pass to a 'neutral' candidate, the Electoral Prince of Bavaria. The French and Austrian candidates, Philip of Anjou and the Archduke Charles, would receive compensation in Italy and the Netherlands.

In other respects, the King and the Junto were now fatally at odds. Resentful of the fact that Sunderland still controlled crown patronage, they demanded a Secretary-ship of State for Wharton when one fell vacant in December 1697. Instead, William promoted the under-secretary, James Vernon. (He did not want a secretary who might interfere in foreign affairs, he disliked Wharton personally, and he feared that the Junto were aiming at a mono-poly of power.) Resentment on both sides was exacer-bated when Sunderland resigned that month in the face of personal parliamentary attacks: with Shrewsbury still a recluse, his essential role as 'link-man' and political manager could not be filled. Blaming the Junto for all his misfortunes, for the reduction of the army, for Sunder-land's resignation and Shrewsbury's refusal to serve, William withdrew his confidence from them almost en-tirely, and the ministry drifted dismasted under continu-ing broadsides.

From the army Parliament turned to war finance, an even greater source of discontent, and one which smacked of necromancy in the eyes of most members. Influenced by the economic thinking of Charles Montague, the govern-ment had made no serious effort, apart from the land tax, to meet the cost of the war (over £5 million a year) from direct taxation. Instead, it had used the income from in-direct taxation to meet the interest payments on massive loans, and Montague's Act of 1693, enabling the public to buy annuities on a million-pound loan to be serviced by new excise duties imposed for ninety-nine years, betrayed the fact that the government envisaged not repaying the capital at all. The Bank of England, established the fol-lowing year to provide a loan of one and a half million

pounds, extended this principle; from the first it issued
paper money in excess of its bullion reserves, an unheard-
of heresy. By the end of the war a National Debt had been
created, standing at over thirteen and a half million
pounds, and though Montague acknowledged that this
must be controlled (he had established a sinking fund as
early as 1696 to pay off part of it), its total liquidation was
not part of his programme. It was unfortunate that in
1698 the Lord Chancellor at last gave judgement in the
long-drawn-out Bankers' Case, confirming the government's repudiation of its debt to the goldsmith-bankers
incurred by the Stop of the Exchequer in 1672; even more
unfortunate that the Lord Chancellor should be the Junto
leader, Somers.

To the less sophisticated landowning gentry in Parliament it seemed immoral not to liquidate the National
Debt, and they resented the fact that perpetual interest
payments extended the financial burden of the war into
peacetime. They may also have understood, however
dimly, that this new system of deficit finance seriously
undermined their capacity to control government by the
imposition of fiscal pressure; to refuse taxation to service
the debt would drive the government to bankruptcy and
wreck the economy of the whole country. There was also
a more generalized resentment of 'the moneyed interest';
to the old apposition between 'Court' and 'Country'
was added a new apposition, between 'Country' and
'City', the stronger in that London, steadily growing
in size, was now breaking its last links with the country-
side.

The boom in trade in the 1670s was the beginning of
what some historians call 'The Commercial Revolution'.
The re-export trade from the colonies and India was
steadily increasing, and a surplus of exports over imports

brought a steady flow of money into the merchant community, the 'spare' money which floated the government
loans of the 1690s and funded the Bank of England. To
those who have, more shall be given, and to the wealthy
entrepreneurs of the City went most of the lucrative contracts thrown off by the war, in clothing, food, arms, stores
and ships. The war itself had remarkably little effect on
English trade; in fact the need for an increasing income
from indirect taxation strengthened the tariff walls which
had been rising round England since the 1670s. The war
even had direct benefits; for instance, William's decision
to winter the English fleet at Barcelona in 1694–5 made the
western Mediterranean safe for English merchant shipping for the first time since the 1650s. Money breeds
money; the Bank of England enhanced London's status
as one of the chief financial centres in the world, and increased the circulation of 'notional' money, the profit on
bills of exchange and exchequer certificates, already an
object of suspicion. The bullion crisis of 1696 conveniently
eliminated the bank's rivals.

It was obvious that the mercantile and financial classes
payed no tax on most of their profits, including the interest
on or annuities from loans to the government, and the
increasing burden of customs and excise could always be
passed on to the consumer. The land tax could not. It
was a burden which most tenants successfully refused to
shoulder, and by the nature of things it was a tax which was
difficult to evade – land is there for all to see, its approxi-
mate value obvious. One class – and this was increasingly
a class question – was making huge profits from the war,
while another was making huge outpayments; and the
class which was suffering was still over-represented in both
Houses.

Even so, with a weak and tottering ministry before

them, and almost complete command of the House of Commons, the 'Country' members achieved little that was radical, novel or constructive. The real solution lay in the taxation of liquid assets, but this was always beyond the scope of seventeenth-century governments. Instead, they launched an old-fashioned attack, reminiscent of Charles I's reign, on royal ministers and favourites. Charles Montague beat off the first accusations of bribery in 1697 and 1698, but succumbed to a more leisurely examination of his conduct of the Treasury. He resigned in 1699, though the following year he went to the Lords as Baron Halifax. Orford also resigned in 1699, in resentment at a similar inquiry into his conduct of the Admiralty. (Obviously both men had improved their fortunes during the war, but a long-drawn-out parliamentary inquisition, continuing into 1705, uncovered no hard evidence of wrong-doing.) The attack on Somers was even more small-minded, concentrating as it did on his unfortunate misjudgement in issuing a privateering licence to the notorious Captain Kidd. Equally obvious and old-fashioned, though not unjustified, was a two-year campaign, ending in 1700, to resume the enormous grants of confiscated Irish land to William's former mistress, Elizabeth Villiers, Countess of Orkney, and his foreign condottiere, Godert de Ginkel, Earl of Athlone, and Henri Massue de Ruvigny, Earl of Galway. To push their Resumption Bill through the Lords in April 1700, the Commons tacked it to the Finance Bill for that year, provoking a constitutional crisis potentially more serious than any since 1680. Somers advised William to give way; William accepted his advice but at once dismissed him.

The dismissal of Somers now forced William to consider the formation of a new government. Hitherto he had relied on makeshift replacements, using men of no defined party attitude or obvious ability. James Vernon laboured on as sole Secretary of State until 1699, when the absentee Shrewsbury was transferred to the Lord Chamberlainship, making way for the Earl of Jersey. (Shrewsbury resigned altogether in 1700, and retired to Italy for his health.) At the Treasury, Montague was replaced by an extraordinary *revenant*, Ford Lord Grey of Werke, Monmouth's cavalry commander at Sedgemoor, now Earl of Tankerville. The Duke of Leeds was belatedly removed in 1699, only to be replaced by the ineffective Earl of Pembroke. Strangest of all, the ailing Lord Lonsdale, described as 'scrupulous and unready', was brought out of retirement to be Lord Privy Seal, though he died within the year. Somers was replaced by a second-rate career lawyer, Sir Nathan Wright, with a Tory reputation.

In peacetime, and with a system in which the financial needs of the government were modest and most officials were paid out of fees anyway, in which ministers were not expected to have a programme nor even to initiate legislation, a monarch could still survive in this fashion for quite long periods, especially if he had foreign policy under his direct control. But in the summer of 1700 two crucial deaths forced William to take action. The death of the young Duke of Gloucester in July meant that the succession, after Anne, must now be formally vested in the Hanoverian line (represented by the Dowager Electress Sophia, only surviving child of James I's daughter Elizabeth). For this important constitutional resettlement a strong government was essential, and perhaps even a new parliament. Then the long-awaited death of Charles II in Spain in September brought into effect the second Partition Treaty, negotiated by William and Louis XIV in 1699, after the death of the young prince of Bavaria. This provided for the roughly equal division of the Spanish inheritance between the French and Austrian claimants. Unfortunately, Charles II left a will bequeathing his dominions entire to the French claimant, Philip of Anjou, or failing him, the Austrian claimant, Charles. Put to an excruciating choice, Louis XIV accepted. Crucial foreign-policy decisions must now be taken, which could lead to war.

William's solution was to send for Godolphin, representing conservative but not Tory interests, and Robert Harley, whom he relied on to control the 'Country' members. As a sop to the Church Tories, Rochester took office again, for the first time since 1687, but only as Lord-Lieutenant of Ireland. Harley demanded a dissolution and got it, but he cannily declined a ministerial appointment, hoping to preserve his independence by standing as Speaker in the new parliament. But events proved that Harley had taken too much on himself, and Godolphin could give him scant assistance. The short-lived parliament of 1701 was the most unruly of the reign.

Thus the Act of Settlement, though it duly vested the succession in the Hanoverians, also proved to be a 'Country' charter and an implied attack on William's conduct as king. On Anne's death, placemen were to be barred from the Commons at last, and all policy decisions were to be taken in the Privy Council. The Hanoverian monarchs were forbidden to leave England without permission of Parliament or to appoint foreigners to government office, and they were specifically obliged to enter into communion with the Church of England. William had to swallow these insults as best he could, and the reduction of his Civil List to £600,000. Meanwhile, his request that Parliament advise him on a new foreign policy was pushed aside by the discovery of his two secret partition treaties, binding on England, which had never been submitted to

Parliament or even communicated to all his ministers. (The second treaty was particularly offensive, in that it had been signed in February 1700, when Parliament was sitting.) Portland, Somers, Orford and Halifax were promptly impeached, but the fact that the charges against Portland were dropped almost at once betrayed the party animosity behind this manoeuvre, which led to a bitter squabble between Lords and Commons.

At the same time, Louis XIV's action in occupying the barrier fortresses in the Spanish Netherlands which had been allotted to the Dutch at Ryswick to protect them against future French aggression caused considerable public alarm. Mercantile interests were also roused by the formation of a French company to exploit the Central and South American trade, formerly closed to all but Spaniards. Fears that Spain under the boy king Philip V would be a mere appendage of France were being realized. In May, a deputation from the grand jury of Kent submitted a petition to the Commons requesting them to grant further supplies and authorize the King to assist his allies by any possible means. They were thrown into prison, but this produced the much more threatening Legion Memorial – signed, 'Our name is legion, for we are many' – presented by Daniel Defoe. After an excoriating review of the Commons' deficiencies, particularly their lack of patriotism, respect for the King or concern for the nation's safety, it denied their right to punish any but their own members. This provoked a full-scale legal and constitutional debate in the public prints, and by 24 June the Commons' reputation was so sunk that William thought it reasonable to prorogue them and depart for The Hague, using a unilateral resolution of the Lords as his authority to negotiate with the Emperor and the Dutch.

He took with him the Earl of Marlborough, who had

steadily climbed back into favour after Queen Mary's death and the subsequent reconciliation between his patron Anne and the King. In 1698 he had been made governor to the young Duke of Gloucester, and a privy councillor; in 1698, 1699 and 1700 he had served as one of the lords justices, or regents of the kingdom, during William's absence abroad. He was now appointed Captain-General of the allied armies in Flanders, since William's health made it unthinkable that he should take the field in person. The Grand Alliance negotiated that August by him and William, which brought England into the War of the Spanish Succession the following year, was strictly limited in its aims. The Emperor was to be bought off by the acquisition of Milan, Naples and Sicily, and the Spanish Netherlands, which would also solve the Dutch barrier problem. The Indies trade was to be opened up, and measures were to be taken to prevent the possible union of the French and Spanish crowns.

The following month, September, William's hand was considerably strengthened. James II died at Saint-Germain, and Louis XIV quixotically recognized his son as James III of England, VIII of Scotland, in flagrant contravention of the Treaty of Ryswick; England was swept by a wave of patriotic revulsion and anger. William returned in November, and after consulting Somers and Sunderland ordered a dissolution; Godolphin resigned. But the parliament which met on the last day of the year, though wholehearted in its support of the King's war policy, was far from being strenuously Whig. The impeachment of the Whig lords, hung over from the previous parliament, was a stumbling-block, and William contented himself with appointing a nondescript collection of peers: the Earl of Carlisle at the Treasury, Manchester as Secretary of State, Pembroke as Lord Admiral and the Duke of

Somerset as Lord President. The Commons patriotically voted a new army of 40,000 men (18,000 of them British), but any further changes which may have been pending were cut off by William's sudden death on 8 March 1702 after a minor riding accident.

This last parliament of William's reign was very much like all the others, with the 'Country' interest still in the ascendant, though perhaps slightly reduced in numbers. It re-elected Harley as Speaker, though only by two votes, and there is probably truth in Godolphin's representations that the previous parliament, in view of the changed situation abroad, would have done the King's business just as well. Yet from now on until 1714, and for some years beyond, the political scene, inside and outside Parliament, was dominated by the clash between Whig and Tory; under these titles quite formidable party organizations emerged, and by 1708, if not before, the great majority of Members of Parliament, apart from placemen and office holders, were voting along strict party lines. Why this sudden change; and was it so sudden?

Probably the change had been gestating ever since the end of the last war. In adversity the Junto leaders had acquired a new popularity, and they attracted fresh support in the country at large from those who were dissatisfied with the policy, or non-policy, of the House of Commons, and its indifference to foreign affairs and the prospect of war. This reached a climax in 1701, when the Commons' continued irresponsibility brought a marked public reaction, when the Junto's warnings were fully justified by events abroad and their spiteful impeachment at the same time gave them the new status of martyrs. The Junto Whigs emerged as a constructive party vowed to support strong constitutional monarchy at home and defend the Settlement and the Protestant Religion abroad.

The years 1698–1702 also witnessed the final break between them and the Country Whigs, and their consequent divorcement from pre-1688 traditions of Whiggism. Of course, they remained a minority movement – until 1715 they never decisively 'won' a general election, as the Tories did in 1702 and 1710 – and they remained open to accusations of rank republicanism on the one hand and compliance with military autocracy on the other. This was the message of Davenant's *True Picture of a Modern Whig* in 1701, one of a number of pamphlets on both sides seeking to define the nature of party in no very charitable spirit. (The Tories, of course, were denounced as francophile, Jacobite and crypto-Catholic.) But the Junto's pragmatic acceptance of the Revolution, without too close an inquiry into its nature, and their recognition of the need to inflict a final defeat on France in order to safeguard the Settlement, had an increasing appeal to the upper classes, and it is significant that from about 1701 right through to 1713 they exercised a control over the House of Lords which no one would have ventured to forecast in the early 1690s.

But the Tories had not been idle; indeed, it was arguably they who took the offensive, and they found a rallying-cry in the defence of the Church. It was soon apparent that the Toleration Act of 1689 had seriously weakened the Church of England, and not only because its claim to a monopoly of English Protestantism had finally been abandoned. The fact that some parishioners could now legally worship elsewhere meant that it was impossible to enforce the church attendance of anyone, and the Uniformity Act became a dead letter. The size, wealth and power of the Dissenting congregations which now emerged to fill the new 'meeting houses', or chapels, was disturbing, especially since church attendance was falling at a faster rate than the withdrawal of the Dissenters alone could explain. Deism and atheism were gaining a hold on the upper classes, and their claims were openly put in books like John Toland's *Christianity Not Mysterious* (1696) and even in Locke's *Reasonableness of Christianity* (1695). The theories of Newton encouraged a natural or scientific approach to religion which many found disturbing; moral offences such as blasphemy, adultery and homosexuality were thought to be on the increase. The theatre had put behind it the worst excesses of the Restoration, but its lightmindedness and irreligion, its preoccupation with the breakdown of marriage, brought down upon it a celebrated philippic from the non-juror Jeremy Collier in 1698. Societies for the Reformation of Manners flourished, though they in turn threatened an ecclesiastical monopoly.

This lamentable state of affairs was freely blamed on the Dissenters, the Whigs and even the bishops. Understandably so. William's bishops could all with truth be described as 'latitude men', and after Mary's death he followed Charles II's example in delegating church patronage to a commission headed by the two archbishops, Tenison and Sharp, who tended to favour pious and learned but uncontentious candidates. As for the Dissenters, they were achieving an alarming position of social prominence, especially in London, and they were qualifying themselves for office in local government by taking the Anglican sacrament on one occasion or at long intervals. This practice of 'occasional conformity' was regarded with loathing on religious grounds, and with alarm on political grounds, and it received spectacular publicity in 1697 by the folly of the new Lord Mayor of London, Sir Humphrey Edwin, in attending an afternoon service at his meeting house in full regalia after worshipping as an

Anglican that same morning. As for the Whig leaders, it was plausible to regard Somers, Halifax and Wharton as freethinkers, or even deists, and there were tie-ups between all these groups. Many bishops and Whig politicians were known to be sympathetic to Dissent; the Dissenters were reputed to be Whig voters to a man; and many prominent apostles of 'Whig finance' were wealthy City Dissenters.

But the Tory cry of 'Church in danger!' also implied a more diffuse but potent sentiment. No one seriously supposed that the Church was in danger of extinction, or even of disestablishment (though the disappearance of the Scots Episcopal Church in 1689 was an awful warning, and relevant to the Union in 1707), but it was facing a crisis common to all hierarchical churches in Europe at this time, including the Roman. The centuries-old identification of Church with State, strengthened by the Reformation and the Counter-reformation, was breaking down, and at the same time the habitual anti-clericalism of the English ruling classes had been encouraged by the Revolution. It was fashionable to assert that the excesses of Charles I and James II had both been provoked by the indiscreet meddling of churchmen in affairs beyond their competence, and Whiggism perfectly represented a state of mind to which religion was a personal matter, irrelevant to politics, and the Church merely a department of state. The High Church Movement, gathering momentum in the late 1690s, passionately defended the Church's central role in politics and the constitution.

The movement surfaced in 1697, when Francis Atterbury published his *Letter to a Convocation Man*, calling for the regular assembly of the Convocation of Canterbury, adjourned since 1689, at the same time as Parliament and with co-equal status. This was an age of great pamphlets, which had a perceptible effect on public opinion; Atterbury's arguments were taken up by the Commons Tories, and Lord Rochester made the meeting of Convocation in 1701 a condition of his adhesion to the Godolphin–Harley government. It met thereafter until 1717, and though it never answered the expectations of its supporters, and succeeded in dividing the Church rather than strengthening it, it certainly brought religion to the forefront of politics and cemented the union between the Church and Toryism.

In the next monarch the Tories looked for a leader and a patron, but many of them stumbled on the very threshold of Anne's reign, and the circumstances are significant. Louis XIV's recognition of James III led to an Act in January 1702 attainting him of high treason, and another imposing on all office-holders and clergy the Abjuration Oath, which acknowledged William as 'rightful and lawful' king (at last), denied that the Pretender had 'any right or title whatsoever' to the Crown, and pledged support for the Hanover succession. But it was one thing to pass the Act of Settlement, and another to swear to uphold its provisions, and it is one of the paradoxes of Toryism that many who were willing to attaint the Pretender were still reluctant to deny his title. The Abjuration Act passed the Commons by one vote, and the Earl of Nottingham told Archbishop Sharp in agony that it was 'like swearing against God's Providence and [his] government of the world'. Sharp urbanely told him, 'I am of opinion that [princes] hold their crowns by the same legal right that your lordship holds your estate, and that they may forfeit their rights as well as you may do yours; and that the legislature is judge in one case as well as the other.' But this was a very advanced Toryism, and a Toryism which strangely enough grew more not less heterodox as the misdeeds of James II retreated into a past not directly experienced by a new generation of clergy and politicians. A few weeks later William was dead, and the Tories could rejoice in a successor who, as a child of James II, had a hereditary as well as a statutory claim to the throne. But the issues raised by the Abjuration Oath were only postponed.

# XIII

# THE WHIG WAR, 1702–10

Queen Anne is a monarch whose character is still being revised at the hands of historians, but certainly she can no longer be dismissed as an unintelligent, *fainéante* figure-head, a puppet in the hands of her squabbling ministers, governed only by her rather dubious passion for members of the same sex.

Of course, she was a woman in a man's world, and servants of Marlborough's stature, or Somers's, or even Bolingbroke's, would have posed serious problems of control even for an aggressive and able male ruler. But she had a mind of her own, and her most successful ministers, Godolphin and Harley, were those who took her most seriously. Persistent eye trouble from an early age hindered her education, though it would be difficult to show that it was more deficient than Charles II's, for instance, or James II's; it was perhaps more important that she could not achieve the mastery of documentation which was now essential for an active chief executive. She had to delegate more work than her predecessor, though this was not necessarily a source of weakness; on the other hand, she continued to preside over the weekly meetings of the Cabinet Council, and without her agreement no important policy decision could be made. In fact, all such decisions in her reign – the war with France, the Union with Scotland, the Peace of Utrecht – were essentially personal to her. It is significant that she resumed Charles II's practice of attending debates in the House of Lords incognito, and she was the last monarch to do so. She took very seriously her role as war leader and defender of European Protestantism, and one of her first acts as queen was to assume Elizabeth I's famous motto *semper eadem*. She had a deep concern for the welfare and happiness of her people, and this governed her actions to an unusual degree. She was willing to sacrifice her own religious convictions for the sake of national unity, and she abandoned her closest personal friendships and jeopardized her political comfort and tranquillity for the sake of the nation.

It was her fate to be misjudged, and the first to do so were the Tories, led by her uncle Lord Rochester. In fact, though historians have joined with contemporaries in labelling her 'High Church', it is not clear on what evidence this is based. She had been brought up with a detestation of Roman Catholicism which had been strengthened by tussles with her father, whom she seems to have disliked on personal grounds too. She clove to the Church of England as a bulwark against Rome and a prop to the social order; she felt a maternal concern for the clergy and took her role as Supreme Governor with great seriousness. But just as she was queen of the whole nation, so she was head of the whole Church, and she rejected those who threatened the unity of either – moreover, those who fomented discord in the Church were guilty in her eyes of blasphemy. Certainly she was opposed to Occasional Conformity, few Anglicans were not, but this does not mean that she accepted the rest of the High Church platform. Her principal ecclesiastical adviser was Archbishop John Sharp of York, who was almost whiggish in his firm belief in the subordination of Church to State, and this was reflected in her moderate episcopal appointments. No High Churchman joined the bench until 1713, when she

advanced Atterbury to the see of Rochester with the greatest reluctance. Others, like Blackall and Dawes, labelled
'High Church' by contemporaries, were in fact conform-
ists in the mould of Sharp; others, like Wake of Lincoln
and Tyler of Llandaff, were downright Whigs.

But contemporaries may be forgiven their confusion.
Her reign opened with a bang, with the dismissal of every
Whig in sight and their replacement by firm Tories;
notably Rochester, who was confirmed as Lord-Lieutenant of Ireland, Sir Edward Seymour, who took Wharton's
Comptrollership, and Nottingham, who was reappointed
Secretary of State after nine years in the wilderness. It
was Nottingham who inserted into her first speech to
Parliament, over Godolphin's protests, the words, 'My
own principles must always keep me entirely firm to the
interests of the Church of England, and will incline me to
countenance those who have the truest zeal to support it.'
In May, Rochester judged the time ripe to publish the
first volume of his father Clarendon's *History of the Rebellion*,
itself a conservative manifesto, with a preface proclaiming
the Tory millennium. In June, a high-flying Oxford don
called Henry Sacheverell published *The Political Union*,
asserting the dual identity of Church and State and denouncing the Dissenters as republicans and concealed
atheists. In the elections by that time in progress, the
Tories won a firm majority in the Commons.

By this time, differences of opinion on the Church had
produced a strong polarization, pulling men into the Whig
or the Tory camp; to these were soon added differences of
opinion on war and foreign policy. The introduction of
'Country' measures, like Place Bills, could still revive the
'Court' *versus* 'Country' axis, cutting across party lines,
but from now on most members voted Whig or Tory with
a consistency which becomes the more impressive the more

the situation is investigated. In 1702, for the first time a party could be said to have 'won' a general election, and its majority could be improved by the avowedly partisan settlement of disputed elections once the House met. It was natural that the Queen's ministers, with their hundred or so placemen, should ally with the prevailing party in the House of Commons to obtain a clear working majority – a luxury rarely enjoyed by their predecessors.

But appearances were deceptive, and the Tories would have done well to pay more attention to the sermon preached by Sharp at Anne's coronation. In an ideal Christian world, said the Archbishop, the Queen's subjects 'would not, for difference of opinion about the methods of public conduct, break out into parties and factions. Much less, in case of such divisions, would they sacrifice the peace of the kingdom to their own private resentments, and mingle Heaven and Earth for the supporting of a side.' Anne consistently deplored the strength and vigour of both parties, and like William she saw in their victory the Crown's defeat. As far as she could she ignored them. By an indication of royal preference, as well as by the use of crown patronage, she was well able to influence the result of elections. In any case, there was no constitutional obligation on her to accept such results and choose her ministers accordingly, as she showed in 1705 and to some extent in 1708; tradition still imposed a duty on all politicians to serve and support her if required to do so. Like William, she preferred to work through a neutral parliamentary manager or managers.

In 1702, her system of management was particularly strong. Marlborough, to whom she was bound by the strongest ties of affection and friendship through his wife Sarah, Groom of the Stole, not only commanded the allied armies in all theatres of war, but had usurped control of foreign policy from the Secretaries of State, stepping into William's shoes. The navy was headed by her husband, Prince George, with a council dominated by Marlborough's brother, George Churchill. Finance, patronage, domestic policy and the affairs of Scotland were the responsibility of Godolphin, the first Lord Treasurer since 1687, and another old friend of hers and the Marlboroughs. Robert Harley, elected Speaker for the third time, was very much part of this government aggregation, and so was William Lowndes, Guy's successor as Secretary to the Treasury. Neither they nor Anne would brook interference, and in the first trial of strength, in May, Rochester's objections to an immediate declaration of war on France were overruled.

But, on the religious front, Anne seemed all Tory. She gave the strongest possible backing to a Bill to outlaw occasional conformity, which passed the Commons by a large majority in December 1701; she forced Marlborough and Godolphin to vote for it, and even her Lutheran husband. The Whig lords dare not reject it, but they amended it so drastically that the Commons disowned it. In all other matters, Marlborough's views prevailed. His first campaign in Flanders in the summer of 1702 was necessarily tentative, though his indulgent mistress gave him a dukedom for it; but, in September, Admiral George Rooke rather luckily surprised and destroyed a Franco-Spanish fleet in Vigo Bay. This encouraged the advocates of a 'blue-water' policy, mainly Tory and 'Country' interests. They argued that England should not waste manpower and resources in a war of siege and manoeuvre in Flanders, for which she had no natural bent; she should carry the war to France and Spain on the sea and in the colonies instead. (It harked back to the policy of the parliamentary majority in the 1620s, but it also looked

forward to the policy of Chatham in the Seven Years
War.) Rochester was the most prominent supporter of
such ideas, in opposition to Marlborough and Nottingham, and even his relationship to the Queen could not
save him; he was dismissed in February 1703, and in
May Anne agreed to a decisive extension of the land war
in Europe.

The Methuen Treaties brought Portugal into the war,
and gave England an all-the-year-round base at Lisbon
from which the navy could dominate the western Mediterranean, a position consolidated by the capture of Gibraltar
(1704) and Minorca (1708). On the other hand, the treaties committed England to conquering Spain, deposing
Philip V and replacing him by the Austrian claimant
Charles III, an enterprise which William III had dismissed as impracticable when he made the Grand Alliance only two years before. The Peninsular War ended in
disaster and frustration, and arguably prevented a final
military decision in northern Europe; Louis XIV never
met his Waterloo. It ruined Marlborough, and ultimately
the Whigs.

Meanwhile, the campaigning season of 1703 only witnessed further brilliant but indecisive manoeuvring in
Flanders. Anne blamed the stalemate partly on the strife
of parties at home, which was increasing in violence; and
the Tories, aggressively critical of the government's war
policy, gave the greatest offence. When Parliament reassembled in the autumn, she made a speech calling for
national unity and an end of faction, and she withdrew
her support from the second Occasional Conformity Bill,
which passed the Commons in December. It was rejected
outright by the Lords, provoking a quarrel between her
and Nottingham which culminated in his resignation the
following May, when she also took the opportunity of

dismissing Seymour and Jersey, the other Secretary of State. Nottingham's place was taken by Robert Harley, increasingly an advocate of patriotic, non-party government.

The campaigning season that followed was resoundingly successful; it was as if God smiled on the Tories' humiliation. In May, the Peninsular War opened with the landing of one British army at Lisbon and another, under the Earl of Peterborough, near Barcelona. In July, Rooke seized Gibraltar, and in August he fought a decisive fleet action off Málaga. (Málaga has been likened to Jutland; the French Grand Fleet was not defeated, but it did not stir out of Toulon again.) Meanwhile Marlborough had marched part of the allied army in Flanders down the Rhine to the Danube; he relieved the Franco-Bavarian pressure on Vienna, which was threatening to pull the Emperor out of the war, and at Blenheim in August he won the greatest victory of his career and one of the most comprehensive in European military history, comparable only with Pavia in 1525.

Having already dug their own grave, in the winter of 1704–5 the Tories jumped into it. With a fanatical desperation they tried to push through a third Occasional Conformity Bill by incorporating it in the Finance Bill for the year, on which the war effort depended. To the Queen, such irresponsibility was almost incredible, especially in view of the success with which God had visited British arms. The Tories split, and the 'Tack' was removed in the Commons by 251 votes to 154. The Bill alone was defeated in the Lords by a larger margin than before, and no more was heard of this issue until 1711. The immediate result was a 'Country' reaction, and an intensification of the long-drawn-out squabble over *Ashby* v. *White*.

This celebrated case dated back to the election of 1700,

when the Tory mayor of Lord Wharton's borough of Aylesbury struck several Whig voters off the electoral list. Wharton financed one of them, a cobbler named Ashby, to bring an action at the Assizes, which he won. The mayor, White, appealed to Queen's Bench, which reversed the judgement 3 to 1 on the grounds that this was a matter for the House of Commons. But the lone dissentient was the Whig Lord Chief Justice, Holt, who held that a vote was a species of property, and therefore came within the cognizance of the courts. By this time it was 1703, but Ashby (and Wharton) took the case on to the House of Lords. Wharton knew that the Lords would reverse the Queen's Bench judgement, which they did, and calculated that this would provoke a quarrel between the two Houses so bitter that it would force a premature general election. The Commons, however, did not rise to the bait, so he engineered further actions against White, loosely known as 'The Case of the Aylesbury Men'. This time the Commons obliged by throwing the Aylesbury men into prison, and the Junto peers moved for a writ of error to bring the matter before the Lords, threatening a clash of jurisdictions even more spectacular than in the great cases of Charles II's reign, *Shirley* v. *Fagg* (1675) or *Skinner* v. *the East India Company* (1670). However, the Triennial Act now obliged Anne to bring this disappointing parliament to an end, and she did not linger; it was prorogued on 14 March 1705 and dissolved on 5 April.

Over the winter, Gibraltar had sustained an epic siege, but the Rock was narrowly held by the Royal Marines, incorporated in 1702. The death of the Emperor Leopold I in April 1705 and the succession of Joseph I caused the allied war effort to hiccup, and Marlborough was frustrated in his aim of outflanking the French armies altogether and striking down into France via the valley of the Moselle. However, he forced the artificial barrier of the Lines of Brabant, and the Spanish Netherlands were at his mercy. In Spain, Peterborough and Charles III took Barcelona, and the provinces of Catalonia, Valencia and Aragón rose against the government in Madrid. Total victory seemed only a matter of time.

Meanwhile, the elections cut back the Tory majority of 1702 and produced a more balanced House of Commons. Godolphin's calculations showed 190 Tories as against 160 Whigs, but he now chose to secure a working majority by allying his 100 placemen with the Whigs. Anne made her own views clear in her opening speech, inveighing against those who declared that the Church was in danger under her governorship. But the Tory peers, led by Rochester and Nottingham, now took another desperate step, by proposing that the Electress Sophia be invited over to England. The Queen was known to be implacably opposed to any such visit, but Sophia was just as eager to come; Godolphin and the Whigs had the choice of alienating the Queen by agreeing, or alienating the next heir (whom they had been assiduously courting since 1701) by refusing. The Whigs did refuse, but they sweetened the pill for Sophia by bringing in a new Regency Bill which would ensure the smooth transfer of power on Anne's death, and protect the interests of the Hanoverians in their absence.

This was in November 1705. In December Wharton forced a full-dress Lords debate on a motion that the Church was in danger, with the Queen present. It was made to appear that the whole High Church campaign arose from mere spleen at the dismissal of Rochester and Nottingham, and that one of its principal aims was to undermine the disciplinary powers of the bishops and the Crown. It ended with a thumping resolution, adopted without amendment by the Commons, which declared that: 'The Church of England, as by law established, which was rescued from the extremest danger by King William III (of glorious memory), is now by God's blessing under the happy reign of her Majesty in a most safe and flourishing condition.' The Tories' discomfiture was completed by the Commons' debates on the Regency Bill, when their 'Country' wing again moved to apply the 'place' clause of the Act of Settlement immediately, which the Queen took as another insult to her. By a series of brilliant political manoeuvres, the Whigs succeeded in emasculating the original clause; men appointed to offices created after April 1705 were henceforth barred from the Commons, but men appointed to pre-existing offices could continue to sit after submitting themselves for re-election, a proviso which did not become a serious disadvantage until the nineteenth century. (The opportunity was also taken to repeal the unrealistic clause in the Act of Settlement which would have obliged the government to take its policy decisions in the moribund Privy Council.) In the same month, February 1706, Anne for the first time intervened in Convocation, notifying the High Church Lower House that she regarded its rejection of the bishops' right to control its proceedings as a threat to her own authority.

In the following summer, the allied war effort reached a triumphant climax. In May, Marlborough smashed the French armies at Ramillies, a victory almost as conclusive as Blenheim, and by September he had conquered the greater part of the Spanish Netherlands and was poised on the vulnerable north-western frontier of France. In September, the Austrian general Prince Eugene relieved Turin and drove the French right out of north Italy. Meanwhile, in May, an Anglo-Spanish army under Peterborough began to advance west from Barcelona while an Anglo-Portuguese army under the Earl of Galway marched east from Lisbon, occupying Madrid in June. Unfortunately the situation then came adrift; Charles III was dilatory in arriving at his capital, and after a quarrel with Galway the unstable and unpredictable Peterborough took himself off home. By September, Galway had advanced right across Spain to the east coast, as if to take Peterborough's place, but Marlborough's nephew the Duke of Berwick, now a Marshal of France (he was James II's illegitimate son by Arabella Churchill) was massing superior forces. All the same, it seemed that the allies were in sight of achieving their war aims; certainly the aims of the Grand Alliance, and perhaps a realistic compromise on the Methuen Treaties. That winter Louis XIV made his first peace overtures, and though they were far from satisfactory they offered a basis for negotiation, and Harley bitterly blamed the Whigs and the 'Duumvirate' (Marlborough and Godolphin) for rejecting them. In fact, the future was to show that 1706 was the last opportunity to achieve a satisfactory settlement of the Spanish problem. The obstinacy of the Whigs can be attributed to over-confidence; they expected that Marlborough would now invade metropolitan France and dictate peace terms in Paris; and Godolphin had to comply because of his over-whelming difficulties in Scotland.

Scotland's intervention in 1638, provoking the Great Rebellion, showed that her political importance was not to be measured by her wealth or size. But the problem thus posed was never solved. Cromwell had practised crude repression, and Charles II and Lauderdale had followed his example, imposing a minority rule by military force, as in Ireland, and artificially reviving the Scots episcopalian church. This system had been broken in 1689, and active Jacobitism perished at Killiecrankie with James Graham of Claverhouse, Viscount Dundee. William III had to acquiesce in the establishment of a Presbyterian state church, and the differing attitude of the Scots is shown by the fact that they made no bones about deposing James VII (James II), and made William's assumption of power – and later Anne's – specifically conditional on a stiff coronation oath.

William's problems were compounded by the abolition in 1689 of the Lords of the Articles, the powerful steering committee which had kept previous Scots parliaments under strict control; on the other hand, the absence of a Triennial Act enabled him to keep the new House elected in 1689 for the rest of his reign. The celebrated Massacre of Glencoe in 1692 added to his troubles, though not in the way usually supposed; by terrorizing the Highland clans for the time being, it removed an important check on the aspirations of the more civilized and politically minded Lowlands. These aspirations were expressed in the Darien Scheme of 1698 for the establishment of a Scots colony and trading base in Spanish Central America. This was Raleigh and the Orinoco all over again. Unable to halt this encroachment on the territory of a friendly power in time of peace, William certainly could not support it, and English trading interests were openly hostile; thus they were blamed for the disastrous collapse of the colony in 1700. The blow to Scots national esteem was as important as the financial loss incurred, and it underlined her dependent position in trade and foreign policy; by the Navigation Acts she was cut off from the lucrative colonial and Indies trade, and in 1689, and again in 1702, war was declared on her behalf without even the pretence of consultation.

The reaction was not long in coming, and it was foreseen by William III and Anne, who both came forward in
1701 and 1702 as strong advocates of Union; William's
endorsement was enough to convert the Junto. In 1702
the Scots Parliament refused to pass an Abjuration Act,
and in 1703 it flaunted its independence by an Act legal-
izing the wine trade with France. Worse still, the Act of
Security in September 1703 declared that Anne's successor
in Scotland should be of the royal line and Protestant, but
not the same as in England. Whom this portended it was
difficult to say; there was still considerable hope that the
Pretender might be converted, but some thought that the
magnificent Duke of Hamilton, with many royal Stuarts
in his ancestry, might make a bid. After a year's agonized
hesitation, Godolphin advised the Queen to give her
assent.

He was now thrown back on the Whigs, and the Whig
solution worked. Facing bluff with bluff, the Junto
brought in the Aliens Act of March 1705, which made
Scotsmen aliens for all purposes unless the Act of Security
were repealed by 1 January 1706. This provoked the celebrated judicial murder of an English merchant captain,
Thomas Green, in Edinburgh, though the action had
the healthy effect of discrediting the new Scottish ministers put in by Anne and Godolphin in 1702; they had to
turn back to the old gang of political fixers favoured by
William III, now headed by the Duke of Queensberry,
whose expertise and toughness made up for their lack of
political morality. They quickly restored order, and in
September they induced the Scots Parliament to open
negotiations for a Union. The Aliens Act was repealed in
December 1705, just before it was due to take effect, and
the English and Scots commissioners assembled in London
in April 1706.

From then on progress was almost precipitous. Agreement was reached and a treaty signed by the end of July; to the general surprise it passed the Edinburgh Parliament in January 1707 and the Westminster Parliament in February. Union Day was 1 May.

This unexpected dénouement was naturally attributed to bribery. It would be unrealistic to suppose that money did not change hands in quite large quantities, as well as favours; it would have been incredible if they had not, and in the case of nobles like Argyll and Queensberry little attempt was made to disguise the fact. But what swayed majority opinion was the favourable terms obtained. Trade with England and the colonies was thrown open to the Scots, and their land-tax commitment was fixed at a generous one-fortieth; a tactful way was also found of compensating the shareholders in the Darien Company. The Scots legal system and code of law were specially protected, and so was the Presbyterian Church, by a separate statute. (Another statute protected the Church of England from an even less likely Presbyterian 'takeover'.) The allotment of forty-five Members of Parliament, elected on the old and almost unbelievably corrupt Scots representative system, and sixteen Scots peers elected for each parliament by the general body of the nobility, may seem niggardly to us, but not to contemporaries. In October, the existing English parliament reassembled with the addition of these Scots representatives, and was declared the first parliament of Great Britain.

The effect of this long-drawn-out crisis was to increase Godolphin's reliance on the Junto peers; it was they who defended him in the Lords for allowing the Act of Security to pass, it was they who framed the Aliens Act, and it was they who dominated the Commission for the Union Treaty

– and not just Somers, Wharton, Halifax and Sunderland, but their allies Archbishop Tenison and Lord Chief Justice Holt. But the Queen, with the support of Harley, firmly resisted the idea that political services automatically guaranteed political office; she cordially hated the Junto, collectively and individually, an emotion it is not easy to explain. True, the moderate Whig, William Cowper, replaced the ineffective Sir Nathan Wright as Lord Keeper in December 1705, but Anne refused to make him Lord Chancellor until 1707. However, there were other signs of the times; in October 1705, Godolphin put the whips on to elect the Junto candidate John ('Honest Jack') Smith as Speaker, against the Tory William Bromley, and several placemen were dismisssed for disobedience, notably Prince George's secretary at the Admiralty, George Clarke. In 1706, with the Union Treaty signed and a year of victories looming, the Junto served notice that unless one of their number were given cabinet office their support would be withdrawn. They chose Sunderland, and after a tense struggle he was appointed Secretary of State in December 1706.

It was a grievous error. Sunderland was designated because he had married Marlborough's favourite daughter Anne, and because he had only been associated with the Junto since 1702, when he succeeded to his father's earldom. (Born in 1674, he was in fact a clear twenty years younger than Somers or Wharton.) 'Driving the nail that would go', Wharton called it in a famous phrase. But the Junto overlooked Sunderland's abrasive temperament, his quarrelsome nature, his indifference to formal proprieties, especially important when dealing with the Queen; in fact, he probably had a contempt for women in general. Even Marlborough found him intolerable. His sins were visited on his associates, and from his entry to the ministry we can date the beginning of an estrangement between those two life-long friends, Sarah, Duchess of Marlborough, and Queen Anne, which was to have vital political implications.

Harley was prepared to support Anne against Sunderland and the rest of the Junto, for he was coming to the conclusion that the war had gone on too long. The campaigning season of 1707 only confirmed him in this view. It began in April with the resounding defeat of Galway's army by Berwick at Almanza, the subject of an outraged parliamentary inquiry the following winter. France and Britain continued to pour troops into the Peninsula, but the campaign was lost. An Anglo-Austrian attempt to open up a 'second front' at Toulon in September was beaten off. The outline of allied gains and French losses was hardening out.

That summer, Abigail Masham displaced Sarah Marlborough in the Queen's affections, and the relationship between Anne and Sarah henceforward steadily deteriorated to the accompaniment of lasting bitterness. Mrs Masham was related to Harley, but whether he needed her help, except as a fetcher and carrier of messages, is to be doubted. His political views coincided with the Queen's, and they had established a relationship of mutual confidence and trust which was not to be shaken until the very last months of her life. In the autumn of 1707 he began to assemble a group of moderate Whigs – the Dukes of Newcastle, Devonshire and Somerset, Henry Boyle, John Smith, even the young Robert Walpole – who were prepared to abandon the Junto and join with moderate Tories like William Bromley, Henry St John and Simon Harcourt, who were equally disillusioned with the extremism of Rochester and Nottingham. Together they could offer a new, bipartisan basis of parliamentary support for the

Godolphin–Marlborough government; or, as it would then be, the Harley–Godolphin–Marlborough government.

All these tensions – over the war, parties and personalities – found a focus in the Bishoprics Crisis of 1707. Needless to say, bishops were important political functionaries, if only because of their vote in the House of Lords, and appointments were anxiously scrutinized. In this respect, Anne had formerly taken the advice of Sharp and sometimes Nottingham, but Sharp's revulsion from the High Church party, coupled with pressure from the Junto, had led to two markedly Whig appointments, at Lincoln in 1705 (William Wake) and Llandaff in 1706 (John Tyler). The Junto were eager for more, but Anne was uneasy, and Harley, in cynical alliance with the High Church spokesman Francis Atterbury, constituted a 'third force'.

In November 1706, Anne suddenly resumed the initiative, and appointed Jonathan Trelawney, the Tory bishop of Exeter, to Winchester. Godolphin and the Junto grudgingly agreed, but claimed a say in the disposition of Exeter, and also Chester, which had now fallen vacant. In April 1707, however, it became known that Anne had promised these sees to two other Tory churchmen, William Dawes and Offspring Blackall. She could not be budged, but she dare not actually fill the sees (Exeter, in fact, stood vacant from November 1706 until January 1708), and the Junto, with their usual aggressive self-confidence, demanded a recantation; they also wanted Norwich, which fell vacant in June. Blaming Harley, perhaps unfairly, for Anne's intransigence, and aware of his secret negotiations for a 'third party', they decided to remove him. In November 1707 they tried to coerce the Queen by launching a parliamentary inquiry into the conduct of the Admiralty, which meant Prince George and Marlborough's brother, George Churchill.

But the move failed. Privateering losses, the main bone of contention, had in fact declined from their high point in 1704, and though the Junto were allied with the Tory peers for the occasion, this was a cynical arrangement which could not be sustained for long. They were also embarrassed by an inquiry into the affairs of Spain. Somers pushed through a resolution refusing to make peace until the Bourbons had been removed from the Spanish throne, but it was not apparent how this could be done; Marlborough resisted the transfer of experienced troops from Flanders, the Dutch refused point-blank, and the Emperor would not release his best general, Eugene. By the new year, the Whig assault had been beaten off, and the Bishoprics Crisis was speedily wound up. The Junto had to be content with the bishopric of Norwich for Charles Trimnell (another count against Sunderland, whose protégé and former tutor he was). Anne had learned that the Whigs could be just as obstructive as the Tories in ecclesiastical affairs.

With a general election pending in the spring of 1708, the time was ripe for Harley's government of moderates. Anne was now understandably bullish, and increasingly disillusioned with Godolphin, whose doubts, tantrums and pathological suspicions, increasing from 1705 onwards, bespoke a deterioration in his character under the strain of war and politics. He had never been a bold man. He could not cooperate in the new order, so he must go; Anne dismissed him early in February. Unfortunately, they could not detach him from Marlborough, who also resigned. And it then appeared that, apart from Newcastle, none of the peers and commoners who would have supported a Marlborough–Godolphin–Harley government, or even, at a pinch, a Marlborough–Harley government, would follow Harley *tout seul*, especially since

315

Marlborough's only obvious replacement as Captain-General was the Duke of Ormonde, High Tory and crypto-Jacobite. Harley's reputation was also lowered by the discovery that one of his clerks, William Gregg, had been selling secrets to France, which at its best was a serious reflection on the secretary's security precautions. Within a week he was forced to resign, Godolphin and Marlborough came back, and the Lord Treasurer, more firmly committed to the Junto than ever, promptly dismissed those of Harley's supporters with junior offices in the government, notably St John and Harcourt. Walpole, henceforward a committed Junto man, replaced St John as Secretary at War.

This was the most notable political defeat sustained by the crown since the Revolution; indeed, it can only be compared with the much-discussed coercion of George II by the Pelhams in 1744 and 1746. Anne had made her views on her choice of ministers unequivocally clear, and they had been thrown back in her face. Moreover, having failed to get the ministry she wanted, she then failed to get the parliament she wanted, though for this she had her half-brother to blame. The Pretender, with 6,000 French troops, set out to invade Scotland in March 1708. Harassed by the navy, plagued by contradictory advice, and finally deterred by violent storms, he never landed, but he did expose a sorry state of military preparedness in Scotland, and some disaffection. It was also noticed that a group of Tory financiers chose this moment to organize a run on the Bank of England. The result was a resounding victory for the Whigs in the elections which followed in May, though exact figures are difficult to establish; according to Sunderland, their representation in the Commons increased by seventy, giving them a clear majority over the Tories.

But the Whigs were never able to capitalize on this success. Anne remained in a smouldering state of rebellion, thoroughly disillusioned now with both parties, and especially, as is the way, with the stronger of the two. Far from acceding to Junto pressure for cabinet office, she demanded Sunderland's resignation in June, and the struggle went on all summer. She was secretly in touch with Harley, and the Duke of Shrewsbury was another sinister figure on the sidelines. Returning from Italy in 1706, he had found himself rejected by his old associates in the Junto; this and personal inclination drove him into a middle position, and his wealth, his experience, his social status, his impeccable Revolution record and his moderate stance on religion made him potentially the ideal head of a 'national' government.

As for the war, victories were now in short supply. The capture of Minorca in September 1708 was not sufficient to divert attention from a general allied retreat on the Spanish mainland. In Flanders, Marlborough was for once outmanoeuvred by Vendôme, who slipped round his flank and occupied Ghent and Bruges in his rear; only his over-confidence allowed Marlborough, and the Austrians under Eugene, to encircle and defeat him at Oudenarde in July. But the defeated French fled north instead of south, and with their rear threatened the allied generals would not invade France. Instead, Marlborough settled down to a five-month siege of Lille, ending in December, which inflicted five times the casualties of Oudenarde, the British losing one third of their strength. Ghent and Bruges did not capitulate until January 1709. But Marlborough was probably glad to be out of England, where the summer and autumn were taken up with a bitter struggle to force more Whig ministers on the Queen. It ended only with the death of her husband, Prince George, on 28 October, which not only left her incapable of further resistance but opened up a game of ministerial musical chairs. The Earl of Pembroke succeeded the Prince as Lord High Admiral, freeing his two offices of Lord President of the Council and Lord Lieutenant of Ireland for Somers and Wharton respectively.

This was the high point of Whiggism in the reign, but it was emphatically a pyrrhic victory. The Queen was soon won over by Somers's charm and address, she was happy with Cowper, and the unacceptable Wharton was safely in Dublin. But Sunderland remained a constant source of friction, and her sleeping resentment was roused by the fierce struggle which now developed to displace Pembroke as Lord Admiral in favour of Orford. The Junto got their way in November 1709, but it was another pyrrhic victory, and a short-lived one. Anne's sense of maternal responsibility for the well-being of the nation was roused by the evident war-weariness of the people, especially during the exceptionally hard winter of 1708–9. The Great Frost of January 1709, followed by heavy rain into the summer, wrecked the harvest and doubled the price of bread; the land tax still stood at 4s. in the pound, the excise was still rising yearly, the depredations of French privateers on English commerce continued. Though Parliament cheerfully added 10,000 men to the British contingent in Flanders, it was not so easy to recruit them. The Recruiting Act of 1704, permitting the conscription of the unemployed, was unpopular enough, and now ineffective. In January 1709 Walpole tried to put through a Bill for selective general conscription, but even a Whig House of Commons would not stomach that; on the contrary, it demanded, and got, a reduction in the land tax on parishes providing recruits. There was a rash of minor mutinies. The purposelessness of the war was numbing; Spain was effectively lost, and in Flanders Marlborough seemed more intent on a war of attrition than the invasion of France. In fact it is doubtful if Marlborough the diplomat, as distinct from Marlborough the general, wanted to reach Paris and inflict so decisive a defeat on France that it must unbalance the whole state system of Europe. In the autumn of 1708 he had even opened secret negotiations with his nephew Berwick, though they came to nothing. Marlborough's growing unpopularity as a symbol of the Moloch war was a far from negligible factor in the general political situation, and the splendid gifts heaped on him after Blenheim by Queen and Parliament now only added to the public frustration.

Tentative negotiations with France in May 1709 revealed that, though Louis XIV was now willing to withdraw from Spain, he could not guarantee the abdication of Philip V. Marlborough and Eugene took the field late, in June, and found themselves facing 'The Last Army of France', hastily thrown together and placed under the command of Villars, much the best French general surviving. Again the allied commanders resisted any temptation to invade France; instead, they sat down for three months to besiege Tournai, for the loss of 5,000 lives, then Mons. The battle of Malplaquet in September was in fact provoked by Villars, and though technically a victory for Marlborough, and not by any means his least brilliant, it must count as a disaster. It was the costliest battle of the whole war, with allied casualties of 16,000 to 18,000 as against 11,000 French. Moreover, Villars withdrew in good order and still barred the way to France. The British losses were in fact light (600 killed and 1,300 wounded, out of a contingent of 14,000), but the battle was reviled in London as a pointless bloodbath, the more pointless because in Spain the allies were everywhere on the retreat, and Charles III was now penned up in Catalonia. Marlborough chose this impolitic moment to request from the Queen confirmation of the captain-generalship for life, which was, of course, refused. The popular cry went up, 'A General for life, and our lives for the General.' The Dutch were even more war-weary than the British, and when Townshend went to The Hague in December 1709 to wind up the long-drawn-out negotiations for a Barrier Treaty, he had to make concessions which were deeply unpopular in London: the Dutch were to share the South American trade with Britain, and to compensate him for the Dutch barrier towns in the Netherlands Charles III was to have Minorca. Marlborough refused to sign.

How long this farce would have continued we cannot say, but it is difficult to imagine that the Whigs could have held on to their parliamentary majority in the elections due in 1711. However, their fall was accelerated by an unexpected domestic crisis.

# THE TORY PEACE, 1710–14

The passions of the High Churchmen had only been excited further by their loss of royal favour in 1704 and 1705. This was an era of the most violent party polemic, in the press and from the pulpit, and none was more violent than Henry Sacheverell, whose *Political Union* in 1702 had set the tone for High Toryism from the beginning. Since then, the debate had increasingly focused on the nature of the Queen's title and the moral validity of the Revolution. Was Anne's title purely hereditary, as the Tories insisted, or was it, as the Whigs argued, dependent on the Bill of Rights and the Act of Settlement? This had important implications for the succession; experience of William III had underlined the danger of a 'Noncomformist' ruler with strong European commitments, and hostility to the Dissenters was steadily increasing, despite regular public affirmations by the Queen of her support for the Toleration Act. The Hanoverians, of course, were Lutheran, and James III, though still a Catholic, was in many ways a more attractive candidate, especially now that his father's aggressive Romanism was fading into past history. He was at the moment tied to Louis XIV's apron-strings, but the peace, when it came, might well bring with it a *rapprochement* between England and France, as in 1698 and 1699. The issue was muddied by the fact that several Whig publicists, glorying in the legal authority conferred on Anne and the Hanoverians by Parliament, now admitted that the Pretender was no doubt legitimate enough.

As for the Revolution, this was a moribund issue revived by High Church preaching. Once William was dead, the High Churchmen abandoned the principle of *de facto* kingship, and did not hesitate to preach the formerly discredited doctrine of absolute non-resistance to constituted authority. The fiction of James II's abdication enabled them to combine this with technical acceptance of the Revolution; on the other hand, the doctrine of strict legitimate succession could only lead them in the end to support the Pretender. The Whigs argued with vigour that the Revolution had in fact involved resistance to constituted authority, and that in the circumstances of 1688 this was its peculiar virtue. Their chief clerical champion, Benjamin Hoadly, turned Scripture on its head (or so it seemed) to justify Whig dogma out of the mouth of St Paul, and this involved him in 1708 and 1709 in a furious pamphlet and pulpit battle, first with Atterbury, and then with the Queen's favourite bishop, Blackall of Exeter. This public debate reached a climax on 5 November 1709, when Henry Sacheverell was invited to preach, at St Paul's, the anniversary sermon commemorating William III's landing at Torbay twenty-one years before. Sacheverell now argued that the Prince's actions, or those of his supporters, had not constituted an act of resistance, and those who said they did were blackening his memory. He also repeated, with the utmost violence, the common accusation, which had caused such offence to Anne in the past, that the government was countenancing and even encouraging a fifth column of Dissenters within the Church and the administration.

No preacher, Whig or Tory, had yet been prosecuted, however inflammatory his utterances, but Godolphin now

THE TORY PEACE, 1710-14

acceded to the Junto's demand for Sacheverell's impeachment. The sermon, published under the title 'The Perils
of False Brethren', had attracted enormous publicity, and
Whig Members of Parliament, as well as ministers, saw this
as a challenge which could not be ignored, as well as an
opportunity to reaffirm their political philosophy in the
most solemn and public manner. Given their existing
majority in both Houses, an acquittal was unthinkable,
and they even agreed that the trial be held in Westminster
Hall, not in the Lords' House itself, where accommodation
for the public was scanty.

From the beginning the affair got quite out of hand. The
long delay in bringing on the trial, from early December
1709 till late February 1710, allowed public feeling to
build up, particularly in London, to a degree which had
not been seen since the early days of the Popish Plot in
1678, if then. Sacheverell himself was a popular hero: not
only a martyr for the true Church of England, but a
symbol of the nation's war-weariness. In the middle of the
trial, on the night of 1–2 March, London was swept by
savage rioting, and the mobs, bellowing 'Sacheverell and
Peace!', destroyed the principal meeting-houses and for a
brief time threatened the Bank of England. As for the trial
itself, Sacheverell was duly convicted, but only by the
shamingly low majority of 69 to 52, and his sentence was
derisory: the offending sermon was suppressed, and he was
forbidden to preach another for three years. Moreover, by
their emphasis on resistance in the Revolution, the Whigs
now laid themselves open to the accusation that they were
championing direct intervention in politics by the common people; indeed, they were directly blamed for the
Sacheverell Riots. On the other hand, Sacheverell's
counsel, led by Simon Harcourt, argued that his doctrine
of non-resistance implied non-resistance to a sovereign

parliament, not to the monarch, and though no one seriously believed him, it was a construction difficult to disprove. One long-term result of the trial was that the next generation of Whig leaders, represented among the Commons managers by James Stanhope and Robert Walpole, learned by bitter experience the danger of meddling with church matters or ventilating political theory. It was also questionable how long the Whigs could continue to protect the Dissenters.

In the aftermath of the trial, the Queen was more anxious than ever to be rid of the Whigs, and she was now more confident than before that it could be done. Marlborough's resignation was no longer a potential blackmail weapon, as in 1708, for she wanted an end to the war anyway. An unpleasant confrontation with the duke over army commissions in January 1710, and one which would clearly not have arisen had she been a man, further enraged her. Her relations with the duchess were now poisonous, and her bitterness spilled over on Godolphin. But she was rightly cautious, and so was Harley; she could not afford a repetition of her defeat in 1708. On 4 April she dismissed the duchess from her post of Groom of the Stole, and a week later she appointed Shrewsbury Lord Chamberlain.

There was still a tenuous convention that court appointments like these were the monarch's private concern; Sarah had few friends, and Shrewsbury had no public affiliations with the Tories. Serious peace talks were proceeding with the French at Gertruydenberg, and the Whigs waited. The crunch came in June, with the abrupt dismissal of Sunderland. But the earl, like Sarah, had few friends; he was replaced by Lord Dartmouth, a very moderate pro-Hanoverian Tory, and Wharton, the Junto's chief tactician, was in Dublin. They hung on, and were lost. They even hung on when Godolphin was dismissed in August, believing that the Whig financiers of the City could force his reinstatement by withholding credit.

The government's hand was forced, but in another way. All the evidence suggests that Anne and Harley wanted to form a moderate bipartisan ministry, as planned in 1708, with Shrewsbury as a figurehead, and retain this parliament until it legally expired in 1711. But the strength of public feeling against the war, the Whigs and Marlborough was too strong for them. On the war front, a conclusive victory seemed as far off as ever. The negotiations at Gertruydenberg broke down on the allies' insane demand that Louis XIV use the French army to remove his grandson from the throne of Spain. The temporary withdrawal of Berwick and the French from the Peninsula did enable Stanhope and Charles III to invade Aragon, win a couple of cheap victories at Almenara (July 1710) and Saragossa (August) and occupy Madrid. But Marlborough, dreading another Malplaquet, spent the summer marching and counter-marching across the Flanders plain, unwilling to attempt the new *Ne Plus Ultra* lines which blocked the road to Paris. The return of a French army to Spain in the autumn restored reality; in December, Stanhope was surrounded and captured at Brihuega, with 4,000 of his troops.

In September, the Queen bowed to Tory pressure and dissolved Parliament. Lord Chancellor Cowper, the Whig she most wanted to keep, at once resigned, and the others – Somers, Wharton, the Duke of Devonshire, Henry Boyle and Robert Walpole – followed as the election results began to come in, revealing one of the biggest swings since the Revolution, with at least 300 Tories as against 150 Whigs. The ministry which resulted was far from the

325

moderate, bipartisan administration Harley had envisaged. Of the leading Whigs, only the Duke of Newcastle
stayed on, as Lord Privy Seal, and he died in 1711. Shrewsbury proved a broken reed, and after two years' indecision
retired to Dublin as Lord Lieutenant. Devonshire's Lord
Stewardship had to go to the unbalanced and eccentric
ultra-Tory John Sheffield, Duke of Buckingham ('John of
Bucks'). Most serious of all, Harley was forced to give the
Secretaryship of State vacated by Henry Boyle to Henry St
John, who already showed a disposition to run with the
Commons right wing. In October 1710, the Commons
ultras organized themselves as the October Club, pledged
to a quick peace and damn the allies, the humiliation of
the monied interests and (it was plausibly rumoured) the
succession of the Pretender. The first fruits of their labours
was an Act of 1711, supported by St John, which imposed
a landed property qualification on Members of Parliament of £600 for county members and £300 for others. (It
was to prove ineffective in practice, but this was not evident at the time.) But the attempt of a French spy, Guis-
card, to assassinate Harley in March 1711 enhanced his
prestige, and led Anne to appoint him Lord Treasurer with
the title of Earl of Oxford.

His first business was peace; the government's mandate
from the electorate was overwhelming, and the Queen
was committed, too. But the Emperor was reluctant to dis-
engage, and by the Barrier Treaty of 1709 the previous
government had exchanged binding agreements with the
Dutch not to make a separate peace. It could be argued
that the allies deserved no consideration; that the meanness
and caution of the Dutch had sabotaged Marlborough's
campaigns in Flanders, and that the Austrians, whose first
target was Italy, had never thrown their full weight into
the Peninsula. This was the burden of Jonathan Swift's

argument in *The Conduct of the Allies*, in 1711, and it proved one of the most influential pamphlets of the century. All the same, if Britain initiated peace negotiations unilaterally she would be laying herself open to charges of bad faith which it would be difficult to counter. The Puritan Lord Oxford, who not only wanted to do right but wanted to be seen to do right, put most of the public responsibility on the more elastic Henry St John.

The insurmountable obstacle was the Elector George of Hanover, the future George I: a close ally of the Emperor, a professional soldier, and a profound admirer of the Duke of Marlborough. He, Marlborough and the Whigs wanted the war to continue beyond Queen Anne's death, so that the Pretender's claims would go by default as an ally of the national enemy; therefore any peace would be Jacobite by implication. The circumstances of the peace itself, as they developed, also made it profoundly anti-Imperial, and therefore anti-Hanoverian. Thus the logic of events drove Oxford and St John inexorably into the Pretender's camp, in which their enemies' propaganda had already placed them from the beginning. To what degree they flirted with the idea of a Jacobite Restoration, and how far Anne wavered in her loyalty to the Protestant Succession, are questions still debatable. The Whigs always professed to believe that the new government was Jacobite; by the winter of 1713-14, there is every sign that they actually did believe it. There was corresponding optimism amongst the Jacobites, and semi-treasonable chatter from ultras like Sacheverell. But James's conversion to Protestantism, or at least his undertaking to consider it, was a *sine qua non*, and this was never forthcoming.

As it was, Harley and Shrewsbury initiated top-secret talks with Louis XIV's foreign minister Torcy in the autumn of 1710 through the Earl of Jersey. From these

emerged the 'Preliminaries' of April 1711, a simple outline structure for further discussion: Philip V was to keep
Spain, the Emperor and Charles III being compensated
in Italy; the Dutch were to have a Barrier, but not the
entrée to the South American trade promised them in
1709 – this was to be reserved for Britain. Shrewsbury
insisted that these terms be made public, and there was a
predictable storm of protest from Vienna, The Hague
and Hanover. But that same month the sudden death of
the Emperor Joseph I made the Spanish issue more meaningless than ever. The titular king Charles III now succeeded his brother as Holy Roman Emperor, and if
Britain went on fighting to keep the crowns of Spain and
France apart in a future contingency which might not
arise, she would only succeed in uniting the thrones of
Madrid and Vienna immediately. St John now took over
the negotiations, though he continued to be closely supervised by Oxford. (If posterity has awarded most of the
responsibility for what followed to St John, it is because
Oxford stayed on in 1714 to face impeachment, and was
able to amend the evidence accordingly.) The basic
assumption was that if the allies would not cooperate,
England and France would work out a general settlement
to be presented at the peace congress. To back up words
with deeds, St John launched an expedition against
Quebec and unleashed Marlborough for his last campaign.
The Quebec expedition failed, but in a virtuoso exhibition
of his mature genius Marlborough forced the *Ne Plus Ultra*
lines without a single casualty and took the fortress of
Bouchain, all without the aid of the Austrians, who had
withdrawn into Germany to safeguard Charles VI's
election.

The result was the 'Preliminary Articles' of September
1711. Britain was guaranteed 'most favoured nation'

treatment in trade with Spain, and sole right to the slave trade between Africa and South America (the 'Asiento'), which would provide the financial underpinning for Oxford's newly founded South Sea Company. Gibraltar and Minorca would tie up the Mediterranean trade; Newfoundland and Hudson's Bay, the cod fisheries and the fur trade. The French privateering base at Dunkirk was to be destroyed. A supplementary paper guaranteed the English Succession, the perpetual separation of the thrones of Spain and France, and the Dutch Barrier; but, on the whole, the Dutch, in Trevelyan's phrase, were left 'to jostle with the Austrians for such broken meats as they could find under the conference table'. It was a peace neatly calculated to appeal to the xenophobia of the Tory squires and the greed of the Whig merchants.

The Whig politicians were enraged. The Junto bid for the alliance of the Earl of Nottingham by agreeing to pass a modified Occasional Conformity Act in November 1711, thus betraying the expediency of their moral and religious principles, and Nottingham's motion of 'No Peace without Spain' passed the Lords on 7 December 1711 by 62 votes to 54. Politics now descended to a new degree of bitterness; charges of peculation were brought against Marlborough, and Walpole, as Secretary at War. Marlborough was dismissed the captain-generalship and soon afterwards went abroad; Walpole was expelled the House of Commons and sent to the Tower. On 1 January 1712, on Oxford's advice, the Queen took the controversial step of creating twelve new Tory peers *en bloc*, thus destroying the Junto's slender majority in the Lords.

The Congress which opened at Utrecht three weeks later was managed by Oxford, St John and Torcy. England's main aim was to wring from Louis XIV a guarantee regarding the thrones of France and Spain; it was made the more necessary by a measles epidemic which ravaged the French royal family in February, removing Louis's grandson and heir, the Duke of Burgundy (the Dauphin had died of smallpox in 1711), and Burgundy's elder son. If Burgundy's younger son, the future Louis XV, died – and he was a sickly babe-in-arms – then the succession would pass back to his uncle, Philip V of Spain. Oxford suggested an exchange of titles and territories between Philip and the Duke of Savoy, Philip being allowed to carry his new dukedom with him if he became King of France. Louis XIV liked the idea, but Philip did not, and Oxford had to accept Louis's simple guarantee for what it was worth. Meanwhile he and St John brought the allies to heel by their famous Restraining Orders to the Duke of Ormonde, Marlborough's successor as commander of the British contingent in Flanders (12 May 1712). The British did not march, and Villars inflicted a heavy defeat on Prince Eugene's German-Dutch army at Denain in July; it was unfortunate for the English ministers that the Elector of Hanover fought alongside Eugene on that day and was nearly killed.

These sorry manoeuvres apart, Britain drove a hard bargain, and the allies, with the exception of Charles VI, grudgingly came in to sign the various treaties of Utrecht in March and April 1713. The Emperor fought on for another year, forcing Louis XIV to further concessions on the Rhine frontier, but his principal gains, the southern Netherlands, Naples and Sardinia, were already awarded him at Utrecht. (He exchanged Sardinia for Sicily with the Duke of Savoy in 1720.) Savoy and Prussia, Britain's favourite allies at this stage, were handsomely compensated; France's most faithful ally, Bavaria, was proportionately disappointed. Britain's projected advantages were wittled down, with serious implications for the South

Sea Company and future relations with Spain, but the rest of her demands were met. The Dutch Barrier, in what were now the Austrian Netherlands, was inferior to that promised in 1709, but superior to that awarded in 1697. (In any case, the military effectiveness of any such barrier was doubtful, and this one failed its first test, in 1745.) It was a good peace for Britain, received with joy and relief by the public; if it was not so good for her allies, this reflected her disproportionate contribution to the war effort, in men, ships and money. The Emperor, who was still the cornerstone of British foreign policy, was the ally with the least real cause for discontent, and in any case his demands, and those of his brother and his father, had always been greedy and unrealistic. Though the Whigs fulminated against the Peace, they did not even try to amend it when they came to power in 1714.

It was St John's peace. Though Oxford had retained overall control of the negotiations, and the Queen's own share should not be underestimated, the Secretary had borne the main burden of the long negotiations. His request for an earldom in July 1712 was far from being impertinent, and he had reason to feel aggrieved when he was given a viscountcy (Bolingbroke) instead. In October, he was again passed over when Anne created twelve new Knights of the Garter, including Oxford.

The reasons are still not clear. Almost certainly Anne disapproved of Bolingbroke's maltreatment of his wife and his general profligacy, yet in the summer of 1712 he seemed as high in her regard as anybody, including Oxford. Oxford may have sabotaged him, as Bolingbroke thought, but it is difficult to see why; the practical difference between the two titles was negligible. It is more likely that Oxford was worried by the festering scandal which clung around Bolingbroke regarding the contracts for the Quebec expedition in 1711, and Anne herself may have considered that his estate was, in any case, insufficient to support an earldom. But whatever the reasons, relations between Oxford and Bolingbroke, which had been a trifle strained since 1710, when he had very obviously been Oxford's second choice as Secretary of State, entered on a precipitate decline. In August 1712, at the height of the final peace negotiations, Oxford haled him before the Queen, accused him of exceeding his instructions, and temporarily displaced him at Utrecht by Dartmouth, technically the senior Secretary of State. He even insisted on censoring Bolingbroke's dispatches abroad, and corrected his prose.

The final signing of the peace, in March and April 1713, was a fillip to Bolingbroke, but in June he suffered a humiliating defeat when he brought before the Commons his crowning achievement: a new commercial treaty with France designed to lower the tariff barriers erected between the two countries since 1670. The Tories split, and the treaty was defeated 194 to 185. This was the first overt appearance of the 'Whimsicals', a group of Tory members led by Sir Thomas Hanmer, who were suspicious of Bolingbroke and the October Club and pledged to defend the Hanover Succession. With a new election due, Oxford shuffled the ministry in order to strengthen his position, and contemporary rumours that he was being overmastered by Bolingbroke can be discounted. In the elections, held in August and September 1713, the Tories profited by the Peace, and somewhat unexpectedly increased their existing majority from 151 to 213.

In December 1713 the Queen fell seriously ill, offering the Jacobites a 'dress rehearsal', as it were. It showed them to be seriously unprepared, but the Queen's attitude on her recovery was ambivalent; she was widely suspected of a leaning towards her half-brother, though this has never been proved. What is indisputable is her aversion for the Hanoverians, and the Hanoverians' aversion for her present ministers. So it was natural that, in February 1714, Oxford and Bolingbroke should secretly inform the Pretender that he must announce his conversion to Anglicanism, with the implication that they would support him if he did. The prince refused point-blank, and from then on the ministry was adrift. At this stage Oxford abruptly forfeited much of the Queen's confidence by requesting the dukedom of Newcastle for his eldest son Edward, who had married Henrietta Cavendish-Holles, principal heiress to the last duke, who had died without heirs. (Again, peerage proved a sensitive matter with Anne.) The Treasurer now lapsed into a lethargy so obvious that even his friends suspected it was caused by drink, but Anne shrank from dismissing him, and if she did she would be left with Bolingbroke, who was no more acceptable, apparently, than he ever had been.

Meanwhile the ministers' predicament was apparent to all, and their approaches to the Pretender widely suspected. On 18 March 1714 the Whig journalist Richard Steele was expelled from the Commons for a pamphlet called *The Crisis*, which openly warned that the Protestant Succession was in danger. A motion to this effect in the Lords on 5 April was defeated by only twelve votes, the exact number of Tory peers created to pass the Peace. Ten days later, on a similar motion in the Commons, the government's majority fell to fifty, with the Whimsicals voting with the Whigs or abstaining. The bishops and archbishops, with only two exceptions, were now ranged against the ministry, and the 2nd Duke of Argyll ('John of the Battles'), whose support for the ministry was now withheld, was dismissed all his offices in Scotland. The ministers' conduct appeared in an even more sinister light when the Hanoverian envoy requested a writ of summons to the Lords for the Electoral Prince (the future George II), who had been created Duke of Cambridge; it was issued, but he was warned not to use it. The best Bolingbroke could do at this stage was to try and reunite the Tories by bringing in a Schism Bill to suppress the Dissenting academies, whose competition with the universities had been causing resentment in the Church for many years. In the short term, he was triumphantly successful; many of the bishops rallied, and so did the Tory leaders in Commons and Lords, except for the eccentrically consistent Earl of Nottingham, who had always limited his demands to an Occasional Conformity Act and continued to vote with the Junto.

But in the long term Bolingbroke failed, of course. When Parliament rose on 9 July, the Queen was already sinking. Shrewsbury had returned from Dublin in June, and was now exercising a certain degree of control, almost certainly in conjunction with the Dukes of Argyll and Somerset. On the 27th Anne was at last persuaded to dismiss Oxford, whose present conduct, in fact, left her with little choice. But she made no move to replace him. Bolingbroke could have gambled on a Jacobite Restoration, but to do so would involve defying the Act of Settlement, and it was not clear how far the army would support him, though its commander, Ormonde, had strong Jacobite sympathies; it was something the Whigs professed to fear rather more than was realistic. On the 29th, with Anne clearly dying, Shrewsbury summoned an emergency meeting of the Privy Council, attended by Argyll and Somerset, who were in disgrace, but whose names were still on the council list. It was they who moved that the council advise the Queen to appoint Shrewsbury Lord Treasurer, and therefore *ex officio* chairman of the Regency

Council, and Bolingbroke offered no opposition. The Queen, *in extremis*, handed the white staff to Shrewsbury, and died in the early hours of the following morning, 1 August. The Regency Council at once proclaimed George I king, and his succession, contrary to all expectation, went through with clockwork precision and the minimum of fuss. Letters from Hanover reappointed Marlborough Captain-General and dismissed Bolingbroke from the secretaryship. The new king landed at Greenwich on 30 September.

# ARTISTIC AND LITERARY
## TRENDS, 1603–1714

In terms of poetry and drama, the Stuart century is a period of inevitable decline from the unmatchable genius of Shakespeare, only temporarily arrested by the emergence of Milton. The period opened with Shakespeare at the height of his powers, with some of his greatest plays still to come. It closed on Addison and Congreve, with Colley Cibber the rising star.

Neither Shakespeare nor his immediate successors enjoyed consistent royal patronage, or very. much of it. *Measure for Measure*, acted at Court on Boxing Day, 1604, was written in James I's honour, and so, obviously, was *Macbeth*. *Macbeth*, *Othello* and *The Comedy of Errors*, together with *The Merry Wives of Windsor*, were all staged at Whitehall in the winter of 1604–5, followed by *King Lear* at Christmas 1606. But it is not surprising that James, who was essentially a light-hearted (not to say light-minded) man found Shakespearian tragedy heavy going, and in many respects not conducive to a respect for kingship; as for the comedies, it is doubtful how far a foreigner, even one fluent in English, could follow them. James's tastes inclined him instead towards the masque, an empty pageant of embodied virtues, couched in simple language or even mimed, and devoid of psychological strain, pain or terror. Ben Jonson wrote several masques for the new king, but their literary value is slight. Indeed, only Milton triumphed in this genre, and who would read *Comus* now if the author of *Paradise Lost* had not written it? The main legacy of the Jacobean and Caroline court masques are the beautiful drawings of Inigo Jones, who master-minded the elaborate stage machinery and scenery for these whimsical confections.

And, of course, the drama had its dangers. James was furious at Jonson's *The Devil is an Ass* (1616), which was a biting satire on monopolies. Thomas Middleton's *A Game of Chess* (1624) was an elaborate parody of the international diplomacy of Spain, and was withdrawn after four nights at the request of the Spanish ambassador. Massinger waited for James's death before putting on *A New Way to Pay Old Debts* (1626), in which the convicted monopolist Sir Giles Mompesson was satirized as Sir Giles Overreach.

Under Charles I it was the same, despite his cultural superiority to his father. 'The Queen's Players' continued to enjoy some kind of shadowy patronage from Henrietta Maria, and Charles was much taken with James Shirley's *The Gamester* (1633), though one would have thought its moral tone rather loose for his taste. Shirley wrote a masque for Charles in 1633, *The Triumph of Peace*, but the following year he departed for Dublin, where he obviously found the new Lord Deputy, Wentworth, more generous. Charles preferred the masque, partly because it made more effective propaganda for Divine Right kingship (see p. 118 above), and partly because it allowed him and his courtiers a greater degree of participation. Charles and his wife were both keen dancers, and Charles had been performing in court masques since 1617.

Thus the drama remained popular entertainment, subject to the law of the market, and the changes it underwent must in some sense reflect changes in public taste. Webster and Tourneur pushed the theme of disruption, perver-

337

sion, torment and catastrophe beyond all normal limits (see p. 45 above), and their success must raise questions about the psychological make-up of the audiences who watched them. Their work was continued, though with slightly less extravagance, by Thomas Middleton in the 1620s, particularly in *The Changeling,* and by John Ford. Ford's plays, notably *'Tis Pity She's a Whore, Love's Sacrifice* and *The Broken Heart,* are less violent and blood-boltered, and display a greater psychological subtlety, but their themes still centre on incest, adultery or sexual frustration.

By the 1620s the public clearly wanted lighter, more cheerful entertainment; satiric comedies or light romances. Ben Jonson, in his closing years, tried to meet this need with *Bartholomew Fair* (1614) and *The Staple of News* (1626), but he was outstripped by Francis Beaumont and John Fletcher, a writing team with the enormous output of more than fifty plays between them, mainly lightweight comedies or romances. Little read today, they dominated the Caroline stage, and many of their plays continued to be performed in the next reign. Indeed, comedy was now passing into the satiric, amoral mode usually associated with the Restoration theatre. The trend can be seen as early as 1626, with Massinger's *A New Way to Pay Old Debts,* followed in 1632 by *The City Madam;* it is even more obvious in the comedies of Shirley, notably *The Witty Fair One* (1628) and *The Lady of Pleasure* (1635). It was this moral looseness, and the dramatists' indifference to religion except as an object of derision, which provoked the wrath of William Prynne. Unfortunately, his violent and wordy assault on stage morals, *Historio-Mastix* (1632), contained indirect aspersions on the King and Queen which brought him before Star Chamber the following year. His savage punishment at Laud's hands created a false association in the public mind between the drama and the political and religious establishment, and it is not surprising that on 2 September 1642, as it girded itself for war, the Long Parliament ordered the theatres to close – not to reopen officially until 1660.

Music, on the other hand, was still in embryo. Outside the Church it was very much a matter of domestic entertainment, consisting of dances, catches and songs, with a little instrumental chamber music. It thus attracted a certain amount of 'automatic' royal patronage. William Byrd, organist of the Chapel Royal to Elizabeth and James I, is probably the most celebrated composer of this era; he died in 1623. His successor, Orlando Gibbons, wrote many songs and chamber pieces, particularly for the viols and virginals, as well as anthems and motets. James and Charles I had quite a large, floating establishment of court musicians, particularly for the masques; but songs were slotted into the masque in an episodic way, without any attempt at a unified score.

This tradition continued. The Puritans had no objection to secular music as such. As Lord Protector, Cromwell had his troupe of court musicians, and Sir William Davenant's *Siege of Rhodes* in 1656 was the first attempt at an English opera. Opera became fashionable under Charles II, but it is doubtful how far it was understood or properly practised; as late as 1684, the King was still importing singers and musicians from France. On the other hand, music at last began to move out of the home in 1672, when the first public concerts were held in London.

Henry Purcell, organist of the Chapel Royal from 1682 until his death in 1695, was rediscovered in recent times, but his contemporary fame is difficult to assess. He was very much a maid-of-all-work, composing a wide variety of anthems, songs and odes, apparently to order. Many of his songs in the early 1680s were firmly loyalist and 'Yorkist' in tone, and reflect the political tensions of the time, though like many fringe professionals he survived the Revolution without apparent difficulty. His only true opera, *Dido and Aeneas*, was composed in 1689 for a girls' school in Chelsea; his *Diocletian* (1690) was a musical setting of a Fletcher and Massinger tragedy; and he was doing the same for Sir Robert Howard's *The Indian Queen* when he died. Perhaps his best-known work is the song 'Fairest Isle', from Dryden's *King Arthur* (1691).

Despite Purcell's work for the stage, opera and the more ambitious choral and concert music continued to be regarded as a foreign specialism, and if Purcell was evolving an indigenous school of music, it died with him. The existing French and Italian influence merely surrendered in the eighteenth century to the German. Handel paid his first visit to England in 1706 – to conduct Italian opera.

In poetry, as in drama, the first half of the century was a period of ambiguous achievement. The poets of this era most admired today were tormented men, a prey to strong religious, and one suspects sexual, frustrations. John Donne, a convert from Catholicism who rose to be Dean of St Paul's, is typical; even in his great love poetry, complex and erotic, he never appears in the guise of a happy man. Similarly, Richard Crashaw, whose tortured and introspective contemplation of divine themes led him first to the famous Anglo–Catholic community established by the Ferrars at Little Gidding, then into the Roman Church itself. George Herbert, an Anglican clergyman whose collection of religious poems, *The Temple* (1633), was an unlikely best-seller, wrote verse whose simplicity and directness conceals an inner tension. He deeply influenced Henry Vaughan, 'The Silurist', one of the few genuine mystical poets in the English language, whose best work was published in the 1650s and 1660s.

In contrast, Robert Herrick, another clergyman-poet, found solace in light, melodious, occasionally bawdy rustic verse. John Milton, who had also been educated for the Church, was still writing fluent but rather dull poems like *L'Allegro* and *Il Penseroso* in the fashionable pastoral-bucolic mode. The direct anger, the harsh brevity of a poem like John Cleveland's on the death of Strafford, strikes us like a blow in the face. In a little-known novel, *They Were Defeated* (1932), Rose Macaulay admirably conveys the fragile, divided spirit of these pre-war years. Unfortunately, and perhaps strangely, the Civil Wars produced no great war poetry, unless we except Marvell's famous 'Horatian Ode Upon Cromwell's Return from Ireland'.

Indeed, the greatest advances were being made in the field of English prose. Bacon's *Essays*, published with successive additions in 1597, 1612 and 1625, established a new prose rhythm and a vocabulary divorced from the classical, which was reinforced by his *History of Henry the Seventh* (1622), and by Sir Walter Raleigh's enormously popular *History of the World* (1614). It is a pity that two of the most admired prose writers of the mid century, Milton and Sir Thomas Browne, returned to a clogging, latinate, involuted style.

But the most far-reaching influence, of course, was exerted by the Authorized Version of the Bible, published in 1611. However, it was not alone; the Bible did not suddenly leap into the vernacular in 1611. The early sixteenth-century translations of Tyndale and Coverdale danced to the same majestic music, and so did the Geneva

Bible of 1560. Nor must we forget Cranmer's Book of Common Prayer, which had been setting the highest standards to the largest public since 1549. The most obvious result was the enormous fluency and grace with which ordinary men spoke and wrote in this century; and, on the whole, the less formal education they had had, the less contact with classical learning, the more capable they were. This is evident most notably in the speeches of many of the Levellers in the famous Putney Debates in 1647, as well as in John Bunyan.

But if literature was in something of a doldrums, art was in a much worse state. Artists were simply imported, mainly from the Low Countries, beginning with Mytens and Van Somer, and continuing under Charles I with Hendrick Gerritz Pot, Van Dyck and Rubens. Even the great topographical artists – Wenceslaus Hollar, whose etchings of Charles I's London are famous, and Leonard Knyff, who later drew his exact perspective views of the mansions of the great Whig noblemen – were born in Prague and Haarlem respectively. As Rubens painted the Whitehall ceilings for Charles I (see p. 118 above), so Verrio painted the ceilings and friezes at Windsor for Charles II, whose court painter was the Fleming Sir Peter Lely. Lely's successor was the German Sir Godfrey Kneller. Kneller and Lely settled in England for life, as did Anthony Verrio, though as a Catholic he had to be specially exempted from the penal laws in 1678 and 1679. He loyally declined to work for William III, but he had no scruple about accepting commissions from great Whig noblemen like the Duke of Devonshire (at Chatsworth) or the Marquess of Exeter (at Burghley), and it was Exeter who induced him to re-enter the service of the monarchy under Queen Anne. He died in 1707 in a grace-and-favour residence at Hampton Court. Not until the very end of the period does a native Englishman break through, in the person of Sir James Thornhill, who executed a series of important mural and ceiling paintings at Hampton Court, Kensington and Greenwich, and then possibly only because Verrio was not available. It is noticeable that Charles I was only once painted full length by an Englishman; by Edward Bower at his trial, when he had no say in the matter. He commissioned busts of himself from Bernini and Dieussart (another Fleming), and Charles II patronized the Frenchman Honoré Pellé.

Was this a failure in patronage? It may be so. It was clearly fashionable to employ foreigners, even foreigners who were not outstanding, like Lely and Kneller. On the other hand, royal patronage was always extended to the miniaturists, in whom England excelled. The greatest of them, Samuel Cooper, worked for Charles I, Cromwell and Charles II in turn. After the Restoration, there are even signs of artistic chauvinism, and Robert Streeter, who executed the *trompe l'oeil* paintings for the ceiling of Wren's Sheldonian theatre at Oxford, was complimented in a remarkable couplet:

> Future ages must confess they owe
> To STREETER more than Michel Angelo.

Yet the foreign invasion continued.

What was lacking, apparently, was the large-scale, bread-and-butter patronage from the upper and middle classes which would have allowed studios to be set up and painters trained at the hands of a master. The very narrow circle of patrons, confined to the royal family, plus a minority of noblemen who were themselves a minority of the upper classes, left no margin for failure. Men had to

343

be fully accomplished to succeed, and they could only acquire this accomplishment on the Continent.

The same trend is evident in architecture, though not to the same degree. James I's Surveyor-General, Inigo Jones, had been to Italy (an unusual feat in those embattled times), and had returned brimful of ideas. The result was the Queen's House at Greenwich, still incomparably the best three-bedroomed house in England, and the great Banqueting House at Whitehall, which he built for King James in 1619–22 as a proper setting for royal ceremonial and the reception of ambassadors. The failing fortunes of the Stuart monarchy meant that this building was never the focus for a new Italianate palace complex as Jones intended; and it is ironic that Charles I was executed in 1649 on a scaffold erected outside the first-floor windows. Miraculously, it was the only part of the old, bug-ridden, tumble-down palace of Whitehall which survived the disastrous fire of 1698, and it is still one of the great buildings of London, if not the greatest. But, apart from this, Jones's commissions were few; he almost certainly designed the interior of Wilton House, notably the famous Double Cube Room, but the exterior was by his pupil, John Webb.

In the second half of the century, the story was very different. Jones's disciple, Christopher Wren, established himself at an early stage in the favour of Charles II and of the authorities at Oxford and Cambridge. This gave him a solid patronage base, and the Great Fire of London was a magnificent opportunity. He held the Surveyorship of Works under five successive monarchs, from 1669 to 1718. During that time he rebuilt St Paul's, which took him until 1711, as well as fifty-two other London churches; he built Chelsea Hospital for Charles II and Greenwich Hospital (now the Naval College) for Mary II; he planned a whole new palace for Charles II at Winchester, and he carried out full-scale alterations to Kensington and Hampton Court for William III and Anne; he also left a decisive mark on Oxford and Cambridge, notably with the Sheldonian Theatre and Trinity College Library. As a result he not only set new fashions in the most commanding way, he also established a workshop-studio where he could train masons, carvers and builders. His great wood-carver was Grinling Gibbons, though if Gibbons fulfilled all the commissions attributed to him he must have worked twenty-four hours a day. His professional heir was Nicholas Hawksmoor, his assistant since 1679.

Wren's influence was all-pervading, and his style quickly copied; many of the great houses built in Charles II and James II's reigns have no known architect, except in some cases their owner. However, William Talman established himself as an important provincial architect; his best-known houses are Chatsworth, for the first Duke of Devonshire, and Dyreham Park, Gloucester, for William Blathwayt.

Sociological factors may have been at work, too; after 1660, except for the brief period 1686–8, the aristocracy were more relaxed in their attitude towards the monarchy. The King might still be a nuisance, but he was no longer a menace, and he could even be an ally; there was no longer the same gulf between court and country, and it was no longer dubious to ape royal fashions or follow the royal lead in matters of taste. Moreover, long before Wren's death the aristocracy were venturing out on their own into the more advanced forms of the baroque. Here the key figure is John Vanbrugh, playwright and man-about-town as well as architect, who built Castle Howard, Seaton Delaval and, above all, Blenheim: great crawling, commanding palaces which owed something to the French example but had an ornate monumentality all their own. The era closes with a return to stark classical forms in Hawksmoor's mausoleum at Castle Howard.

As for literature, it is strange that after the Restoration the main burden was carried by Puritans or ex-Puritans. John Milton sacrificed his eyesight in the service of the Republic, and produced a series of violently anti-monarchical tracts in 1649 for which he narrowly escaped retribution in 1660. Yet in his years of blindness and distress he produced the greatest epic poem in the English language, *Paradise Lost* (1669). Andrew Marvell, another ex-Puritan, wrote what is arguably the greatest love lyric in the language ('To His Coy Mistress'), as well as an important corpus of political satire. Hobbes, who was a rebel in another sense, was not only a master of political theory (see p. 188 above), but of English prose.

But perhaps the most commanding, and in retrospect the most influential writer of the century was John Bunyan, the tinker turned hedge-preacher, who spent the first twelve years of Charles II's reign in prison under the Clarendon Code. In him the prose rhythms of the Authorized Version were triumphantly wedded to vernacular speech. The result was *Grace Abounding to the Chief of Sinners* (1666), which has been described as 'the greatest spiritual autobiography since St Augustine's', and the immortal *Pilgrim's Progress*, in 1678. The Church itself did not produce devotional literature of the highest class, though this was a great age of preaching; after *Pilgrim's Progress*, the great religious best-seller of the eighteenth century was *A Serious Call to a Devout and Holy Life* (1729), by the non-juror William Law.

In contrast, all the literary associations of the restored

monarchy were with the new 'Restoration' theatre; up
to 1679, the King and his brother the Duke of York were
the sole patrons of the two theatres which bore their
name. In fact, the new drama was not entirely new (see p.
338 above), and the term 'Restoration' is applied right
up to 1714. At its best, the new drama was a prodigy of
wit and timing, and its dialogue sparkled, but it is in the
second rank of dramatic literature, perhaps even the third.
A sideways glance at Corneille and Racine in France, even
Molière, gives us a more exact assessment. Its themes
made a mockery of accepted moral standards, derided
the institution of marriage, and reduced all human motivation to a desire for sex or money. Worse still, the Restoration saw the advent for the first time of female actresses,
many of whom became the immediate sexual toys of
the King and his leading courtiers. It is not surprising that
the playwrights should be attacked, as they were by Jeremy
Collier, in *A Short View of the Immorality and Profaneness of the
English Stage;* what is strange is that the attack should
come so late, in 1698. (Collier was another non-juror, by
the way.) Collier's criticisms had more effect than contemporaries liked to think; the great days of Congreve
were yet to come, but Collier drove the drama sideways
into a comedy of manners, then into 'sentimental comedy',
and in the transition it lost its way. The attempt to harness
it to political propaganda, beginning with Addison's
*Cato* in 1713, eventually brought down upon it a firm
government censorship under Walpole.

Meanwhile a great deal of good verse was being written; by John Dryden, by John Wilmot, Earl of Rochester,
and then by Prior and Swift. How much of it was poetry is
another matter. Pat Rogers points out that while the preoccupation of the Jacobeans had been a fear lest the world
fall apart, the Augustans feared that its components would

merge, or come together. Therefore the stress was increasingly on regularity, apartness, as well as order. This had a deadening effect, as did Dryden's adoption of the rhyming couplet, and his great satires, *MacFlecknoe, Absalom and Achitophel* and *The Medal*, must be regarded as a triumph of feeling over form. Dryden turned Catholic under James II (a decision he stuck to), and produced a rather laborious poem on the matter, *The Hind and the Panther* (1687), which was bitingly satirized by the young Charles Montague in *The Story of the Country Mouse and the City Mouse*, as well as a poem on the birth of the Prince of Wales in 1688, *Britannia Rediviva*. Some of his best poetry was written in his later years: famous odes to Congreve and Purcell, *Alexander's Feast* (1697) and his charming *Fables Ancient and Modern* (1700).

In prose, the field was led by the witty, elegant George Savile, Marquess of Halifax, who in some sense set himself up as the English La Rochefoucauld. (He is not to be confused with Charles Montague, later Lord Halifax and Earl of Halifax, who was a great patron of the arts under Queen Anne and had modest literary pretensions of his own.) He wrote some of the most polished political propaganda in the language, though he was so anxious to get his jokes across and balance his antitheses that his pamphlets lack bite. He was the first of the great Augustan social moralizers, and it is often forgotten that *Advice to a Daughter* (1688), now the least regarded of his works, was in print throughout the eighteenth century, and was translated into Italian and French. He is now best remembered for his witty and perceptive character sketch of Charles II, not published until 1750. Clarendon, whose *History of the Rebellion and Civil Wars in England* was posthumously published in 1702–4, was a great prose stylist who could not pace his narrative; though each sentence is a jewel, the overall effect is one of intense tedium. And though his *History* is of vital importance as a contemporary record, its effect on the development of historiography was slight; a combination of history and autobiography, it is best compared with the various works of 'history' produced by twentieth-century statesmen like Lloyd George and Winston Churchill. Finally, in the diary of Samuel Pepys the period gave us one of the masterworks of our society and literature, which ensured its author a deeper and more complete immortality than any of his contemporaries.

But, in one sphere of literature, political journalism, England took an early lead, largely owing to the inability of the government to control the press. Censorship by Privy Council and Star Chamber collapsed in 1640, and the Civil Wars and Interregnum spawned an almost incredible number of pamphlets, sermons, broadsides and books on political or religious affairs – over 22,000 items survive in the British Library, and this is not the whole – despite periodic attempts by the Long Parliament, the Commonwealth government and the Lord Protector to stem the flow by legislation, executive order and the use of the courts. The Civil Wars also saw the emergence of several weekly or twice-weekly newspapers, notably the royalist *Mercurius Aulicus* and the parliamentarian *Mercurius Britannicus*. Cromwell suppressed all except his own official *Mercurius Politicus*, and Charles II sustained the tradition of a tame government organ, which after various fluctuations of title emerged in 1665 as the *London Gazette*. Meanwhile censorship was reimposed, with mixed success, by the Licensing Act of 1662; important pamphlets like Moulin's *England's Appeal* (see p. 208 above) got published, however hostile to the government, and in 1679 the Act lapsed, allowing a flood of polemics, and a rush of ephemeral newspapers and journals, during the Exclusion

Crisis. The Act was renewed in 1685 and 1690, but objections to the monopoly it conferred on the Stationers' Company and the university presses (rather than any abstract love of press freedom) caused it to be abandoned for good in 1695.

So there was little to restrain the expression in print of the mounting political and religious partisanship which distinguished the closing years of this century and the first two decades of the next. Political propaganda steadily increased in volume and violence. Nor was the violence merely verbal: Defoe was sentenced to the pillory in 1703 for *The Shortest Way with Dissenters*, John Tutchin was indicted in Queen's Bench for seditious libel in 1704, and was lucky to get off on a technicality. A young Jacobite printer, John Mathews, was not so lucky; he was found guilty of high treason in 1719 and hung, drawn and quartered. Tutchin himself was beaten up more than once in the street, and died of his injuries after the last such attack, in 1707.

Anne's reign saw the emergence of nineteen newspapers of various kinds, though only one daily (*The Daily Courant*, founded in 1702). But in 1702 Tutchin introduced the Whig *Observator*, a twice-weekly journal of a new kind, offering political discussion and comment rather than straight news. Its success led to the appearance in 1704 of Defoe's *Review*, with a strong economic bias and under clandestine government patronage, and the ultra-Tory *Rehearsal*, edited by the non-juror Charles Leslie. In 1711, Jonathan Swift was taken on by Harley to edit the *Examiner*, the most skilful of these political journals. The *Review* and the *Observator* folded soon after the passing of the Stamp Act of 1712, which reintroduced indirect censorship by imposing heavy duties on printed periodicals, but the traditions they established continued down the eighteenth century. Meanwhile the *Tatler*, published by Richard Steele in 1709–11, and the *Spectator*, 1711–13, by Steele and Joseph Addison, were the first examples of a more general kind of periodical, dealing not only with politics but with literature and manners. They were 'magazines', in fact, the precursors of the famous *Gentleman's Magazine* (founded 1731).

The literary standards of these Augustan journalists was not high, though their enormous output, grist to university Ph.D. mills, has earned them a disproportionate amount of attention. But the frenetic conditions of Anne's reign were a forcing-ground for some remarkable literary advances in the next generation: Defoe's *Robinson Crusoe*, for instance, in 1719, and Swift's *Gulliver's Travels*, in 1726. The path to England's future literary greatness was to lie not through drama, or poetry, but through the new form of the novel.

# CONCLUSION

For Britain, the seventeenth century was a period of almost unequalled material progress comparable only with the century of the Industrial Revolution, from 1760 to 1860. From being a poor, peripheral, backward country in 1603 she had now blossomed into one of the wealthiest nations in the world, with an expanding maritime and colonial empire. She had displaced the Netherlands as the chief trading nation, and London was a serious rival to Amsterdam as the banking and credit capital of the world. In two major wars, she had first dragged France to a standstill, then pulled her down. She could never permanently overcome France's inbuilt advantages, a large population and an abundant agricultural base, nor could she expect to overcome the French army in the future without Marlborough's unique genius; this point was rammed home by Maurice de Saxe at Fontenoy in 1745. But her navy was now paramount, and in the Peninsular War she had shown, in the capture of Gibraltar, Barcelona and Minorca, that she had mastered the difficult technical feat of mounting amphibious expeditions. Her agricultural system, much studied and improved, now enabled her to feed all her population all of the time, which could be said of few other European nations. Not until the nineteenth century was she to rival France's cultural ascendency in Europe, but in Hobbes and Boyle, Newton and Locke, and to a less extent Francis Bacon, she had produced scientists and philosophers of world stature. Indeed, Newton's *Principia Mathematica* (1687), followed by the *Opticks* (1704), and Locke's *Essay Concerning Human Understanding* (1690) dominated the thinking of eighteenth-century Europe. So, too, did Locke's treatises *Of Civil Government* (1689), though their immediate influence, on his own generation and the next, has been exaggerated.

In the political or constitutional sphere, however, England's progress was more equivocal, and less easy to assess. If she did set an example to the world of constitutional liberty and good order, this was largely by accident. It is conventional to assume that 1649 and 1688, and even 1660, represent the triumph of parliamentary over monarchical institutions. With the benefit of hindsight this may seem obvious; it was not so at the time, and it is to be doubted if it ever was. The noisy advocacy of those who represent the events of the 1640s as a revolution has battered us into the belief that the events of 1660 and 1688 were a mere epilogue, their eventual outcome preordained. In fact, weak and disorganized as the monarchy often was, Parliament was more so, and at the two crucial turning-points of the century, in 1640 and 1688, the monarchy only succumbed to overwhelming outside intervention, from Scotland and the Netherlands. In 1660 monarchy was triumphantly restored, not on its own initiative, at a time when it was penniless and powerless; and in 1678–81 it withstood a sustained assault from a series of parliaments whose mandate was renewed at three successive general elections.

The Exclusion Crisis, in fact, illustrates Parliament's inability to exert sustained pressure or enforce anything that might be called the popular will, and the settlements of 1660 and 1689 illustrate its unwillingness to face basic problems. They are both a patchwork of compromises,

353

for the most part concerned with peripheral detail. The two key questions of the seventeenth century, the reform of the electoral system and the relations between the executive and parliament, were never settled. Similarly, despite a continual rumble of criticism, the antiquated and eccentric English legal system was allowed to creak on unreformed.

As a result, the monarchy after 1688 proved unexpectedly powerful and independent, while Parliament was its old chaotic, disorganized and ineffectual self. Had Queen Anne been a man, or if she had been a more intelligent and aggressive woman, or if Marlborough had really harboured the megalomaniac dreams his enemies credited him with, then the future might have been very different; for, protestations to the contrary notwithstanding, the regular army after the Revolution steadily increased in size and efficiency, and so much of England's 'liberties' or 'liberty', indeed the whole constitution, depended on the willingness of the monarch and his ministers to observe conventions which were strictly non-enforceable – the Triennial Act is a good example. The advent of party brought with it some hope that here was a means of organizing and controlling Parliament, but long before 1714 the excesses committed in the name of Whig and Tory had disgusted the public, and many hailed the end of the Succession Wars and the death of Anne as signalling a new, more moderate order, which meant essentially a conservative, authoritarian oligarchy, subject after 1716 to a veto only at seven-year intervals.

If we are to find an element of continuity or control, we must seek it in the Lords. In the second half of the century the high prestige and exclusiveness of the English peerage were accentuated by economic factors working to the advantage of the large, as against the small, land-owner, and in favour of the large investor in funds and stocks. Yet, at the same time, the relaxation of central government control over the localities after 1660 increased the stature of the lord lieutenant, and made county society more hierarchical than ever; class feeling which might have operated against the aristocracy was vented on the 'monied interest' instead.

There is a school of thought which sees the House of Lords as the key to the constitutional situation even before 1640; after 1660 there is no doubt of it. In the Long Parliament of Charles II the Lords were the only element of continuity, and during the Exclusion Crisis, of stability. It was the House of Lords which threw down the first challenge to James II, in November 1685, after the Commons had been browbeaten into submission; in 1688 it was a series of individual peers who by their actions (or inaction) defeated him. Under William III and Anne they still claimed a monopoly on national leadership. The growing corruption of the electoral system increased the government's power over the composition of Parliament, and at the same time the peerage's. The system of deficit finance which evolved during the Succession Wars eroded the importance of the Commons' control of taxation, and impeachments, inquiries into the conduct of war and 'state-of-the-nation' debates like the Church in Danger debate of 1705 or the 'No Peace without Spain' debate of 1708, emphasized the fact that the House of Lords was now the forum of the nation. In major crises responsibility tended to be focused much more narrowly, not even on the peerage, but on the dukes; it was the opposition of Somerset and Devonshire, and the coolness of Newcastle, which frustrated the attempt to get rid of Godolphin in 1708; Shrewsbury, Somerset and Newcastle made it possible

355

to ditch the Whigs in 1710; and it was Shrewsbury, Somerset and Argyll who ditched the Tories in 1714. What was founded in 1688 and confirmed in 1701 and 1714 was not parliamentary monarchy but aristocratic monarchy.

# BIBLIOGRAPHY

To facilitate cross-referencing, I have numbered the paragraphs which follow. All books are published in London unless otherwise stated.

[1] The standard bibliography is the Royal Historical Society's *Bibliography of British History: Stuart Period* (2nd edn., 1970), ed. Mary Frear Keeler, but this is designed for specialist use. For 1660–89 there is a more modest and useable compilation by William L. Sachse, *Restoration England* (1971), but for the general reader the best guide, at least to work published since 1945, is G. R. Elton's mordant survey, *Modern Historians and British History 1485–1945* (1970).

[2] The way to a deeper study of the period is through various published collections of documents, with commentary. J. P. Kenyon, *The Stuart Constitution* (1966) is continued beyond 1688 by E. N. Williams, *The Eighteenth-Century Constitution* (1960). Andrew Browning, *English Historical Documents 1660–1714* (1955) is on an altogether larger scale, but its companion volume for 1603–60 has not yet been published. There are a number of more specialized collections for the period 1640–60. The best known is *The Good Old Cause*, ed. Christopher Hill and Edmund Dell (2nd edn., 1969), but Stuart E. Prall, *The Puritan Revolution* (1968), is in many ways better.

*Chapter I* (Introduction)

[3] The classic picture of Elizabeth I and her achievement is contained in J. E. Neale, *Queen Elizabeth* (1934), and *Elizabeth I and her Parliaments* (2 vols., 1953, 1957), though Neale himself painted a much more sombre picture of the last decade of the reign in 'The Elizabethan Political Scene', reprinted in *Essays in Elizabethan History* (1958). The classic statement on the reigns of James I and Charles I is S. R. Gardiner's *History of England 1603–42* (10 vols., 1883–4) and his *History of the Great Civil War 1642–49* (4 vols., 1893), a work which is still unrivalled as a source of information. Gardiner's historical methods were severely criticized as early as 1915 by the

357

American Roland G. Usher, in *A Critical Study of the Historical Method of Samuel Rawson Gardiner* (Washington University Studies, vol. 3, St Louis), but it is only quite recently that his whole approach has come under fire; to some extent from Kenyon [2], more notably from Conrad Russell, in 'Parliamentary History in Perspective 1604–29', *History*, 61 (1976), and in a volume he edited on *The Origins of the English Civil War* (1973). Russell's approach is foreshadowed in his *Crisis of Parliaments 1509–1660* (1971) and this is now the best short treatment of the period from 1603. On the other hand, Lawrence Stone, in *The Causes of the English Revolution 1529–1642* (1972), still abides by what is essentially an updated version of the Gardiner thesis. What does seem to be finally discredited is the rigid constitutionalist approach typified by Margaret Atwood Judson, *The Crisis of the Constitution* (Rutgers 1949), a book once regarded with reverence (and still far from valueless, of course). The emphasis now is on the view of the past enshrined in the doctrine of the Ancient Constitution; see J. G. A. Pocock, *The Ancient Constitution and the Feudal Law* (1957).

[4] The sociological aspect of early seventeenth-century history was dominated for two decades after the Second World War by the great controversy between historians on the 'rise (or the fall) of the gentry'. The controversy is very fairly summed up by one of the leading participants, Lawrence Stone, in *Social Change and Revolution in England 1540–1640* (1965), reprinted in revised form in Stone, *Causes* [3]. An epilogue is provided by G. E. Mingay in *The Gentry: the Rise and Fall of a Ruling Class* (1976). Stone's *The Crisis of the Aristocracy 1558–1641* (1965), supplemented by *Family and Fortune* (1973), covers the nobility.

[5] Carl Bridenbaugh, in *Vexed and Troubled Englishmen 1590–1642* (1967) and Wallace Notestein in *The English People on the Eve of Colonisation 1603–30* (1954), are up-to-date examples of the attempt to analyse English society in a sentimental, literary sort of way (Trevelyan's *English Social History*, is, of course, the most notorious example of this trend). In both cases, their work is distorted by the fact that, to them, English history is but a prelude to American history.

[6] Streets ahead of either is Alan Everitt's questing, speculative essay, *Change in the Provinces: the Seventeenth Century* (Leicester University Press, 1969). Indeed, the way ahead lies through detailed examination of the localities, and in recent years there have been several helpful and discerning studies of individual counties; notably Thomas G. Barnes, *Somerset 1625–40* (1961),

and J. T. Cliffe, *The Yorkshire Gentry from the Reformation to the Civil War* (1969). See also Fletcher, *Sussex* [30], and others cited in that paragraph.

[7] In recent years historians, demographers and sociologists have been actively employed in trying to reconstruct a picture of the working class in the seventeenth century. Peter Laslett, *The World We Have Lost* (1965), was a highly influential exploratory essay in this genre. 'Family history' is now a fashionable field of research, but even if it were pushed to much greater lengths than it is now, it is difficult to see how it could affect our general picture of the seventeenth century.

[8] The economic history of the period is covered by Charles Wilson, *England's Apprenticeship 1603–1763* (1965), which has an admirable chapter on the economic causes of the Great Rebellion; see also L. A. Clarkson, *The Pre-Industrial Economy 1500–1750* (1971), and D. C. Coleman, *The Economy of England 1450–1750* (1977). Two important monographs are, *Commercial Crisis and Change 1600–42* by B. E. Supple (1959), and *The Crown and the Money Market 1603–40* by Robert Ashton (1960). But on the crucial point of royal taxation and finance we are still dependent on F. C. Dietz, *English Public Finance 1558–1641* (1932), a pioneering work of the greatest value which is badly in need of supplementation and perhaps emendation. However, Menna Prestwich's *Cranfield* [20] provides a first-class analysis of these matters under James I.

[9] We are not well provided with books on the history of the Church as such, though Claire Cross, *Church and People 1450–1660* (1976), is a good introduction to the subject. R. G. Usher's books on *The Reconstruction of the English Church* (2 vols., New York, 1910) and *The Rise and Fall of High Commission* (1913) are valuable, but to be used with caution. Usher exaggerates the cohesion and aggressiveness of the Puritan movement; so does S. B. Babbage, *Puritanism and Richard Bancroft* (1962). Christopher Hill, *Economic Problems of the Church* (1956), is a seminal book, and the only one on this subject. H. R. Trevor-Roper, *Archbishop Laud* (2nd edn., 1965) is the best biography of any churchman in this century.

[10] As for Puritanism, of making books on this subject there is no end, and any bibliography must be selective. The old-fashioned, romantic-dynamic concept of Puritanism was formulated by William Haller in *The Rise of Puritanism* (New York, 1938), a classic book, beautifully written, which still has much to offer. Haller has been followed by Christopher Hill in a number of books, of which *Society and Puritanism in Pre-Revolutionary England* (1964) is the best as well as the most

359

representative. The extreme concept of Puritanism as a true revolutionary movement is persuasively, but not convincingly argued by Michael Walzer, *The Revolution of the Saints* (1966).

[11] Charles H. and Katherine George, *The Protestant Mind of the English Reformation 1570–1940* (Princeton, 1961), can detect no difference between Anglicanism and Puritanism; J. F. H. New, *Anglican and Puritan* (1964), emphatically can. That is the way. Arminianism, which everybody thought a dead letter, has been revived by Nicholas Tyacke, in Russell, *Origins* [3], who argues, just like contemporary Puritans, that it was a distinct counter-revolutionary movement within the Church. Unfortunately, this short, dogmatic essay has not been followed up.

[12] On the Roman Catholics we are fortunate to have two first-class general histories: *The English Catholic Community 1570–1850* by John Bossy (1975) and *The Handle and the Axe* by J. C. H. Aveling (1976). Aveling has a useful bibliography. John Bossy also examines the Catholics under James I in Smith [14], and Martin J. Havran covers *The Catholics in Caroline England* (Stanford, 1962). The definitive study of the Gunpowder Plot is by Joel Hurstfield, reprinted in his *Freedom, Corruption and Government in Elizabethan England* (1973). Other books on the plot are to be regarded with caution, especially if they are written by members of the Society of Jesus.

[13] Finally, there have been attempts in recent years to relate the crisis in England to contemporaneous events in Europe. *The Crisis in Europe 1560–1660*, ed. Trevor Aston (1965), reprints important articles by H. R. Trevor-Roper and E. J. Hobsbawn on 'The General Crisis'. See also Trevor-Roper's 'Religion, the Reformation and Social Change', in his volume of the same name (1967), and Theodore K. Rabb, *The Struggle for Stability in Early Modern Europe* (New York, 1975). Foreign policy in this period is very much a desert, apart from J. R. Jones's short survey, *Britain and Europe in the Seventeenth Century* (1966). G. M. D. Howat, *Stuart and Cromwellian Foreign Policy 1603–88* (1974), is shallow and unperceptive; Paul Langford, *The Eighteenth Century 1688–1815* (1976), is rather better.

*Chapter II* (1603–18)

[14] James I is an extraordinarily difficult man to analyse, despite, or perhaps because of, all we know about him. The best attempt is D. H. Willson's *James VI and I* (1956), stodgy and

humourless as it is. David Mathew's *James I* (1967) is on the whole disappointing, though it makes a few shrewd points, as does his earlier book, *The Jacobean Age* (1938). G. P. V. Akrigg, *Jacobean Pageant* (Harvard, 1962) is undeservedly neglected. A. G. R. Smith (ed.), *The Reign of James VI and I* (1973), is a collection of papers of varying worth. For those who prefer to reach their own conclusions, there is *James I by his Contemporaries* (1969), ed. Robert Ashton.

[15] James's relations with Parliament are covered very thoroughly in a series of monographs which reflect the interest of a previous generation of American historians in early seventeenth-century English history. Wallace Notestein, *The House of Commons 1604–10* (Yale, 1971), was left unrevised on the author's death. It is conceived on the Neale plan, in that it is more concerned with confrontation than cooperation. The same can be said, with more excuse, of Thomas L. Moir, *The Addled Parliament* (1958). This was old-fashioned the moment it was published, and evades certain issues which even Gardiner recognized as important. Robert Zaller, *The Parliament of 1621* (Berkeley, 1971), and Robert E. Ruigh, *The Parliament of 1624* (Harvard, 1971), are much more in the trend of modern historical thinking, and can be supplemented by Prestwich [20]. D. H. Willson, *The Privy Councillors in the House of Commons 1604–1629* (Minnesota, 1940), is also useful.

[16] For elections and electioneering, much of J. E. Neale's *The Elizabethan House of Commons* (1949) is still relevant, but Derek Hirst, *The Representative of the People?* (1975), is a pioneering attempt to explore these questions to a greater depth, with surprising results.

## Chapter III (1618–29)

[17] This section is largely a nil report. There is no satisfactory study of the key figure of Buckingham, nor of the parliaments of 1625–9. We are still reliant for our picture of parliamentary politics and war after 1624 on Gardiner and Dietz [8].

[18] Similarly with the parliamentary opposition. C. V. Wedgwood, *Thomas Wentworth, first Earl of Strafford: A Revaluation* (1961), is eminently sane and sensible; Harold Hulme, *Life of Sir John Eliot* (1957), is absurdly uncritical. Conrad Russell is writing a life of Pym which it is hoped will shed new light on the matter.

[19] Nor is the Common Law well served. There is no acceptable modern study of Bacon or Coke, and Catherine D. Bowen's

biography of the latter, *The Lion and the Throne* (1957), is to be used with caution; so is Sir Charles Ogilvie, *The King's Government and Common Law 1471–1641* (1958). However, *Politics and the Bench*, by W. J. Jones (1971), is strongly recommended, together with his article in A. G. R. Smith [14]; he also contributes a useful study of Lord Chancellor Ellesmere to *Early Stuart Studies*, ed. H. S. Reinmuth (Minnesota, 1970). Two other monographs on specialized subjects may also be noted; Colin Tite, *Impeachment and Parliamentary Judicature* (1974), and J. S. Cockburn, *A History of English Assizes 1558–1714* (1972).

[20] Finally, there are two good modern biographies of Lionel Cranfield, an embarrassment of riches: R. H. Tawney, *Business and Politics under James I* (1958), and Menna Prestwich, *Cranfield: Politics and Profit under the Early Stuarts* (1966).

## Chapter IV (1629–40)

[21] Charles I, one of the most complex of English kings, has successfully defied the biographers; the best attempt is by John Bowle, *Charles the First* (1975). However, his chief servants, Laud and Strafford, are well handled by Trevor-Roper [9] and Wedgwood [18] respectively. Martin J. Havran, *Caroline Courtier* (1973), is a sound study of a lesser figure, Francis Cottington.

[22] Charles I's Court, however, has been intensively studied in recent years, notably by Roy Strong, in *Splendour at Court* (1973), ch. 6, and *Van Dyck: Charles I on Horseback* (1972); by Oliver Millar, *The Age of Charles I* (1972); and by Peter Thomas, in Conrad Russell, *Origins* [3], and in *The Courts of Europe*, ed. A. G. Dickens (1977), ch. 9. David Mathew, *The Age of Charles I* (1951), also retains a certain value. G. E. Aylmer, *The King's Servants* (1961), is an exhaustive study of the royal civil service, in but not of the Court.

[23] What we most obviously lack is any satisfactory assessment of Charles's domestic policy, though in a short pamphlet, *The Eleven Years' Tyranny* (Historical Association, 1962), Hugh Kearney suggested how it might be done. The polarization of 'Court' and 'Country' is recounted rather conventionally by C. V. Wedgwood, *The King's Peace 1637–41* (1955), and more analytically by Peres Zagorin, *The Court and the Country* (1969). Manning [26] and Morrill [30] are also useful here.

[24] Though technically the history of Scotland is beyond the scope of this book, the Scots Rebellion was so important that it deserves more attention than it usually gets. See Gordon

Donaldson, *Scotland: James V–James VII* (Edinburgh, 1965), and David Stevenson, *The Scottish Revolution 1637–44* (1973); also Trevor-Roper's brilliant short study of the matter in his *Religion, the Reformation and Social Change* (1967). For Ireland, see Hugh Kearney, *Strafford in Ireland* (Manchester, 1959) and Aidan Clarke, *The Old English in Ireland 1625–42* (1966).

*Chapters VI–VII* (1640–60)

[25] Ivan Roots, *The Great Rebellion 1640–1660* (1966), is a sound 1-vol. treatment of the whole period, reasonably up-to-date.

[26] The membership of the Long Parliament has been analysed by D. Brunton and D. H. Pennington, *Members of the Long Parliament* (1954), and described by Mary Frear Keeler, *The Long Parliament 1640–41* (Philadelphia, 1954). The crisis which led to the outbreak of war is discussed in Conrad Russell, *Origins* [3], in Brian Manning, *The English People and the English Revolution 1640–49* (1976), and in some of the essays in *The English Civil War and After*, ed. R. H. Parry (1970). Manning has also edited a similar collection entitled *Politics, Religion and the English Civil War* (1973). However, having exposed historians' neglect of lower-class unrest at this time, Manning is now in danger of exaggerating it.

[27] What is lacking is any attempt to deal with the outbreak as a politico-military problem; the nearest to this is Zagorin [23], and Valerie Pearl, *London and the Outbreak of the Puritan Revolution* (1961). Otherwise we must draw our own conclusions from the detailed narrative in Gardiner [3]. B. H. G. Wormald, however, analyses (very densely) the constitutional royalist position in *Clarendon* (1951), and Ruth Spalding deals with the conservative parliamentarian outlook in her life of Bulstrode Whitelocke, *The Improbable Puritan* (1975).

[28] The campaigns of the civil wars are a focus for continuing research and debate, which is of little concern to any save military historians. C. V. Wedgwood, *The King's War 1641–47* (1958), is a useful summary. Meanwhile, we still know very little about the organization of the war effort. C. H. Firth, *Cromwell's Army* (1902), is still the standard authority, though the earlier parliamentary armies receive attention from Clive Holmes, *The Eastern Association* (1974). Ian Roy is writing a much-needed study of the royalist armies; in the meanwhile, he contributes an interesting essay on 'The English Civil War and English Society' to *War and Society*, ed. Brian Bond and Ian Roy (1975).

[29] The political intrigues in the Long Parliament are analysed

by J. H. Hexter, *The Reign of King Pym* (Harvard, 1941), continued in John R. McCormack, *Revolutionary Politics in the Long Parliament* (Harvard, 1973). See also Valerie Pearl on London in the 1640s in Aylmer, *Interregnum* [38]. Violet A. Rowe, *Sir Henry Vane the Younger* (1970), is a distinct disappointment.

[30] The best discussion of the impact of the war on the country is J. S. Morrill, *The Revolt of the Provinces* (1976). See also Ian Roy [28]. Alan Everitt has produced two fine studies of individual counties, *Suffolk and the Great Rebellion* (Suffolk Records Society, 1960), and *The Community of Kent in the Great Rebellion* (Leicester University Press, 1966); also a useful essay on *The Local Community and the Great Rebellion* (Historical Association, 1969). Anthony Fletcher, *A County Community in Peace and War: Sussex 1600–1660* (1975), is also excellent. Underdown [33] has an interesting analysis of the situation in the provinces 1649–50, and has recently produced a detailed study of *Somerset in the Civil War and Interregnum* (1973). Other histories of individual counties in the civil wars, of which there are many, are merely narrative and descriptive.

[31] The all-important county committees are examined in two instances: by D. H. Pennington, *The Committee at Stafford* (Manchester, 1957), and by Everitt again, in *The County Committee of Kent* (Leicester University Press, 1957). But the only light shed on Parliament's finances, a burning issue at the time, is by Pennington, 'The Accounts of the Kingdom 1642–49', in *Essays in the Economic and Social History of Tudor and Stuart England*, ed. F. J. Fisher (1961).

[32] It is strange that the history of Puritanism has not been carried through the 1640s, though there are plenty of books on the Levellers [34]; some would say too many. For attempts to reform the Church we are still very dependent on an older work, W. A. Shaw, *A History of the English Church during the Civil Wars and under the Commonwealth* (1900). William L. Lamont examines the Presbyterian position in *Marginal Prynne* (1963) and *Godly Rule; Politics and Religion 1603–60* (1969). William Haller, *Liberty and Reformation in the Puritan Revolution* (New York, 1955), is primarily concerned with the literary aspect of Puritanism, but is still useful. As I have said, I doubt if the strenuous debate in recent years on the identity of the Presbyterians and Independants in politics is very fruitful; it can be followed in the works cited by Elton [1], nn. 373–6.

[33] Two recent books have revolutionized our view of the crisis of 1649: *Pride's Purge*, by David Underdown (1971), and *The*

*Rump Parliament,* by Blair Worden (1974), which goes on until 1653. Otherwise, our principal authority is still S. R. Gardiner, who ploughed on until 1656 in his *History of the Commonwealth and Protectorate* (4 vols., 1903).

[34] The Levellers are well served by H. N. Brailsford, *The Levellers and the English Revolution* (1961), Joseph Frank, *The Levellers* (Harvard, 1955; New York, 1969), and Perez Zagorin, *A History of Political Thought in the English Revolution* (1954), to mention only a few. G. E. Aylmer, *The Levellers in the English Revolution* (1975), is an excellent short study, with selected documents. A. L. Morton, *Freedom in Arms* (1975), is another easily available selection of Leveller writings, and Christopher Hill performed a similar service for the Diggers in *The Law of Freedom and other Writings* (Pelican Classics, 1973). A. S. P. Woodhouse edited the famous Putney Debates under the title *Puritanism and Liberty* (1938).

[35] However, twentieth-century socialists, beginning with Harold Laski, have tended to exaggerate the importance of left-wing Puritan thought, especially in its more extreme aspects; this trend is continued by Christopher Hill, in *The World Turned Upside Down* (1972), A. L. Morton, in *The World of the Ranters* (1970), and B. S. Capp, in *The Fifth Monarchy Men* (1972). Many think that this line of research has been pursued too far. The real preoccupations of the New Model Army are exposed by Leo F. Solt, *Saints in Arms: Puritanism and Democracy in Cromwell's Army* (Stanford, 1959), and Ian Gentles, 'Arrears of Pay and Ideology in the Army Revolt of 1647', in Bond and Roy [28]. See also J. S. Morrill, 'Mutiny and Discontent in the English Provincial Armies 1645–47', *Past and Present*, 56 (1972).

[36] *The Trial of Charles I* by C. V. Wedgwood (1964) is a straightforward if rather sentimental account. Charles is the only English monarch to leave a substantial political testament, and it is strange that the *Eikōn Basilikē* has not received more attention from historians. The best edition, which also deals with the vexed problem of its authorship, is by Philip A. Knachel (Cornell, 1966). *The Letters of Charles I*, ed. Sir Charles Petrie (1935), is also useful.

[37] Charles's great adversary, Oliver Cromwell, remains something of an enigma. Sir Charles Firth's biography, *Oliver Cromwell and the Rule of the Puritans in England* (1900), was always over-praised, and is now out of date. Even its title begs at least one important question, and Firth never intended it as more than a popular summary of Gardiner. Antonia Fraser, *Cromwell: Our Chief of Men* (1973), is the most detailed

STUART ENGLAND

biography; it has many shrewd insights, but it is sprawling and undiscriminating. At the other extreme is Christopher Hill, *God's Englishman* (1970); really a series of very good essays which do not add up to a biography. Many will prefer the pamphlet Hill wrote for the Historical Association on Cromwell's tercentenary in 1958. There is still much to be said for John Buchan, *Oliver Cromwell* (1934). The one indispensable book is *The Lord Protector: Religion and Politics in the life of Oliver Cromwell*, by Robert S. Paul (1955).

[38] Gardiner's history was carried from 1656 to 1658 by his pupil Firth, in *The Last Years of the Protectorate* (2 vols., 1909), and on to 1660 by Firth's pupil Godfrey Davies, in *The Restoration of Charles II* (San Marino, 1955); they are both stupefyingly dull, but informative after their fashion. For new light on the Protectorate we must turn to *The Interregnum: The Quest for a Settlement*, ed. G. E. Aylmer (1972), a stimulating symposium. Maurice Ashley's *Cromwell's Generals* (1954) is useful, and so is his extended study of *General Monck* (1977). Ashley has also produced the best study of economic policy in the 1650s, *Financial and Commercial Policy under the Cromwellian Protectorate* (1934).

*Chapters VII–VIII* (1660–85)

[39] David Ogg, *England in the Reign of Charles II* (2nd edn, 1955), is really a continuation of Gardiner, though on a smaller scale, and in a more analytical vein. It is decidedly Whiggish, but enormously valuable, and it has worn well. Which is fortunate, because there is no satisfactory biography of Charles II; the best is still Arthur Bryant, *King Charles II* (2nd edn. 1955), but it is much too uncritical, and based on a wrong interpretation of the crown's financial situation. (See Chandaman [44].) K. H. D. Haley's brief sketch (Historical Association, 1966) is one of the best things in print. See also the famous contemporary assessment of Charles by Lord Halifax, in *Halifax: Complete Works* (Pelican Classics, 1969).

[40] The political and constitutional implications of the Restoration have scarcely been explored. Apart from Ogg [39], see the documents and commentary in Kenyon [2]. Joan Thirsk, *The Restoration* (1976), though essentially a textbook, is nevertheless valuable. *The Restoration of the Stuarts: Blessing or Disaster?* (Folger Library, Washington, 1960) is an interesting collection of speculative papers by leading historians.

[41] In contrast, the Restoration of the Church is quite well covered, notably in R. S. Bosher, *The Making of the Restoration*

*Settlement: the Influence of the Laudians 1649–62* (1951). In fact, Bosher rather exaggerates the ultimate success of the Laudians; for a corrective see Anne Whiteman, 'The Re-establishment of the Church of England 1660–3', *Transactions of the Royal Historical Society*, ser. 5, vol. 6 (1955) – also important articles by Whiteman and others in *From Uniformity to Unity 1662–1962*, ed. G. F. Nuttall and O. Chadwick (1962). Norman Sykes, *From Sheldon to Secker: Aspects of English Church History 1660–1768* (1959), carries the story on, as do some of the articles in Nuttall and Chadwick. Post-Restoration Dissent is covered in two books by G. R. Cragg, *From Puritanism to the Age of Reason 1660–1700* (1950), and *Puritanism in the Period of the Great Persecution 1660–88* (1957). See also Douglas R. Lacey, *Dissent and Parliamentary Politics 1661–89* (Rutgers, 1969).

[42] The relationship between Puritanism and the scientific spirit is now as much debated as the relationship between Puritanism and capitalism was a generation or so ago. For the background, see A. R. Hall, *The Scientific Revolution* (1954), H. F. Kearney, *Science and Change 1500–1700* (1971), and Robert K. Merton's classic *Science, Technology and Society in Seventeenth-Century England* (2nd edn. New York, 1970). The theme is carried further by Christopher Hill, *The Intellectual Origins of the English Revolution* (1965), and Charles Webster, *The Great Instauration 1626–60* (1975). Webster has also edited an important collection of specialist articles from the journal *Past and Present: The Intellectual Revolution of the Seventeenth Century* (1974) – valuable, too, for more than science.

[43] For Hobbes, see *Hobbes and His Critics*, by John Bowle (1951), and Samuel L. Mintz, *The Hunting of Leviathan* (1962). There is an attractive edition of *Leviathan* in the Pelican Classics series, with a good introduction by C. B. Macpherson; less easily available, but well worth tracking down, is *Behemoth*, Hobbes's idiosyncratic analysis of the Great Rebellion, ed. Ferdinand Tonnies (repr., 1969).

[44] The political history of the 1660s is surprisingly obscure, though D. T. Witcombe, *Charles II and the Cavalier House of Commons 1663–74* (Manchester, 1966), is a great help. The lack of a modern life of Clarendon, apart from Wormald's analytic study [27], is a serious gap. Meanwhile Keith Feiling, *British Foreign Policy 1660–72* (1930), and Charles Wilson, *Profit and Power* (1957), do much to elucidate war and foreign policy. Ralph Davis provides a useful summary of his researches into English trade in *A Commercial Revolution* (Historical Association, 1967); see also Davis on *The Rise of*

*the English Shipping Industry* (1962) and G. D. Ramsey, *English Overseas Trade during the Centuries of Emergence* (1957).In *The Army of Charles II* (1976), John Childs looks at an institution too often taken for granted. But the key book, whose revisionist lessons have still to be incorporated in the historiography, is C. D. Chandaman, *The English Public Revenue 1660–88* (1975).

[45] In the 1670s we are on firmer ground, with Andrew Browning's *Thomas Osborne Earl of Danby* (3 vols., Glasgow, 1944–51), K. H. D. Haley, *The First Earl of Shaftesbury* (1968), and Maurice Lee, *The Cabal* (Illinois, 1965). Browning's article, 'Parties and Party Organization in the Reign of Charles II', *Transactions of the Royal Historical Society*, ser. 4, vol. 30 (1948), is also valuable. For the Popish Plot and the Exclusion Crisis, see John Miller, *Popery and Politics in England 1660–88* (1973), J. R. Jones, *The First Whigs* (1961) and J. P. Kenyon, *The Popish Plot* (1972), as well as Haley's *Shaftesbury*. Haley also contributes an interesting paper on '"No Popery" under Charles II', to *Britain and the Netherlands V*, ed. J. S. Bromley and E. H. Kossmann (1976). For the aftermath, J. R. Western, *Monarchy and Revolution* (1972), is of the first importance. The survival of underground political radicalism through the reign is glimpsed in Iris Morley, *A Thousand Lives* (1954), and Maurice Ashley, *John Wildman* (1947); but we need an authoritative study of this whole subject.

[46] The closing years of the reign are also covered in various important biographies, of Halifax, Jeffreys, Sunderland and James II himself, which are listed in the next section [48].

### Chapters IX–X (1685–90)

[47] For the reign of James II and the Revolution, the fullest and in many ways the best account is by Macaulay, in his classic *History of England* (the Everyman edition is as good as any). It is too often avoided because of its Whig bias, which is obvious enough and easily discounted. David Ogg continues his history of late seventeenth-century England in *England in the Reigns of James II and William III* (1955). His antipathy to James II, however, is as deep as Macaulay's, and his sensitive and perceptive account of William's reign is to be preferred.

[48] For the rest, we are heavily dependent on biographies, like H. C. Foxcroft, *Life and Works of Halifax* (2 vols., 1898), J. P. Kenyon, *Sunderland* (1958), G. W. Keeton, *Lord Chancellor Jeffreys* (1965), and F. C. Turner, *James II* (1948); also the

standard lives of William III [51]. John Miller on Popery [45] is also directly relevant.

[49] On the Revolution itself there has been almost an embarrassment of monographs in recent years: Lucille Pinkham, *William III and the Respectable Revolution* (Harvard, 1954), Maurice Ashley, *The Glorious Revolution of 1688* (1966), John Carswell, *The Descent on England* (1969), J. R. Jones, *The Revolution of 1688* (1972), and J. R. Western, *Monarchy and Revolution* (1972). Apart from Ashley, which is a conventional account of received fact, they all have new contributions to make; on balance Western is the best. Pinkham's violent animosity to William III makes it necessary to use her with caution; the rest are well-balanced, with Jones attempting a revision of our view of James's abilities, if not his character.

[50] For the political settlement in 1689, see also *Britain After the Glorious Revolution*, ed. Geoffrey Holmes (1969), and the documents and commentary in Williams [2] and Browning [2]. The religious settlement is discussed by Henry Horwitz in *Revolution Politicks* (1968) – a bizarre title for a biography of Daniel Finch, Earl of Nottingham – and by George Every, *The High Church Party 1688–1718* (1956). See also G. M. Straka, *Anglican Reaction to the Revolution of 1688* (Wisconsin, 1962). However, all these are to some extent superseded by G. V. Bennett, *The Tory Crisis in Church and State 1688–1730* (1975).

*Chapters XI–XII* (1690–1702)

[51] John Carswell, *From Revolution to Revolution 1688–1776* (1973), is a ,very superior textbook, which provides the best short account of events through to 1714. The best analyses of political society in this period are provided by Ogg [47], J. H. Plumb, *The Growth of Political Stability 1675–1725* (1967), and by Plumb again in *Sir Robert Walpole*, vol. I (1956). The best life of *William III* is by Stephen B. Baxter (1966), but *William of Orange: the Later Years* by Nesca A. Robb (1966) is also of value. Macaulay [47] continues to provide a detailed factual narrative, with rather dubious interpretations, up to 1698.

[52] The politics of party in William's reign has been the subject of animated discussion for some years. The best guide now is B. W. Hill, *The Growth of Parliamentary Parties 1689–1742* (1976), which gives an informed consensus. Meanwhile, in *Parliament, Policy and Politics in the Reign of William III* (Manchester, 1977), Henry Horwitz offers the most detailed

account we have for any reign. Geoffrey Holmes and W. A. Speck provide an interesting selection of documents in *The Divided Society 1694–1716* (1967). The biographies of Danby [45] and Sunderland [48] already cited are of continuing use after 1688. We lack a study of the Whig Junto, but see William L. Sachse, *Lord Somers* (Manchester, 1975). Keith Feiling's pioneer *History of the Tory Party 1640–1714* (1924) is a book of elegance and distinction whose usefulness is far from exhausted, though it needs to be used with care.

[53] Political ideas are not so well served, though Straka [50] and Bennett [50] deal with the conflict in the Church of England. However, J. G. A. Pocock subtly analyses the 'Country' ethos in essays collected in *Politics, Language and Time* (1972) and in the last section of *The Machiavellian Moment* (Princeton, 1975); and in *Revolution Principles* (1977), J. P. Kenyon tries to assess the contribution of the Revolution itself to party ideologies in the next two generations. John Dunn, *The Political Thought of John Locke* (1969), deals with the man usually considered the arch-theorist of Whiggism; see also Peter Laslett's introduction to his definitive edition of Locke's *Two Treatises* (1960).

[54] Financial developments through to 1714, and beyond, are incomparably expounded by P. G. M. Dickson, *The Financial Revolution in England* (1967), but for one crucial aspect, see also E. A. Reitan, 'From Revenue to Civil List 1689–1702', *Historical Journal*, 13 (1970). There is a fine book on the navy, John Ehrman, *The Navy in the War of William III* (1953), but nothing comparable for the army.

*Chapters XIII–XIV* (1702–14)

[55] G. M. Trevelyan, *England under Queen Anne* (3 vols., 1930–34), retains most of its value as a detailed history of the reign in all its aspects. David Green's biography of *Queen Anne* (1970) is acceptable, though not outstanding. (His *Sarah Duchess of Marlborough* (1967) is a much better book.)

[56] Trevelyan covers the war very well, and more detail on the Flanders campaign can be gleaned from Winston Churchill's *Marlborough* (4 vols., 1933–8). See also Corelli Barnett's essay *Marlborough* (1974), and R. E. Scouller, *The Armies of Queen Anne* (1966). (However, there has never been a satisfactory life of Marlborough, covering all aspects of his career, and the same can be said, with greater emphasis, of Godolphin.) David Francis, *The First Peninsular War 1702–13* (1975), calls our attention to an undeservedly neglected theatre.

[57] On parliamentary and political history, the leading authority is Geoffrey Holmes, in *British Politics in the Age of Anne* (1967), one of those rare books which are not only first-class history but works of art. See also Hill [52] and Plumb, *Stability* [51]. The religious aspect of politics is magisterially handled by Bennett [50], and there is a useful summary by Geoffrey Holmes, *Religion and Party in Late Stuart England* (Historical Association, 1975). Holmes also analyses the key crisis of the reign in *The Trial of Doctor Sacheverell* (1973). Elections are discussed by W. A. Speck, *Tory and Whig: the Struggle in the Constituencies* (1970), and in two important papers: J. H. Plumb, 'The Growth of the Electorate 1660–1715', *Past and Present*, 45 (1969), and Geoffrey Holmes, *The Electorate and the National Will* (Lancaster University Press, 1976).

[58] *Robert Harley: Puritan Politician*, by Angus McInnes (1970) though really a preliminary study, is the most successful attempt so far to come to grips with this difficult man. The standard life of Bolingbroke is now H. T. Dickinson's *Bolingbroke* (1970). The important issue of the peace negotiations is to some extent dealt with by Francis [56] for the Spanish theatre, and more generally by A. D. MacLachlan in Holmes, *Glorious Revolution* [50]. MacLachlan is preparing a book on Utrecht which is badly needed; in the meanwhile, see B. W. Hill, 'Oxford, Bolingbroke and the Peace of Utrecht', *Historical Journal*, 16 (1973).

*Chapter XV* (1603–1714)

[59] The new Revels *History of the Drama* is open to many objections, but provides the best coverage for the relevant periods (vol. III, 1576–1613, appeared in 1975, and vol. V, 1660–1750, in 1976).

[60] As for the literary giants, there is no acceptable life of Defoe, but *The World of Defoe*, by Peter Earle (1976), is a penetrating analysis of his mind as displayed in his writings. The standard life of Jonathan Swift is being compiled by Irvin Ehrenpreis in three massive volumes, of which two have appeared (1962, 1967); the best short introduction is *Focus on Swift*, ed. C. J. Rawson (1971). An incredible amount of rubbish has been written on these two, and other Augustan writers. Michael Foot, *The Pen and the Sword* (1957) is a racy, but accurate and lively account of the politico-literary battle, 1710–13. *The Augustan Vision*, by Pat Rogers (1974) attempts, with considerable success, a total vision of the years 1688–1740 – art, morals, literature and politics.

[61] On art and architecture, the appropriate volumes in the Oxford History of English Art and the Pelican History of Art remain our best standby, viz. Eric Mercer, *English Art 1553–1625* (1962), and Margaret Whinney and Oliver Millar, *English Art 1625–1714*; Ellis Waterhouse, *Painting in Britain 1530–1790* (1953), and John Summerson, *Architecture in Britain 1530–1830* (rev. edn. 1977). Mercer is particularly good on the social implications of architecture, and this theme is explored to a much greater depth by Judith Hook, *The Baroque Age in England* (1976).

### ADDENDA

The following books either appeared after this bibliography went to press, or were inexplicably and undeservedly forgotten.

[6] To the list of county histories, here or in [30], should be added: M. E. James, *Family, Lineage and Civil Society . . . in the Durham Region 1500–1640* (Oxford, 1974), Peter Clark, *Religion, Politics and Society in Kent 1500–1640* (1977), and J. S. Morrill, *Cheshire 1630–1660* (Oxford, 1974).

[8] A vital addition to this section is *The Agrarian History of England and Wales*, vol. iv: *1500–1640* ed. Joan Thirsk (Cambridge, 1967).

[9] R. A. Marchant has also written two excellent monographs on specialized aspects of the Church: *The Puritans and the Church Courts in the Diocese of York* (1960), and *The Church under the Law* (1969).

[38] Add G. E. Aylmer, *The State's Servants: the Civil Service of the English Republic 1649–1660* (1973).

# INDEX

(NOTE: this index does not embrace the bibliography.)

Abbott, George, archbishop, 72, 77, 97, 99, 105, 114
Abjuration Act (1702), 296
d'Adda, Ferdinand, nuncio, 236
Addison, Joseph, 336, 347, 351
Adwalton Moor, 149
Agriculture, 15, 16, 17, 188–9
Ailesbury, Thomas Bruce, 2nd earl of, 269
Aliens Act (1705), 310
Almanza, 313
Alresford, 151
Ancient Constitution, the, 29–30
Anne, Queen, 26, 244, 249, 250, 261, 273, 281, 291, 312, 318, 331–2, 333
  character and style, 297, 298 ff., 301
  title, 321
  and the Church, 299–300, 306–7, 314 ff.
  and the Junto, 312, 314–15, 316, 317, 318
  and the succession, 306, 327, 332–3
  and peace, 326, 327
Anne of Denmark, Queen, 55, 117
Answer to the Nineteen Propositions (1642), 34, 42, 143, 164
Argyll, Archibald Campbell, 8th earl of, 133
Argyll, John Campbell, 2nd duke of, 311, 333, 334
Arlington, Henry Bennett, earl of, 189, 197, 199, 203, 204, 206, 209
Arminianism, 23, 98, 99–100, 104
Army, the, 43–4, 196; First Army Plot, 125, 128; under Charles II, 262; under James II, 226, 229
Irish Army, the, 122, 126, 127, 149, 223, 232, 250
Arundel, Thomas Howard, 14th earl of, 49, 105, 117
Ashby v. White, 189, 304–5
Ashley, lord, see Shaftesbury
Assassination plot (1696), 261, 269, 279, 280
Atterbury, Francis, 295, 296, 300, 314

Bacon, Francis, 40, 53, 58, 69, 76, 85, 186
  works, 341, 352
Bancroft, Richard, archbishop, 25, 53, 62, 83
Bank of England, 279, 280, 284, 286, 323
Bankers' case, 285
Barfleur, 269, 273
Baronets, order of knights, 69, 78
Barrier treaty (1709), 320, 326
Bastwick, John, 113
Bate's case (1606), 65
Bath, John Grenville, 1st earl of, 251
Beachy Head, 269
Beaufort, Henry Somerset, 1st duke of, 251
Beaumont, Francis, 338
Bennett, Henry, see Arlington
Berkeley, Sir Robert, 41
Berwick, James Fitzjames, duke of, 235, 308, 319, 325
Bible, Authorized Version, 61, 341–2
Bishoprics' crisis (1707), 314 ff.
Blackall, Offspring, bishop, 300, 314, 322

373

Blake, Robert, admiral, 168, 175, 178

Blenheim, 304, 307

Bolingbroke, Henry St John, viscount, 189, 298, 313, 316, 326, 327, 328, 329, 330, 331–2, 334, 335

Book of Orders, the, 110

Booth, Sir George, 178

Boscawen, Hugh, 257

Bower, Edward, 343

Boyle, Henry, 313, 325, 326

Boyle, Robert, 187, 352

Boyne, the, 269, 283

Breda, Declaration of, 179; Peace of, 200

Brihuega, 325

Bristol, John Digby, 1st earl of, 72, 88, 93, 98, 105

Bristol, John Digby, 3rd earl of, 251

Bromley, William, 312, 313

Brooke, Robert Greville, 2nd lord, 139

Browne, Sir Thomas, 341

Buckingham, George Villiers, 1st duke of, 40, 68, 75–7, 78, 79, 89, 120
 in parliament, 1621, 84–5; and 1624, 90; and the benevolence of 1621, 88
 at Madrid, 88–9
 war leader, 92, 97–8
 impeachment, 97, 101
 death, 104

Buckingham, George Villiers, 2nd duke of, 197, 199, 203, 204, 209, 210

Buckingham, John Sheffield, 1st duke of, 326

Buckinghamshire election case (1604), 58

Bunyan, John, 342, 346

Burnet, Gilbert, 268

Byrd, William, 339

Byron, Sir John, 137

Cabal, the, 203–4, 210

Cádiz Expedition, the (1625), 96–7

Carleton, Sir Dudley, 40, 101

Carlisle, Charles Howard, 3rd earl of, 291

Carmarthen, marquess of, see Danby

Catherine of Braganza, Queen, 198, 203

Catholics, the Roman, 28, 50, 51, 62–3, 202–3, 207, 212–13, 223
 under James II, 224, 230

Chapman, George, 45

Charles I, 7, 10, 34, 39, 47, 50, 56, 75, 85, 169
 character, 75, 93–4, 134
 life style, 117–18
 taste, 337, 339, 342, 343
 religious policy, 62, 98–9, 104, 105
 war and foreign policy, 79, 88, 95–6, 116–17, 134
 and parliament, 40, 46, 90, 96, 101, 107, 136
 and Scotland, 120, 132–3, 160–1, 162
 in the Civil Wars, 146, 148, 149, 151
 imprisonment, 155, 156, 158, 160
 trial, 163, 164–5
 posthumous influence, 165, 194, 255

Charles II, 8, 43, 119, 132, 166, 168, 171, 176, 299, 343
 restored, 179–80
 character and interests, 187, 188, 193–7, 199, 222–3, 225
 marriage, 198, 200, 203
 Catholicism, 202–3, 206, 211, 224–5, 294
 foreign policy, 200, 204–6, 211–12, 213, 215, 216, 217–19
 finances, 198, 207, 210, 218
 death, 223–4

Charters, borough, 221, 238, 263; see also Corporation Bill

Churchill, Arabella, 308

Churchill, George, 302, 314

Churchill, John, lord, see Marlborough

Church of England, 23–7
 before the Civil Wars, 98–100, 105, 112–13
 in the Interregnum, 129, 130–1,

133, 134-5, 150, 153-4, 169-70

at the Restoration, 183-4, 194, 219, 224

under James II, 225, 229, 231-2, 237-8, 244-5, 248-9

and Dissent, 228, 245-6

after the Revolution, 265, 268

the High Church movement, 293-6, 295 ff., 314 ff., 321 ff.

Convocation, 295-6, 307

Civil List, establishment of the, 283

Civil Wars, the, 146-54 *passim*, 162-3

effects, 181-2, 188-9

Clarendon, Edward Hyde, 1st earl of, 36, 56, 73, 76, 143, 189, 194, 195, 196, 199, 203

disgraced, 201, 202, 224

*History*, 300, 348-9

Clarendon Code, the, 199

Clarendon, Henry Hyde, 2nd earl of, 232-3, 250, 254, 268, 269

Clarke, George, 275, 312

Cleveland, John, 341

Clifford, Thomas, lord, 197, 199, 203, 204, 206, 207, 209

Cloth industry, the, 14, 80-81, 109

Cockayne Project, the, 80

Coke, Sir Edward, 30, 35, 71, 82-5, 87, 108, 158

and the judiciary, 83

and Parliament, 82-3, 85-6, 90, 97

Coleman, Edward, 212-13

College, Stephen, 220

Collier, Jeremy, 294, 347

Cologne Election, the (1688), 241, 247

Colonization, 16, 190, 191-2, 279

Commission for Ecclesiastical Causes, 231, 234, 248; *see also* High Commission

Compton, Henry, bishop, 229, 231, 235, 243

Conventicles Acts, 184

Cooper, Anthony Ashley, *see* Shaftesbury

Cooper, Samuel, 343

Cornbury, Edward, lord, 250

Corporation Act (1661), 31, 183, 221

Corporation Bill (1689), 263, 264

Cottington, Francis, lord, 105, 116

Country Interest, the, 73, 202, 210, 272, 275-6, 282-3, 285, 287, 289-90, 300-1

Coventry, Sir William, 195, 199, 202

Cowell's *Interpreter*, 66

Cowper, William, lord, 312, 325

Cranfield, Lionel, 76-8, 85, 91

Crashaw, Richard, 340

Cromwell, Oliver

character, 170-71

military career, 149, 150, 151, 152, 158-9, 162, 167, 168

aims, 150-51, 158-9, 169, 176-7

as Protector, 170, 173-5, 176-7

death, 177

achievements, 170-71, 178

posthumous reputation, 7-8, 204

Cromwell, Richard, 176, 177, 178

Cropredy Bridge, 151

Crown, the

position in 1603, 17, 34, 39-41, 43

finances, 38-9, 43, 54-5, 63-4, 198, 210, 226, 266-7, 283

at the Restoration, 181-2, 197

after the Revolution, 260-62, 264, 274-5

Culpeper, Sir John, 135, 139, 143

Customs duties, 38, 96, 101, 110, 129

Danby, Thomas Osborne, earl of Danby, marquess of Carmarthen, duke of Leeds, 189, 207

Lord Treasurer, 209, 210, 211-12

impeached, 213, 214, 278

and the Revolution, 243, 249, 251, 258, 260

after the Revolution, 270, 274, 275, 276, 288

Darien Scheme, the, 309, 311

Dartmouth, George Legge, 1st lord, 224, 237, 248, 252

Dartmouth, William Legge, 2nd lord, 324, 332
Davenant, Charles, 293
Davenant, Sir William, 339
Dawes, William, bishop, 300, 314
Declaration of Indulgence (1672), 207, 208; (1687), 236, 242, 244, 249
Defoe, Daniel, 290, 350, 351
Delamere, Henry Booth, 2nd lord, 251, 257, 266
Demise of the Crown Act (1696), 261
Denain, 330
Derby, William Stanley, 18th earl of, 251
Dering, Sir Edward, 135
Derwentdale Plot (1663), 185
Devonshire, William Cavendish, 1st duke of, 220, 243, 249, 251, 256
Devonshire, William Cavendish, 2nd duke of, 313, 325, 326
Digby, George, 130, 131, 137
Digby, Sir John, see Bristol, 1st earl of
Digby, Sir Kenelm, 117
Diggers, the, 167
Digges, Sir Dudley, 101, 107, 108
Disbrowe, John, 177
Dissenters, the, 184, 199, 220
and James II, 233, 236, 237, 245–6
and the Revolution, 265
under Queen Anne, 293–4, 322, 334
Distraint of knighthood, 59
Donne, John, 45, 340
Donnington Castle, 151
Dorset, Thomas Sackville, earl of, 53, 61, 64, 69
Dover, Treaty of (1670), 205–7
Downing, Sir George, 203
Dryden, John, 347–8
Dunbar, 168
Dundee, James Graham, viscount, 309
Dunkirk, 176, 200
Dutch Wars, the, 191–2
first, 169, 172, 200
second, 200, 204

third, 207–8, 209
Dykeveldt, Everard van der Weede, lord, 235–7, 274

East India Company, the, 14, 110, 192, 278
Eastern Association, the, 149, 151
Economy, the English, 14–17, 80–82, 161
inflation, 16–17, 43
revival, 189 ff., 285–6, 352
Edgehill, 148
Edwin, Sir Humphrey, 294
Eikon Basiliké, 93, 165
Eliot, Sir John, 46, 73, 82, 100, 101, 103, 104, 105–6, 107, 108
Elizabeth, Queen
reputation, 7, 13, 33, 48, 56, 68, 72, 96
policy, 26, 32, 33
Elizabeth of Bohemia, 46, 69
Ellesmere, Thomas Egerton, lord, 53, 58
Elton, G. R., 41
Essex, Arthur Capel, earl of, 214, 221
Essex, Robert Devereux, 3rd earl of, 71, 139, 144, 145, 147, 148, 149, 151
Eugene, prince, 307, 315, 317, 319, 330
Exclusion Bills, 189, 214

Fairfax, Sir Thomas, 149, 152, 159, 163, 167, 168
Falkland, Lucius Carey, viscount, 139, 143
Fenwick, Sir John, 280
Feversham, Louis Duras, earl of, 250, 252
Fifth Monarchists, the, 167, 169, 171
Filmer, Sir Robert, 219
Finch, John, lord, 123, 126, 144
Fitzharris, Edmund, 220
Five Knights' Case, the, 41, 102
Five Members, the, 139
Five Mile Act (1665), 184
Fleetwood, Charles, 177, 178

Fletcher, John, 338
Forced loans, 40, 101–2
Forest Laws, the, 110, 128
Form of Apology, the, 42, 52, 58, 59–60
Frederick V, Elector Palatine, 69, 78, 82

Galway, Henri Massue de Ruvigny, earl of, 308
Gardiner, S. R., 9, 22, 35, 42, 46, 70, 93, 111
Gentry, the, 9, 12, 17–21, 29
George Augustus of Hanover, 334
George, Elector of Hanover (later George I), 327, 330, 335
George, Prince of Denmark, 250, 279, 302, 312, 317
Gibbons, Orlando, 339
Gibraltar, 303, 304, 305
Gifford, Buonaventura, 234
Ginkel, Godert de, earl of Athlone, 273, 274, 287
Glencoe, 309
Gloucester, William, duke of, 261, 288, 291
*Godden* v. *Hales*, 230
Godfrey, Sir Edmund Berry, 212
Godolphin, Sidney, 1st earl of, 189, 215, 216, 222, 223, 237, 239, 258
  under William III, 266, 270, 274, 275, 277, 280, 291, 292, 298
  Lord Treasurer, 300, 302, 306, 308 ff., 311–12, 315, 322, 324
  dismissed, 325
Gondomar, don Diego Sarmineto de Acuña, count of, 37, 69, 70, 72
Goodman, Godfrey, bishop, 116
Grafton, Henry Fitzroy, 1st duke of, 250
Grand Alliance, the, 291, 303, 308
Grand Remonstrance, the, 59, 134–6
Great Contract, the, 65–8
Gregg, William, 316
Gunpowder Plot, the, 50, 61–2
Guy, Henry, 275, 277, 278, 302

Halifax, Charles Montague, 1st lord, 189, 277, 279, 280, 282, 287, 288, 290, 312, 348
  financial policy, 284–5
Halifax, George Savile, 1st marquess of, 189, 193, 210, 214, 215, 216, 223, 225, 229, 235, 243, 251, 258, 260, 266, 270, 348
Hamilton, James Douglas, 4th duke of, 310
Hampden, John, 120, 130, 139, 141, 150
*Rex* v. *Hampden*, 112, 128
Hampton Court Conference, the, 50, 61
Handel, George Frederick, 340
Hanmer, Sir Thomas, 332
Harcourt, Simon, 313, 316, 323
Harley, Robert, 1st earl of Oxford, 189, 279, 282, 289, 292, 298, 302, 350
  peace policy, 304, 308, 313–14, 326
  fall, 316, 333, 334
  Lord Treasurer, 326, 327, 328, 330, 331–2
Harrington, James, 188
Harrison, Thomas, 169, 171, 175
Harvey, William, 187
Haslerigg, Sir Arthur, 139
Hawksmoor, Nicholas, 345
Hay, James, 56, 77
'Heads of the Proposals', the, 160, 161, 173
Henrietta Maria, Queen, 92, 95, 116, 120, 125, 140, 147
Henriette-Anne, duchess of Orleans, 206
Henry, Prince of Wales, 51, 63, 68, 76, 117
Herbert, Arthur, admiral, 233, 246
Herbert, Sir Edward, 245
Herbert, George, 340–41
Herrick, Robert, 341
High Commission, Court of, 83, 114, 124; abolished, 128, 184
Hoadly, Benjamin, 322
Hobbes, Thomas, 44, 182, 187–8, 194, 346, 352

Holland, Henry Rich, 1st earl of, 139
Hollar, Wenceslaus, 342
Holles, Denzil, 106, 108, 126, 139, 141
Holloway, Sir Richard, 245
Holt, Sir John, 258, 305, 312
Hopton, Sir Ralph, 146, 149
Hotham, Sir John, 142
Howards, the, 53, 62, 64, 69
Hull, 132, 142, 149, 151, 251
'Humble Petition and Advice', the, 176
Hyde, Lawrence, see Rochester

Impositions, 64, 65, 67, 83, 88, 110, 129
Independants, the, 154-5
'Instrument of Government', the, 173
Invitation of the Seven, the, 243-4
Ireland, 120, 149-50, 223, 232-3, 235, 256, 266, 267, 269
Ireton, Henry, 159, 160, 161, 162, 163

Jacobitism, 269, 327, 332
James I
  character, 47, 48-52, 54-5, 75-6, 87, 92-3
  views on government, 40, 48, 66, 67, 94
  tastes, 336-7
  and the Church, 25, 27, 28, 49-50, 60-62, 98, 184
  and Parliament, 33, 37, 40, 45, 50, 56, 58, 67, 85-7, 91-2, 94
  foreign policy, 63, 69, 78-82, 85, 88-9
  finances, 54-5, 63-4, 65-6, 69, 72, 76-8, 79
James II, 8, 31, 166, 187, 189, 192, 197, 218, 264
  Duke of York, 199-200, 202, 206, 208, 209, 222-3; conversion, 206; exclusion crisis, 212-16
  King: character, 224 ff.; aims, 225, 229-32; finances, 226, 266

and William, 227, 234-6; relations with the Church, 224-5, 231; and the Dissenters, 233, 236; and the courts, 245, 251-3, 263
  foreign policy, 226, 234-5, 240-42
  electoral campaign, 238, 242-3, 246, 248
  collapse, 239, 240, 244-5, 252-3
  deposition, 254-5, 258-9
  exile, 269
  death, 291
James Francis Edward, Prince of Wales (later James III), 243, 249, 252, 255, 259, 291, 296, 316, 321, 327, 333
Jeffreys, George, lord, 185, 221, 228, 239, 245, 257
Jenkins, Sir Leoline, 222
Jersey, Edward Villiers, 1st earl of, 288, 304, 327
Johnstone, James, 239
Jones, Inigo, 86, 337, 344
Jones, J. R., 242
Jonson, Ben, 336-7
Judges' Bill, 264
Judiciary, the, 83, 245, 251-3, 263-4
Junto, the, see Whig Party
Justices of the Peace, 30-31
Juxon, William, bishop, 115, 126

Keppel, Arnold Joost van, earl of Albemarle, 274
Ker, Robert, see Somerset
Killicrankie, 309
Kirke, Colonel Piercey, 250
Kneller, Sir Godfrey, 342, 343
Knighthood fines, 110, 128
Knyff, Leonard, 342

La Rochelle, 96, 103, 104
Lambert, John, 171, 173, 177, 178
Landen, 273
Langport, 152
Laud, William, archbishop, 120, 122, 123, 129, 130, 138, 338
  policy, 99-100, 112-15, 183
  death, 154

Lauderdale, John Maitland, 1st duke of, 203, 204, 308
Law, William, 346
Law reform, 186, 354
Lawson, John, admiral, 168, 178
Leeds, duke of, see Danby
Lely, Sir Peter, 342, 343
Leslie, Alexander, 120
Leslie, Charles, 350
Leslie, David, 151
Levellers, the, 108, 157–8, 160, 162, 166, 167, 175, 264
  Agreement of the People, 162
Leyburn, John, 230
Lilburne, John, 113, 158, 167
Lindsey, Robert Bertie, 1st earl of, 139
Littleton, Edward, 108
Locke, John, 8, 187, 220, 255, 294, 352, 353
London
  importance, 15
  Fire of, 190, 201
Lonsdale, John Lowther, 1st viscount, 288
Lostwithiel, 151
Louis XIV, 192, 204, 205–6, 209, 211, 217, 218, 226, 234, 240, 269, 281
  and the Revolution, 241–2, 247–8, 256
  and the Spanish Succession, 283, 289, 290, 291, 296, 303, 308, 325, 330
Lowndes, William, 302
Ludlow, Edmund, 175, 255
Lumley, Richard, 1st lord, 243, 251
Lunsford, Sir Thomas, 137

Macaulay, T. B., 242
Magdalen College, Oxford, 233–4, 236, 248
Magna Carta, 30
Málaga, 304
Malplaquet, 319
Manchester, Charles Montagu, 4th earl of, 291
Manchester, Edward Montagu, 2nd earl of, 139, 151
Mansfeld, Ernst von, 91, 92, 95, 96
Manwaring, Roger, 42, 102, 104

Marlborough, John Churchill, earl and duke of, 189, 193, 237, 250, 273, 290–91, 298, 301–2, 303, 312, 315, 319–20, 324, 335
  campaigns, 30, 304, 305–6, 307, 317, 319, 326, 328, 352
  dismissed, 329
Marlborough, Sarah, duchess of, 301, 313, 324
Marvell, Andrew, 341, 346
Mary II, 211, 219, 235, 246, 254, 258, 259, 268, 273, 278, 291
Mary Beatrice of Modena, queen consort, 209, 219, 224, 239, 244, 252
Masham, Abigail, 313
Masque, the, 118, 336–7
Massey, John, 233
Massinger, Philip, 337, 338
Melfort, John Drummond, 1st earl of, 204, 223
Merchant Adventurers, the, 14, 80, 109
Methuen Treaties, the, 303, 308
Middleton, Charles, 2nd earl of, 223, 237, 239, 248, 269
Middleton, Thomas, 337, 338
Militia Act (1661), 181, 196
Militia Ordinance (1642), 136, 140, 142
Milton, John, 167, 186, 336, 341, 346
Mingay, G. E., 20
Minorca, 303, 317, 320
Mitchell, Sir Francis, 84
Mompesson, Sir Giles, 84
Monarchy, the, see Crown
Monck, George, 1st duke of Albemarle, 168, 178, 179, 182
Monmouth, James Scott, 1st duke of, 213–14, 215, 217, 221, 222
  Rebellion, 185, 226, 228–9, 288
Monopolies, 78, 84, 90, 109
Montagu, Edward, 1st earl of Sandwich, 178
Montague, Charles, see Halifax
Montague, Richard, 98, 105
Mutiny Act, 262

Namur, 278

Nantes, Edict of, 234
Naseby, 152, 165
Naval Discipline Act, 262
Navigation Acts, 169, 190, 200, 309
Navy, the Royal, 168–9, 191–2, 201, 202, 262, 286
Neale, Sir John, 7, 13, 33, 35
Neile, Richard, archbishop, 115
New Model Army, the, 152, 156–60, 161–3, 177–8
Newbury, 149, 151
Newcastle, John Holles, 1st duke of, 313, 315, 326
Newcastle, Thomas Pelham-Holles, 1st duke of, 242
Newcastle, William Cavendish, 1st marquess of, 144, 146, 149, 151
Newcastle, Propositions of, 155, 160, 161
Newspapers, 349–50
Newton, Isaac, 294, 352, 353
Nijmegen, Peace of, 212
Northampton, Henry Howard, 1st earl of, 53, 62, 64, 69, 71
Notestein, Wallace, 33, 35
Nottingham, Charles Howard, 1st earl of, 77
Nottingham, Daniel Finch, 2nd earl of, 189, 235, 243, 265, 268, 270, 271, 276, 296, 300, 303, 306, 313, 314, 329, 334
Noy, William, 108

Oates, Titus, 212
Oblivion, Act of, 195, 265, 267
Occasional Conformity, 294–5, 299
  Bills, 302, 303, 304
  Act, 329
October Club, the, 326
Oldfield, Thomas, 243
Orford, earl of, see Russell, Edward
Orkney, Elizabeth Villiers, countess of, 287
Ormonde, James Butler, marquess, 1st duke of, 149, 194, 222, 223, 237

Ormonde, James Butler, 2nd duke of, 250, 316, 330
Oudenarde, 317
Overbury, Sir Thomas, 71–2
Owen, John, 170
Oxford, earl of, see Harley
Oxford, propositions of, 149

Parliament, 10, 39–41, 45–7, 70–71
  Commons: elections, 30–31, 160, 173, 264–5; composition, 31, 286; management, 56–7, 58–9, 66, 270–71, 274–5, 300–1
  Lords, 189, 209–10, 305, 355–6
Parliament, the Long, 36, 39, 109–10, 122
  circumstances, 125, 146; composition, 114; policy, 123, 127–8, 142, 145; reforms, 128–9
  Civil Wars, 146–8, 150–52; peace party, 147, 149; purged, 159, 163, 164, 165–6, 167–9; dispersed, 170, 171–2, 174; recalled, 178; dissolved, 179
  later effects, 181, 195
Partition Treaties, the, 189, 282–4, 288–9
Pelham, Henry, 242
Pellé, Honoré, 343
Pembroke, Thomas Herbert, 8th earl of, 288, 291, 318
Pembroke, William Herbert, 3rd earl of, 97, 103
Penn, William, admiral, 168
Penn, William, Quaker, 233
Pennington, Isaac, 125
Penruddock's Rising, 175
Pepys, Samuel, 187, 199, 263, 349
Peterborough, Charles Mordaunt, 3rd earl of, 304, 307–8
Peters, Hugh, 192
Petition of Right, the, 103–4, 107 123
Petre, Edward, 232
Place Bills, 275, 276, 277
Plague, bubonic, 14, 16, 81, 95 plague of 1665, 184, 190, 201
Popish Plot, the, 212 ff.

Porter, Endymion, 117
Portland, Hans Willem Bentinck, 1st earl of, 272, 281, 283, 290
Portland, Richard Weston, 1st earl of, 104, 115, 118
Portsmouth, Louise de Kéroualle, duchess of, 215-16, 218, 222
Powell, Sir John, 245
Presbyterianism, 154, 155
Preston, John, 98
Preston, Richard Graham, viscount, 224, 269
Pride's Purge, 163, 178
Prynne, William, 113, 338
Purcell, Henry, 339-40
Puritanism, 12, 22-3, 27, 61-2, 112 ff., 185 ff.
Purveyance, 162
Putney Debates, the, 162
Pym, John, 42, 47, 73, 106, 107, 184
 leader of Commons, 124, 125, 126-7, 130, 131-2, 133, 136, 139
 war leader, 140, 141, 143, 147, 150
 death, 150, 154

Quakers, 167, 233
Quebec Expedition, the, 328, 332
Queensberry, William Douglas, 1st duke of, 250
Queensberry, William Douglas, 2nd duke of, 250, 310, 311

Raleigh, Sir Walter, 53, 72-3, 309, 341
Ramillies, 307
Recruiting Act, 318
Regency Act, 261-2, 306, 307
Revolution, theory of, 7, 12
Revolution of 1688
 causes, 228, 231, 244
 course, 243-4, 246-8, 249-53
 settlement, 257, 261-5
 constitutional implications, 255-6, 259-60, 261-2, 270-73
 ideological debate, 268-9, 293, 322
Rights, Declaration (Bill) of, 260-65, 266
Robinson, John, 242

Rochester, John Wilmot, 2nd earl of, 347
Rochester, Lawrence Hyde, 1st earl of, 189, 215, 218, 221, 223, 224, 225, 232, 248, 249, 271, 275, 277, 289, 299, 300, 302, 303, 306, 313
Rooke, George, admiral, 302, 304
Root and Branch Petition, 125, 129, 130
Royal Society, the, 187
Rubens, Peter Paul, 118, 342
Rudyard, Sir Benjamin, 40
Rupert, Prince, 148, 151, 152
Russell, Conrad, 41
Russell, Edward, 1st earl of Orford, 243, 269, 273, 277, 281, 287, 290, 318
Russell, William, lord, 214, 221
Rye House Plot, 185, 221
Ryswick, Peace of, 281, 282, 291

Sacheverell, Henry, 300, 321, 322, 327
 impeachment, 323 ff.
St John Henry, see Bolingbroke
St John, Oliver, 36, 126
Salisbury, James Cecil, 3rd earl of, 210
Salisbury, Robert Cecil, 1st earl of, 37, 49, 52-3, 54, 56, 58, 62-3, 64-7, 69, 82
Sancroft, William, archbishop, 231, 244, 248, 258, 259, 265
Sandys, Sir Edwin, 82
Savoy Conference, 182
Saye & Sele, William Fiennes, 1st viscount, 97, 111, 126, 139
Schism Act, 334
Schomberg, Frederick Herman, duke of, 246
Science, the New, 185-6
Scotland, 48-9, 52, 204, 223
 Rebellion, 42, 112, 119-21, 122
 Civil Wars, 132, 150, 151, 163, 166
 annexed, 168
 Revolution of 1689, 260, 309
 Union with England, 51, 52, 64, 73, 206, 295, 296, 308-11, 312

Security, Act of, 310
Sedgemoor, 228, 288
Selden, John, 108
Sequestration Ordinance, 147
Settlement, Act of, 289–90, 307
Seven Bishops, trial of, 244, 265
Seymour, Sir Edward, 222, 271, 275, 277, 282, 300, 304
Shaftesbury, Anthony Ashley Cooper, 1st earl of, 8, 182, 189, 199, 203, 204
    Lord Chancellor, 207; in opposition, 209, 210, 214, 215, 217; fall, 220
Shakespeare, William, 45, 336
Sharp, John, archbishop, 231, 294, 296, 299, 300, 301, 314
Ship money, 41, 111–12
Shirley, James, 337
Shrewsbury, Charles Talbot, duke of, 235, 236, 243, 256, 270, 275, 276, 277, 279, 280, 284, 288
    under Queen Anne, 317, 324, 326, 327, 334–5
Sibthorpe, Robert, 102
Sidney, Algernon, 221
Sidney, Henry, 239, 243
Skippon, Philip, 139
Smith, John, 312, 313
Smyrna Convoy (1693), 193, 273
Solemn League and Covenant, 150, 155, 183
Solms, Heinrich Maastricht, count de, 273, 274
Somers, John, lord, 31, 189, 207, 257, 268, 277, 279, 280, 285, 287, 290, 291, 298, 312, 315, 318, 325
Somerset, Charles Seymour, 6th duke of, 291–2, 313, 334
Somerset, Robert Ker, earl of, 64, 69, 71, 76
Sophia, Electress of Hanover, 288, 306
Southampton, Henry Wriothesley, 3rd earl of, 49, 84
Southampton, Thomas Wriothesley, 4th earl of, 194, 198, 203
Spanish Succession, the, 281, 288–9

war of, 302, 303, 304, 307–8, 313, 315, 319–20, 325
Spencer, Robert, 1st lord, 97
Stanhope, James, 324, 325
Star Chamber, 101, 104, 109, 113, 115, 117, 124; abolished, 128
Steele, Richard, 333, 351
Steenkirk, 273
Stone, Lawrence, 9, 18, 44
Stop of the Exchequer, 207, 285
Strafford, Thomas Wentworth, 1st earl of, 39, 97, 103, 104–5, 107, 120–22, 144, 337
    impeachment, 123, 124–5, 126–7, 147
    death, 128
Strangeways, Sir John, 130
Strode, William, 139
Suckling, Sir John, 127
Suffolk, Thomas Howard, 1st earl of, 49, 53, 69, 71, 77
Sunderland, Charles Spencer, 3rd earl of, 312, 315, 316, 318
Sunderland, Robert Spencer, 2nd earl of, 215, 216, 222, 223, 242, 249, 277, 279, 280, 281, 283, 291
Swift, Jonathan, 326–7, 356, 351

Talman, William, 345
Tankerville, Ford Grey, earl of, 288
Tawney, R. H., 9, 17
Taxation, direct, 38–9, 54
    assessment, 111, 142, 147
    land tax, 272–3, 286
Temple, Sir William, 204
Tenison, Thomas, archbishop, 294, 312
Test Act, of 1673, 208, 210, 229, 261; of 1678, 213
Theatre, the, 45, 336–8
    Restoration theatre, 294, 346–7
Thornhill, Sir James, 343
Toland, John, 294
Toleration Act, 265, 293, 321
Tonson, Jacob, 239
Tory Party, the
    origins, 215; reaction, 219; in the Revolution, 257; and

after, 271–2, 282; under Queen Anne, 297, 300–1, 303 304
blue water policy, 302–3; church toryism, 293–7, 306–7; and the Succession, 332
Tourneur, Cyril, 45, 337–8
Townshend, Charles, 2nd viscount, 320
Townshend, Horatio, 1st viscount, 220
Treby, Sir George, 257
Trelawney, Colonel Charles, 250
Trelawney, Sir Jonathan, bishop, 314
Trenchard, John, 257, 277
Trevor, Sir John, 278
Trevor-Roper, H. R., 9
Triennial Act, of 1641, 124, 125, 163; of 1664, 181, 211; of 1695, 276, 277, 278
Triennial Bill (1694), 275
Triple Alliance, the, 205
Tunnage and poundage, see Customs
Turnham Green, 148
Tyler, John, bishop, 300, 314
Tyrconnell, Richard Talbot, earl of, 232–3, 235, 239

Uniformity Act (1662), 183, 184, 293
Utrecht, Peace of, 200, 298, 326, 327–31
Uxbridge, Propositions of, 152, 154, 155

Valentine, Benjamin, 106, 108
Van Dyck, Sir Anthony, 118, 342
Vanbrugh, Sir John, 345
Vane, Sir Henry, 150, 166, 192
Vaughan, Henry, 341
Venner's Rising, 182, 185
Vere, Sir Horace, 79
Vernon, James, 284, 288
Verrio, Anthony, 342–3
Vigo, 302

Wake, William, bishop, 300, 314
Waller, Sir William, 151

Walpole, Robert, 242, 313, 316, 318, 324, 325, 329
Wardship, 59, 128
Warwick, Robert Rich, earl of, 100, 111, 139, 142
Webster, John, 45, 337–8
Wedgwood, C. V., 9
Wentworth, Sir Thomas, see Strafford
Westminster, Treaty of, 209, 212
Wharton, Philip, 4th lord, 97, 139, 210
Wharton, Thomas, 5th lord, 277, 280, 284, 300, 305, 306, 312, 318, 324, 325
Whig Party, the
origins, 215, 219; at the Revolution, 257, 322; and after, 271–2, 279–8c
Whig Junto, 277, 280–81, 282, 283, 284, 290, 292–3, 300–1, 311–12, 324; war policy, 308, 319, 327, 329; and the church, 295, 314 ff., 323 ff.; and Scottish Union, 310–12
Whitelocke, Bulstrode, 159
Whitgift, John, archbishop, 24, 27, 53, 62
William III, 200, 205, 211, 219, 227, 234
Prince of Orange: in the Revolution, 239–40, 241–2, 243 ff., 246–7, 249–50, 252–3
and the Convention, 254, 256–7, 258–9
character, 252
religious views, 236–7, 261, 265, 268
made king, 259, 260
King: finances, 266–7, 272–3, 283
domestic policy, 269, 273–4
war policy, 273, 303
and Scottish Union, 310
death, 252
Williams, John, bishop, 40, 54, 87, 97, 138
Windebank, Sir Francis, 116, 124
Windsor Castle, 218, 342
Winnington, Sir Francis, 257
Winstanley, Gerard, 167

Winwood, Sir Ralph, 70
Worcester, 168, 171
Worcester, Henry Somerset, 1st marquess of, 144
Wren, Sir Christopher, 201, 343, 344-5
Wright, Sir Nathan, 288, 312

Wright, Sir Robert, 245

York, Anne Hyde, duchess of, 199
York, duke of, see James II

Zuylestein, William Henry Nassau de, 235